Doctoral Study in Contemporary Higher Education

Doctoral Study in Contemporary Higher Education

Howard Green and
Stuart Powell

Society for Research into Higher Education
& Open University Press

Open University Press
McGraw-Hill Education
McGraw-Hill House
Shoppenhangers Road
Maidenhead
Berkshire
England
SL6 2QL

email: enquiries@openup.co.uk
world wide web: www.openup.co.uk

and Two Penn Plaza, New York, NY 10121-2289, USA

First published 2005

A catalogue record of this book is available from the British Library

ISBN-13: 978 0335 21473 0 (pb)   978 0335 21474 7 (hb)
ISBN-10: 0335 21473 8 (pb)   0335 21474 6 (hb)

Library of Congress Cataloging-in-Publication Data
CIP data applied for

Typeset by RefineCatch Limited, Bungay, Suffolk
Printed in the UK by Bell & Bain Ltd, Glasgow

Dedicated to Our Parents

Contents

Foreword

Studying for a doctorate in the UK may take many forms and result in different kinds of award. For example, a student studying full-time for a PhD and funded by a research council grant is likely to have a very different experience of study from the student working full-time in a demanding professional job while studying 'part-time' towards a Professional Doctorate. Between these two cases there may, among other things, be differences in modes of study, levels of direct instruction, kinds of supervision, notions of the 'contribution' that is made and the research training that is provided. Yet as doctoral candidates both should be operating at doctoral level and both will, if successful, have comparable awards.

The authors of this book have brought together a rich range of material on doctoral study, including an account of the various forms of doctorate and the student population. They have set themselves a challenging task. However, the breadth of their considerations does allow them to highlight similarities and differences in doctoral study and to focus on the central purpose of the doctorate and the implications of its diverse characteristics. They provide some important ideas about what might count as consistencies in principle and practice. In short, by considering doctoral study in the UK in all its manifestations and by referencing it against such study elsewhere, the authors challenge us to reconsider what we engage in when we train students towards doctoral awards. Their suggestions of ways forward make an important contribution to the kind of critical debate about doctoral study that is now required within the UK Higher Education sector.

April 2005

Professor Robert G Burgess
Vice-Chancellor
University of Leicester

Preface

This book considers critically the current state of doctoral study in the UK. It encompasses the range of routes available to candidates seeking to achieve a doctoral award whether that is the 'traditional' PhD, in the professions, in practice-based domains, via published works or in modes described in terms such as 'new route'. Drawing all forms of doctoral study into one context in this way enables comparison between them and subsequent analyses of their commonalities as well as their distinctions. The consideration of UK doctoral awards is referenced against similar awards in other parts of the EU as well as world wide; this referencing serves to inform some of the arguments about accepted practices.

Aspects of doctoral study are considered from recruitment through examination to the destination of doctoral candidates. Such study is reviewed in terms of its place in a changing higher education sector where fitness for purpose, cost and effectiveness are priorities and where the challenge from international competitors is ever present.

Each chapter of the book ends with summarizing issues. These are revisited in the final chapter where consideration is given to the future direction of doctoral awards in the UK. The authors argue for a particular framework in this respect that offers consistency and is underpinned by a series of statements of purpose. Here there is an attempt to step back from the detail and reconsider the purpose of the Doctorate and the necessary features of doctoral study.

In consideration of the multi-faceted nature of doctoral study that is current in the UK, the book is intended to shed some light on various idiosyncrasies and point to a re-evaluation of purpose and practice.

Howard Green and Stuart Powell
January 2005

Acknowledgements

The authors wish to acknowledge all those colleagues who have contributed in one way or another to the writing of this book. It would be invidious to single out individuals for mention because influences have been wide-ranging and pervasive. We have learned from colleagues with whom we have worked in our respective institutions; from participants at conferences and workshops we have attended and run, both in the UK and far beyond; from colleagues within the UK Council for Graduate Education (UKCGE) and other national bodies such as the Quality Assurance Agency (QAA); and from our many research students who were supposed to be learning from us.

Having avoided the naming of names, we do however wish to acknowledge our indebtedness to Kathryn Brown from Leeds Metropolitan University who has not only kept us in order but undertook much of the data collection and managed the final processes of putting together the manuscript for submission to our publishers in such a way that it resembled a book rather than a collection of writings.

Finally we wish to acknowledge the QAA for kind permission to reproduce sections of the revised *Code of Practice – Postgraduate Research Programmes* (QAA 2004) and the UKCGE for kind permission to make use of material from the Council's report into *The Award of PhD by Published Work in the UK* (Powell 2004).

List of abbreviations

ACS	Academic Cost Centre
AHRB	Arts and Humanities Research Board (NB now a council – AHRC)
AMusD	Doctor of Musical Arts
BBSRC	Biotechnology and Biological Sciences Research Council
BPS/UCoSDA	British Psychological Society and Universities and Colleges' Staff Development Unit
BRRG	Better Regulation Review Group
CBI	Confederation of British Industry
CDP	Committee of Directors of Polytechnics
CEQ	Course Experience Questionnaire
CMRST	Committee for Manpower Resources for Science and Technology
CNAA	Council for National Academic Awards
CQFW	Credit and Qualifications Framework, Wales
CRAC	Careers Research and Advisory Centre
CVCP	Committee of Vice Chancellors and Principals [now Universities UK (UUK)]
DArt	Doctor of Art
DBA	Doctorate in Business Administration
DBA	Diploma in Business Administration
DClinPsy	Doctor of Clinical Psychology
DD	Doctor of Divinity
DES	Department for Education and Science
DfES	Department for Education and Skills
DLitt	Doctor of Letters
DMus	Doctor of Music
DNurse	Doctor of Nursing
DPhil	Doctor of Philosophy
DProf	Professional Doctorate
DSc	Doctor of Science

DSocSc	Doctor of Social Sciences
DTA	Doctoral Training Accounts
DTI	Department of Trade and Industry
EdD	Doctor of Education
EngD	Doctor of Engineering
EPSRC	Engineering and Physical Sciences Research Council
ESRC	Economic and Social Research Council
FHEQ	Framework of Higher Education Qualifications
GTA	Graduate Teaching Associate
HEFCE	Higher Education Funding Council for England
HEFCW	Higher Education Funding Council for Wales
HEI	Higher Education Institution
HEIF	Higher Education Innovation Fund
HEQC	Higher Education Qualifications Council
HESA	Higher Education Statistics Agency
HMSO	Her Majesty's Stationery Office
ILT	Institute of Learning Teaching
IP	Intellectual Property
IPR	Intellectual Property Rights
JISC	Joint Information Systems Committee
LEA	Local Education Authority
LLD	Doctor of Law
MA	Master of Arts
MD	Doctor of Medicine
MPhil	Master of Philosophy
MRC	Medical Research Council
MRes	Masters by Research
MSc	Master of Science
NERC	Natural Environment Research Council
NICATS	The Northern Ireland Credit Accumulation and Transfer System
NPC	National Postgraduate Committee
NUCCAT	Northern Universities Consortium for Credit Accumulation and Transfer
OECD	Organization for Economic Co-operation and Development
OST	Office of Science and Technology
PgCert	Postgraduate Certificate
PgDip	Postgraduate Diploma
PGR	Postgraduate Research
PGT	Postgraduate Taught
PhD	Doctor of Philosophy
PI	performance indicator
PPARC	Particle Physics and Astronomy Research Council
PREQ	Postgraduate Research Experience Questionnaire
QAA	Quality Assurance Agency for Higher Education
QR	Quality Research

RAE	Research Assessment Exercise
RDA	Regional Development Agency
SEEC	Southern England Consortium for Credit Accumulation and Transfer
SERC	Science and Engineering Research Council [now EPSRC]
SHEFC	Scottish Higher Education Funding Council
TAPPS	Training and Accreditation Programme for Postgraduate Supervisors
THES	*The Times Higher Education Supplement*
UKCGE	UK Council for Graduate Education
UoA	Units of Assessment

Part 1
Context

Part I

1

The origins, issues and recent development of doctoral study in the UK

Introduction

This chapter identifies and explores many of the developments and issues that have arisen since the Harris report (Harris 1996) in order to provide a questioning context for the rest of the book. Our argument is that doctoral education is at a cross-roads that is not fully recognized by several of the agencies and many of the Higher Education Institutions (HEIs) that are involved in its financing and delivery.

Before going further we should identify, if not define, what we mean by 'Doctorate'. Our purpose in this book is to describe and analyse the several awards that now bear the title 'Doctorate' in the UK, and here we mean awards that are at Doctorate level – whether this be defined in the UK Framework of Higher Education Qualifications (FHEQ), or more loosely by universities' own definitions and standards. Our discussion will include a clutch of awards: PhD, Professional Doctorate, Practice-Based Doctorate, PhD by Published Work and the so-called New Route PhD. In later chapters we distinguish these kinds of doctoral awards and compare and contrast their respective purposes as well as modes of delivery and types of outcome.

This chapter sets the scene and raises some of the issues that are addressed throughout the book. First, we map some of the recent events that have characterized the development of doctoral education in the UK. Second, we consider briefly the kinds of evidence that are commonly taken to inform debates about that education. Third, we map out the arguments, in terms of themes, that seem to us to underpin the future development of doctoral level teaching and awards.

We recognize that since devolved responsibilities were given to Scotland and to a lesser extent Wales, there have been divergences in the way in which higher education has developed, in particular with regard to funding. We have not devoted specific attention to these differences, noting them only for comparative purposes where appropriate. We do, however, acknowledge that generalization about doctoral education in the UK is increasingly difficult because of these developments.

Influences on the current state of doctoral education

The range of influences – direct and indirect

Within this section we review the way in which recent developments in the field have impacted upon the current situation by considering some of the national reports and initiatives that have shaped policy and practice in relation to doctoral education in UK universities, including here the Framework of Higher Education Qualifications. Clearly, all aspects of higher education have been exposed to significant change over the past 20 years or so and doctoral level study is no different in this respect. But it does seem that much change at this level has been driven by factors at undergraduate and, to a lesser extent, at taught postgraduate levels. This has meant that doctoral education has been affected by change that initially was focused on other parts of the system. There has therefore been both direct and indirect influences. An example is the Research Assessment Exercise (RAE) where the original driver was an intention to improve UK research; there is now a situation where that exercise is used by the Higher Education Funding Council for England (HEFCE) as a vehicle for assessing research *training*. The exercise itself made no assessment of training facilities or quality of training outcomes – yet it is now used to determine whether or not particular departments should be funded for training. Doctoral education is in this instance being controlled by a measurement system that was not designed for the purpose and offers no direct evidence of its quality. We suggest that such an incidental approach permeates the field of doctoral education.

We also open up below one of the themes that runs through the book: the way in which the nature of the award itself has changed without controlled deliberation from any of the parties and the significant shifts that have occurred – generally without review – in, for example, the volume of doctoral candidates and in their modes and patterns of study. We consider here the notion of 'training' doctoral candidates in a manner in excess of what might be expected to occur in the traditional apprentice–master relationship. Again, this may be seen as a development that has been introduced largely without the benefit of evidence as to efficacy.

National reports and initiatives in the UK

In 1996 the UK Council for Graduate Education (UKCGE) noted that 'doctoral education was frequently regarded as a cottage industry, a prestigious yet somehow fringe activity in higher education' (UKCGE 1996b). We suggest that the movement from a cottage industry to one that provides excellence in an increasingly mass-production environment continues to challenge universities and their regulators.

The Harris report in 1996 was a landmark document in the debate about quality issues in research awards, recommending, in the now famous Box 3, the conditions in which quality could be delivered at PhD level (Harris 1996). Several themes and actions flowed from the Harris report: the CSU directory of research and postgraduate qualifications in the form of the Prospects Directory; the Quality Assurance Agency (QAA) Code of Practice: Section 1 Postgraduate Research Programmes (QAA 2004); QAA finally agreed its qualifications framework, including definitions of doctoral level outcomes; the HEFCE modified its funding model for PhD students to ensure that they are, in theory at least, located in departments with a 3 plus RAE rating; and the Economic and Social Research Council (ESRC) requires outlets to identify how they develop and monitor supervisor capability (ESRC 2001). Most universities have now reviewed the organizational aspects of their provision and have introduced graduate schools or similar structures (UKCGE 1998a). These changes represent a fundamental shift in the way in which the Doctorate is thought about and the provision of research training in the UK.

The debate is far from over as developments in the PhD continue apace. The ESRC has implemented a 1+3 model for the PhD to include the essential elements of research training expected from social science PhDs, while the Joint Research Councils (Research Councils/AHRB 2001) have published their seven broad categories of research skills expected of the PhD. In the outcomes of their fundamental Review of Research (HEFCE 2001), HEFCE identified the need to examine the practice of research training in order to produce thresholds of provision and good practice guidelines, eventually to be linked to funding. This is included in the revised QAA Code (QAA 2004). The Treasury examined the provision for the training of future scientists and engineers in a working group led by Gareth Roberts (Roberts 2001). The HEFCE has just announced the establishment of a new funding model (HEFCE 2004), and the list goes on.

These debates and changes are taking place not only in the UK. The Bologna declaration has created a climate in which postgraduate and doctoral work is increasingly being examined across Europe. In France, for example, the Government has introduced the *Ecoles Doctorales* to act as the focus for PhD work, concentrating significant resources on programmes in such educational establishments (Ministère de la Recherche 2001). Similar reviews are taking place in the USA and Canada (see, for example, Walker 2001).

The QAA Framework of Higher Education Qualifications and doctoral study

The place and role of QAA in the context of doctoral study is explored elsewhere in this book. For the purposes of this introduction it is perhaps important to note that the Harris report (Harris 1996) and later the Dearing report (Dearing 1997) both commented critically upon the confusion of awards and award titles available within the UK higher education sector, and doctoral study was not immune from these criticisms. In early forms of the Framework of Higher Education Qualifications, which sought to resolve some of the issues raised by Harris and Dearing, the PhD was differentiated from the Professional Doctorates in that the latter was required to be credit rated while the former was not (credit rating is considered more fully in Chapter 5). For the most part, however, the Framework of Higher Education Qualifications does not impact greatly on how HEIs in the UK conceive of, and deliver, their doctoral programmes. The one significant feature is perhaps the qualification descriptor for doctoral level awards, which is referred to in relevant chapters. In summary, the UK now has a description set down for what should constitute a level of doctoral achievement.

HEIs may interpret that in different ways in their criteria for doctoral awards, but the qualification descriptor acts as a standard to which those criteria may lead. There is very little evidence that the descriptors have had any significant impact on the more traditional forms of PhD, their definitions or assessment criteria. Is the PhD being assumed to be above or beyond the scope of the rather mechanistic structures of the Framework?

The Framework of Higher Education Qualifications also impacts on the field of doctoral study by defining (i) that the title 'doctor' should only be used for qualifications that meet the 'full expectations of the qualification at doctoral level', (ii) that the titles of PhD and DPhil should only be used where 'assessment is solely by final dissertation or published work' and (iii) that, where doctoral programmes contain substantial taught elements, the title of the discipline should normally be included in the title (e.g. EdD for Doctor of Education). There is therefore some level of national guidance in the UK about the quality of work required for particular kinds of doctoral award and the way in which those awards can be named in relation to the content of delivered programmes of study.

In one sense the above strictures are non-problematic. However, there is a danger of tying in a nomenclature of research degree to elements of the 'taught' component. A candidate for a PhD might undertake his/her research studies entirely in the field of education, say in the investigation of children's specific reading difficulties and their relationship to pedagogy, and might negotiate and follow a programme of supervised research training in this respect. Similarly, a candidate might follow a predetermined curriculum involving various investigations and training in research methodology, produce a final dissertation on the same kind of topic as in the above example and be awarded an EdD. The distinction, therefore, is almost entirely in the process followed to a similar end. The question arises as to whether or not the candidate in the first example should have been awarded an EdD rather than a PhD on the grounds that the work is focused within the area of education and indeed within a specific aspect of the professional practice of teachers. This is a dilemma that remains unresolved in the current climate of the use of doctoral titles.

One could construct an argument for declaring that all Doctorates should be titled PhD, whatever the process of learning involved – after all, at first degree and Masters degree levels, awards are not differentiated by process but rather by outcomes. An alternative argument would be that all doctoral studies should be differentiated by discipline (e.g. DPsych, DPhys, DLing, DHist, etc.) – clearly a potentially confusing and untidy solution. This question of use of doctoral titles is revisited in the chapter relating to Professional Doctorates, but for our purposes it is important to note that doctoral study in the UK is not perhaps convincingly demarcated by nomenclature and that contrary to Harris's attempts to limit or curtail the use of different nomenclature, particularly in relation to the Professional Doctorate, there is a blossoming of creativity in title designation.

The changing nature and volume of doctoral awards offered in the UK

The context for our discussions in this book is in the changing nature and volume of doctoral awards offered in the UK and the numbers of candidates engaged.

The growth in the postgraduate population has created a sector that is out of all recognition to that of the 1960s when the Robbins report (Robbins 1963), the first major study of Higher Education in the UK, noted a population in 1961/62 of 19,400 full-time and 6,300 part-time students. By 1994/95 at the time of the Harris report, there were 128,300 full-time and 187,100 part-time postgraduate students. The relative position of postgraduate student numbers similarly changed during this period. In 1979, 13% of the total student population were postgraduate (100,900 postgraduate in a total population of 787,000) yet in 1994/95 the comparable figure was 21% (315,400 out of a population of 1,528,600). By the end of the millennium, the total population of postgraduates was 151,330 full time and 257,290 part time (HESA 2001).

Similarly, structural changes were observed in the mode of programmes with a growth in the number of part-time students and equalization of the gender balance, and, more recently, a significant growth in the numbers of overseas students. In 1992/93 there were 25,100 international postgraduate students in HEIs in the UK, 8% from the EU and 92% from the rest of the world. By 1997/98 this figure had risen to 81,000, of which 33% were from the EU and 67% from the rest of the world, theoretically making a major impact on the funding of programmes. The global market, and in particular the UK's position in that market, has been a key factor in the discussion of quality (Spagnold 1994).

If we look simply at the doctoral awards, the importance of this growth is further emphasized with 13,670 doctorates awarded by 129 HEIs in the year 2000. Table 1.1 illustrates the trend since the mid-1990s.

The distribution of awards is highly skewed across universities, as is clearly seen in Table 1.2. Five universities – Cambridge, Oxford, Birmingham, Manchester and University College London, all located in England – accounted for 25% of the total awards in 2000. This concentration is further emphasized by the figures (Table 1.3) for the constituent nations of the UK. These figures do not of course take into account the number or size of the HEIs in each of the nations or the total number of students from each of the nations who are being awarded Doctorates because of transnational

Table 1.1 Total number of Doctorates awarded by UK HEIs, 1996–2002

Year	Total	Annual growth (%)
1996	10,800	
1997	11,860	9.8
1998	12,660	6.7
1999	13,140	3.8
2000	13,670	4.0
2001	14,115	3.2
2002	14,210	0.6
2003	14,875	0.95

Source: HESA (2004a: Table 12)

Table 1.2 The distribution of Doctorates awarded by institution (2000)

Quartile	Number of universities
Upper	5
Second	9
Third	18
Lower	97

Source: Millichope (2001)

Table 1.3 National distribution of Doctorates awarded 2002/03

England	12,270
Wales	605
Scotland	1,605
Northern Ireland	390
Total	14,875

Source: HESA (2004a: Table 12)

movement, and hence should be interpreted with some care. Nevertheless they do clearly demonstrate the dominance of English universities in the UK doctoral education market.

The figures also conceal the variety of awards. While the PhD may remain the most important of the doctoral awards, the last ten years has seen the development of awards such as the Professional Doctorate, Practice-Based Doctorate, PhD by Published Work, New Route PhD and others. Interestingly, we have no national data that allows us to differentiate these new awards in total numbers as HESA combines them all into the broad category of *Doctorate*. Again, this seems to be an example of lack of clarity that necessarily inhibits national planning or informed local development.

Increases in the training element of doctoral study

The criticisms and pressures noted above were also part of an increasing focus on the training element of doctoral study. Success rates of only one-third of candidates prompted those engaged in organizing doctoral study in universities to consider ways of supporting student learning about research (see Part 3 for further details regarding attrition and completion rates). That support has implied going beyond the provision of the right resources and adequate supervision to the inclusion of access to (a) courses dealing with subject specific skills and knowledge regarding research methods and (b) courses addressing the perceived needs of doctoral students with regard to generic skills and general issues of research methodology (see Chapter 3 for further details of skills training courses). One key difference between the picture of doctoral study in the twentieth century and the current situation is the introduction of taught elements and an increased focus on the doctoral student as a learner needing to develop definable, advanced skills. This is not a wholly new phenomenon since, in its earlier manifestations, doctoral study was largely a taught affair. There is now a sense in which doctoral study may be seen to be returning full-circle to its roots.

In part at least the move towards more taught elements within doctoral study is a reaction to students moving into doctoral study from a first degree and being deemed ill-prepared for the independent investigations required of them. In some of the social sciences and humanities it has become commonplace for a period of PhD study to be preceded by a Masters programme. The 1+3 model encouraged by Research Councils such as the ESRC is an example of the trend to see a one-year (or part-time equivalent) course as a prerequisite for a doctoral programme. This in turn mirrors the kinds of programme available in the USA. Indeed, the 1993 Government White Paper (DTI 1993) introduced the notion of a Masters of Research (MRes) award. This award was intended to give candidates structured experience of research methods and methodology. According to UKCGE (2002) this award has not proved universally popular and many HEIs have retained or introduced the awards of MA or MSc by Research, as will be noted in Chapter 3.

There has been considerable discussion about the need for, and type of, skills training. The inclusion of skills training in doctoral programmes raises questions about the fundamental importance of skills within the Doctorate itself and in approaches to doctoral assessment. Typically, though not universally, generic and specific skills are not assessed directly within the final doctoral examination. Skill learning is assumed to be evidenced within the submitted work and the way in which the candidate defends his/her work in the oral examination.

At an institutional level, there may be questions over the funding of skills training programmes. While there has been general agreement that such skills training is important, there has been little questioning of 'for whom?'. Without the research evidence, it may be suggested that the universal 'need' is predicated on a science model undertaken by 21-year-old graduates. As we have already noted, this kind of graduate and research programme is no longer the norm – if indeed it ever was.

Graduate schools

One of the significant changes in the last ten years in the management and organization of doctoral programmes has been the establishment of graduate schools. Unlike many aspects of doctoral education it is particularly fortunate that there have been two surveys of graduate schools which document both their initial development in the early years of the 1990s and their maturation in 2004 (UKCGE 1995; Woodward *et al.* 2004). In 1995 a significant number of universities had established graduate schools: 33 universities and one college of higher education had done so, with a further 23 universities having definite plans to establish such systems. Graduate schools were less common in the new (post-1992) universities, one-sixth of which had them, and in the colleges of higher education, one-tenth of which had them. By 2003/04 the graduate school had become the dominant model for the organization of graduate education across the sector. Two-thirds of the universities who responded to the UKCGE survey now had graduate schools while six other universities were considering establishing one.

Beneath the headline figures given above there is a range of models of what constitutes a graduate school and what role it performs. The model adopted depends, in part at least, on the size of the university and its number of doctoral students. In cases where there is a large number of doctoral students, the graduate school tends to be at faculty or departmental level. In a university with relatively few doctoral students, the graduate school will tend to be at university level. Also, the resources, facilities and responsibilities of graduate schools vary widely between the different models adopted. Many have dedicated accommodation for their staff with associated teaching and learning space for other staff and students. Many are responsible for research training programmes and in some cases for the training of supervisors. Particularly in the university-wide graduate school, quality assurance and student monitoring, the management and support for higher degree committees and institutional returns to the various agencies are often vested in the graduate school.

While this focus on the management and organization of doctoral programmes in graduate schools is, in our view, a very welcome addition to the internal structure of universities and may bring associated improvements in the quality of delivery of doctoral programmes, it is not without its tensions. Perhaps most important of these is the severing of any existing links between research students and the broader student population and the potential disenfranchising of departments and faculties from the research degree process in general.

Evidence

We have already noted the significant changes that have taken place in doctoral education in the last ten years. In writing this book we have become increasingly aware of the lack of UK research evidence for many of the changes. There are exceptions that we note; however, it remains true that in respect of many aspects of doctoral education the evidence that underpins the need for and direction of change is limited. Nor is acknowledgement given to the richer research evidence coming from North America and Australia. This is certainly true for the introduction of skills and supervisor training, and a point that is well exemplified by recent discussion about the issue of complaints and appeals.

A great deal is made of the number of complaints and appeals relating to research degree study as evidence that the doctoral process is not working properly. Wakeford's article (*The Guardian*, 16 March 2004) typifies some of the attitudes of those in and around academia and is used here solely as an exemplar of a prevalent view. His article appeared to be based on a 'number of complaints'. Clearly, all complaints are serious (albeit some may be spurious); however, institutional reaction to them in terms of policy must reflect their frequency and severity. There is an absence of any national data that allows us to state with any certainty how many complaints are dealt with annually with respect to doctoral students. Indeed, Wakeford (2004) does not give any indication of the size of his sample, how it was selected or whether or not it was representative. Similarly, he talks of failure due to bad supervision, yet currently there is no hard evidence about attrition in UK PhD programmes. Recent work in Canada and the USA has begun to shed some light on the issue, but currently no systematically gathered information is available in the UK – certainly nothing that allows a correlation, let alone a causal link between the quality of supervision and attrition.

The work that the Wellcome Trust (Wellcome Trust 2001; Frame and Allen 2002) has undertaken over the last four years, looking at the attitudes of students and supervisors in receipt of their bursaries, suggests that for this group many of our worst fears are *not* found. They did not find supervisors with vast overloads of students or students who were not receiving appropriate support. It is important then to get all this into perspective so as not to create antipathy in the academic community lambasted for its poor performance. It would also be unwise to instigate subsequent national and institutional regulation that is manifestly out of step with the real nature of the issue. Clearly, there have been complaints from research degree students and some HEIs in the UK have had to pay compensation to dissatisfied candidates, but while this is regrettable for both sides we suggest that this is not the angle from which to approach supervision and support for supervisors themselves. The HEFCE Improving Standards in Postgraduate Research Programmes document argued for the training of supervisors and this is reflected in the revised QAA Code of Practice (QAA 2004). However, this training should not be driven by a belief that all supervisors are poor. Clearly, they are not. Certainly, one would need to consider the number of complaints made against the (approximately) 14,000 doctoral awards that are made in the UK each year. Instead, training should be seen as a positive step in personal and professional development, helping all to improve understanding and performance of the task in hand. And in this context many UK universities have already moved a considerable way.

Themes in the future development of doctoral education in the UK

A *thematic approach*

This section sets out some of the themes that run throughout the book. Within these themes we subsume arguments about the advantages and disadvantages of different ways forward. Our original intention was to put down some specific issues – but more appropriate perhaps is to try to identify in broader terms the interrelationships between those issues. Our thematic approach consider the interplay between the international, national, institutional and personal issues related to the development of doctoral study.

A *two-tier structure of doctoral education*

There are ominous danger signs that doctoral education will develop into a two-tier structure in which, for a variety of reasons that we explore below, some students are treated differently and are therefore disadvantaged.

It is already clear that the levels of funding that currently go to universities vary significantly because of the funding model currently in place. For departments with significant 'QR funding' (funding directly from HEFCE to fund research – rated on the quality of research outputs), there is the potential for a well-funded student environment. For those students working in departments in which little or no QR funds are available, it is likely that support will be less generous. Indeed, it is arguable that without QR funds, universities should not be encouraging research degree students unless of course there is other significant external income to support them. The new funding model in England may exacerbate this position (HEFCE 2004).

This question is highlighted more specifically in the implementation of the Roberts recommendations on research training in which the Treasury has agree to allocate on average £850 per year per student to support skills training. This funding is, however, only currently available to students funded through the Research Councils. For those who are not funded through the Research Councils, research training will not be available, unless of course it is paid for directly by the sponsors or provided by the institution, regardless of funds available.

In a culture that stresses the need for equality of opportunity we have a situation where, within a single university, some students are entitled to more support than others. This division is open, publicly declared, virtually unchallenged and Government driven. Apart from the ethical consideration, this situation forces questions about the perceived purposes of the provision of doctoral study. The Government sets up research councils to filter funds down for the support of research in general, and research students form a specific part of that generality. Yet universities recruit research students without necessarily the support of that filtered down funding. The governmental view would seem to be that, in terms of the kinds of quality reviewing undertaken by QAA, all students should be equal yet, in terms of the funding mechanisms, some students will be 'more equal' than others. One theme of this book is therefore an exploration of the dissonance between the intentional and unintentional effects of national strategies in relation to the purposes and practices of doctoral education.

Levels of diversity

There is a danger of focusing the argument about standards of doctoral supervision and study on the full-time PhD student and his/her programme of work. Table 1.4 highlights the importance of part-time students across

Table 1.4 PGR students mode of study 2002/03

	Full-time	Part-time	Total
Old universities	49,600	44,370	93,970
Post-92 universities/Colleges/ Institutes	5,670	8,970	14,640
Grand total	55,270	53,340	108,610

Source: HESA (2004a: Table 9C)

the sector. While there is some ambiguity in the definition of part time – including in many cases, as it does, those students in writing-up mode, and often the destitute cast off from their Research Council grant – it is clear that there are large numbers of part-time students across the sector. While HESA records a 'writing up' category, which in 2002/03 included 18,740 students (HESA 2004a, Table A), many individual universities do not have such a category and simply transfer to part time those full-time students who have not submitted within the period of their stipend. Nor are part-time students simply a characteristic of the 'Modern Universities'. It seems, then, that if discussions relate to full-time mode only, there is a failure to take account of over 50,000 students. This is all the more concerning because it fails to recognize the contribution made to the furtherance of research by those studying in part-time mode. It would be naïve to think that only full-time students benefit from doctoral level study and, in turn, benefit society by their efforts. The tenets of lifelong learning hold true at doctoral level and, similarly, society is enriched by the contributions made in industry, commerce and the professions by those engaged in doctoral study whether they be registered full time or part time.

What, then, might be the differences between these two populations? Are there indeed two distinct groups or should we be referring to a continuum of involvement, from full time through part time to spare time? As with most part-time students, we are faced with the immediate questions of how much time they can devote to the project, what resources they have to support the work, and what other commitments they have to manage as well as the Doctorate.

These variables will affect all aspects of provision, from availability of supervisors in the evenings to the maximum period of registration. How do we transpose the expectation of full time to part time while recognizing the essential differences across the continuum of mode of study? It may be that it is not enough to simply make part time pro-rata twice as long as full time for many aspects of research degree study and to decide on what is best for full-time students and then, as a second thought, to translate that notion of 'best' to 'as appropriate' for those in part-time mode. There are differences of what is required as well as differences simply in terms of time on task.

The chapters in this book seek to explore the diversity inherent in doctoral study. In so doing it becomes ever more apparent that the concept of 'the doctoral student' is one typified more by heterogeneity than by homogeneity. Table 1.5, which presents the age structure of the population of first-year UK residenced doctoral students, highlights the importance, both for full-time and part-time provision, of those students over the age of 30. We argue that the differences within the doctoral student population are significant in terms of implications for what is required of supervision, provision of resources, monitoring and assessment. In short, we consider if, by treating all research students in the same way in terms of policy and/or practice, we misunderstand the situation and necessarily disadvantage some individuals, institutions and perhaps disciplines.

Table 1.5 Age structure: first-year UK students 2002/03

Age	Postgraduate research student	
	Full-time	*Part-time*
Under 21	50	5
21–24	6,250	600
25–29	1,755	925
30 plus	2,115	3,980
Total	10,170	5,510

Source: HESA (2004a: Tables 1d and 1h)

Diversity and awards

As well as diversity in kind and mode of study within the student population noted above, there is clearly a growing diversity of doctoral awards available in UK universities, although we do not as yet have the data to differentiate the Doctorate to make any statements about the relative importance of each. These levels of diversity within and across students and their programmes of study are acknowledged by QAA in their revised Code of Practice; however, the implications for the management and delivery of awards are not addressed in that Code. The matter is summarily dealt with in the section on Definitions.

Research Students
The precepts and explanations below are intended to be appropriate for the many different types of students undertaking research programmes in the UK, including full- and part-time students of all ages and with different needs, UK and international, and from all backgrounds.

Research Programmes
This document is intended to apply to a wide range of research qualifications. Specifically, it covers the PhD (including the New Route PhD and PhDs awarded on the basis of published work), all forms of taught or professional Doctorate, and research master's degrees that include a requirement for the student to produce original work.

(QAA 2004: 4)

Whether one Code, no matter how flexibly applied, can reflect such a diverse provision is surely debatable and one might legitimately ask whether such inclusiveness is driven by a simple Treasury expedient based on the fact that, in theory at least, all such programmes are eligible to receive funding council grant for research.

In summary, the situation in the UK is that there is a range of different doctoral awards each with its own distinctive, and in some ways idiosyncratic, interpretation of (i) ways of learning and 'content' to be learned and

(ii) ways of assessing and knowing what is to be assessed. This theme of distinctiveness of awards within the overall doctoral frame of reference is explored in later chapters.

International recruitment

We note in later chapters the increasing importance of overseas students to UK universities and their importance to both university finance and, in some subjects, to the UK research effort. While welcoming overseas students to the UK, there are risks to both the students and to the UK research effort from such a growing number. In some areas overseas students dominate research groups; and while they may not be taking places from UK students, they may distort the long-term research market by deviating attention, at institutional level at least, from the longer-term research deficit in the UK. For many who do not return to their home country, this negates the original intentions of sponsor countries in home country capacity building. In some cases sponsor countries and universities are recognizing the value of joint delivery where a significant part of the award is delivered in the sponsor country.

An underpinning theme to later chapters is, then, the impact of an ever-diversifying culture in the field of doctoral study. In our own view, increasing the cultural diversity of the research student population brings great strengths to the general development of research in the UK – the interplay of ideas from different cultures and different disciplines across cultures may be judged as essential to the pushing back of the boundaries of knowledge. In respecting this strength there is also a need to take account of the range of impact factors when overseas recruitment becomes an essential, and in some areas a predominant, aspect of the changing research degree student population. We would endorse the views of Triggle and Miller when, speaking of the USA, they suggest that 'they (overseas students) should not be used to cover the failings of the (research degree) enterprise, which is becoming increasingly unattractive to US students' (Triggle and Miller 2002: 290).

UK doctoral provision within a global context

Students referred to in the above section come to the UK to study at doctoral level for a range of reasons. Two prime reasons might be the status of the UK award and the use of English as the language of delivery and examination. Of course, it would be unwise for the UK to be complacent on either count. Research degree provision continues to develop in other countries and English is the common language of study beyond the UK's borders (e.g. in some Scandinavian countries English is the language used for academic study in universities). The UK's place within Europe, the increasing ease of travel and communication world wide and the extension of English as a common academic language mean that the UK is a competitor in a global market in a way that was not the case some ten years ago. Similarly, the Bologna process now includes the Doctorate and hence the UK's way of delivery and the kinds of award offered at doctoral level are coming under scrutiny in the context of other European provisions in these respects. Some of the idiosyncrasies of the UK system may therefore become more apparent and more open to challenge. In the light of the above, our consideration of aspects of the Doctorate in this book needs to be referenced within a context that extends beyond the UK's borders. Space does not permit us to develop an international perspective and in this sense perhaps it is not a 'theme' as such, but nevertheless the issues to be discussed need to be considered within a global rather than a parochial perspective, and that is what we have attempted to do.

The role of doctoral study in the development of knowledge

This book discusses the way in which doctoral study is organized and delivered in the UK. In this sense the book is concerned with matters of teaching and learning; universities take on students and train or teach them to an academic standard that is described as doctoral. But there is another dimension that is reflected in various chapters: the role that doctoral study plays in extending the knowledge base of the UK and beyond. In the education system doctoral work is perhaps unique in that it necessarily (if it is successful) contributes to knowledge. Doctoral study contributes then to the mission of universities in a way that transcends the teaching of skills and knowledge to students. Clearly, the reference here is to that part of a university's mission that relates to 'undertaking research'. A theme of the book is therefore the interplay, and sometimes tension between, the need to 'teach' and the need to 'research'. Outcomes in these two respects may be different within a single case of the interrelationship between student, supervisor, institution and project.

Research degree-awarding powers and university status

Many within the UK would see university status and research degree-awarding powers as inextricably linked. This view is coterminous with the notion that a university necessarily requires active researching and, further, that active researching involves students operating at doctoral level. Of course, these necessary linkages are not universally accepted; in Germany, for example, only some universities have research degree awarding powers, yet those without such powers are still considered universities. A similar situation arises in the USA. The importance of research degree-awarding powers was recognized by many of the former polytechnics in the UK during the period of regulation by the Council for National Academic Awards (CNAA) during which many institutions sought, and obtained, such powers. Some, such as Leeds Metropolitan University, did not however seek such powers; they continued to use the committees and sub-committees of the CNAA for the approval and award of Doctorates.

In later chapters we discuss in more detail the relationship between such powers and university status. This is related to the discussion in the Higher Education White Paper (DfES 2003) concerning the concentration of research awards in the UK, the fact that for many universities the number of awards made annually is very small and the questionable economics of research degree production. The theme here, therefore, is the way in which the place of individual institutions in the 'marketplace' of doctoral provision may be changing and the implications of such change for the sector.

Stipends

It is expected that the recent welcomed rise in stipends for research students, and the more flexible approach to allocation of funds, will make a significant impact on the recruitment of high-quality research students. However, the stipend has not addressed all the issues with which quality candidates should be concerned. Nor has it really clarified the status of the research student (student or employee?), exacerbated by the presence of research assistants or Graduate Teaching Associates (GTAs) working side by side with research students on research projects. New stipend levels are based on a relationship with net average starting salaries of new graduates. As we note later, this begs the question of average as opposed to good salaries and the other benefits of being employed and salaried, as opposed to receiving a stipend. These other benefits include National Insurance and Superannuation Contributions of both employer and employee plus the years of reckonable service and pension levels. We will argue that a move towards regarding the doctoral student as an employee for those in receipt of a stipend resolves many of these tensions.

As well as these issues, the rise in stipends will ultimately reduce the number of fully funded researchers unless more funds are fed into the system. This will increasingly be the case for universities offering their own bursaries and for whom the funding pot is finite and – in some cases within the new funding model – diminishing. This will ultimately impact on the number of Doctorates awarded annually and the growth of UK research. This highlights the general lack of clarity on the total number of Doctorates required more generally in the economy and takes us back to the 1993 White Paper, *Realising our Potential* (DTI 1993), in which the link was made between the quality and capability of research students and the national economy – *but not the number required*. Again, this tension is a theme that is explored and revisited throughout the book.

The quality regime

We began this chapter with the quote from the UKCGE report that discussed the cottage industry nature of the doctoral process. This has certainly changed with the growth in graduate schools and the more systematic regulatory environment that has been provided by the QAA. The new, revised, Code of Practice (QAA 2004), discussed in more detail later in this book, will further enhance the quality of doctoral education. The key to success of the Code will of course be in its implementation and the manner in which audit teams interpret and monitor at institutional level. Evidence from audit to press is not very encouraging (HEFCE 2001). It will be vital that the selection and training of auditors reflects the need to enhance further the quality of doctoral provision.

Of particular interest will be the way in which universities respond to the demands of the Code. As we have noted elsewhere (Green and Powell 2004) the increased complexity of the Code may create problems for many of those universities that have relatively small numbers of research students – probably over 50% of the total number of universities – and cause them to reconsider the financial viability of delivering Doctorates at all. We return to this particular issue later in the book. Throughout the book a theme is the effect of the increasing emphasis on the overt monitoring of the quality of doctoral provision both within institutions and by Government agencies.

Doctoral students and institutional performance

The Doctorate has not escaped from the quest for measures of institutional performance and the performance indicator analysis adopted by the funding councils in recent years (HEFCE 2004). In addition to the Research Assessment Exercise – which assesses the quality of research, including doctoral students – the performance indicators concern themselves with the quantity of research outputs relative to the resources consumed, and hence are supposedly an indication of the efficiency of production. It is notable that the funding councils appear to be rather coy about the use of the indicators in research. The discussion of the overall use of indicators in the HEFCE document *Guide to Performance Indicators in Higher Education* (HEFCE 2003c) for example, explains in some detail how the indicators are calculated for all aspects – except research and research degrees – of the work of the HEIs.

In the case of doctoral students the performance indicators (PIs) are expressed in terms of: (i) proportion of PhDs awarded per proportion of academic staff costs and (ii) proportion of PhDs awarded per proportion of funding council QR funding allocation.

The institutional tables derived from this data make interesting and at times challenging reading, throwing some light on the many contradictions and inconsistencies in the current system and institutional approaches to doctoral education. For example, they highlight that several universities greatly exceed the sector average in terms of output per unit QR input. Initially this might appear to suggest that those institutions are very efficient in Doctorate production relative to the sector as a whole. However, more detailed scrutiny of the data shows that, for many, the level of QR and hence institutional funding for research is very low, raising questions about the quality of the student experience or the level of institutional cross-subsidy required to deliver doctoral programmes.

One of our themes in this book is therefore the relationship between individual students, institutions and Government agencies in terms of performance, cost and efficiency.

Conclusion

When one tries to set out some context for considering doctoral study, it becomes clear that such study is ill-defined because the awards to which it leads are often ill-defined. There is little national let alone international consensus on what we mean when we talk about doctoral awards, how they relate to each other and how their attainment can be judged. Yet the award has a common currency; there is a sense in which people understand what the term 'doctor' means, even if a closer definition may be elusive. In this sense the devil is in the detail, and it is some of this detail that this book seeks to explore.

It is important when considering the future of doctoral study to take account of the totality of the situation. There is a tendency, as exemplified by the Wakeford article discussed above, to judge the whole from an element of its parts. Conclusions about the best ways forward in terms of provision of doctoral programmes, criteria for doctoral level awards, supervisory procedures, examination processes and all the other doctoral-related issues need to be made with a view to overall coherence. The student experience, institutional rigour in applying standards of academic achievement, the advancement of knowledge in all intellectual spheres, and national and international concerns about a doctoral level of application within society need to be considered in relation to each other and with a view to a unified notion of what the doctoral award means and what can be achieved by the continuing development of doctoral programmes of study.

This reflection can only be undertaken when the full range of issues influencing the future of the Doctorate are fully understood. The remainder of this book will examine in more detail the many questions that we have raised in this chapter. A holistic approach to the current text provides a starting point from which to better understand both the direction being taken by doctoral education in the UK and how it fits into the wider context of national and international research agendas.

Summary issues

- Postgraduate research has changed and continues to change with an increasing number of students, studying in a small concentration of universities.
- Many of the issues identified as contributing to quality have been addressed but we are in danger of developing a two-tier system of delivery.
- The student body is becoming increasingly diverse with part-time, mid-career students making up a significant proportion. But have universities and funders fully recognized this fact and responded appropriately?
- To what extent do we simply respond to changing patterns of demand? Should we be setting targets for the number of Doctorates awarded? Do institutions plan research student numbers within a context of research need, lifelong learning or knowledge transfer?

2

Doctoral study, Government and the workplace

Introduction

While the individual university is the guardian of the Doctorate in the UK and assures its standard and quality, Government and other agencies have a significant influence on the nature of doctoral programmes. This influence might be exerted directly through the advice and recommendations that push the award in a particular direction or less directly through manipulation of the funding regimes, reporting structures or regulatory requirements. Government in particular is anxious to ensure that public money is spent appropriately in the pursuit of doctoral education and that its research objectives are achieved. At times these external influences are at odds with the views of universities for whom academic freedom and the pursuit of knowledge, free of regulation and influence, is an overriding requirement. In this chapter we look at the nature of some of these external influences, some of their outcomes and the tensions they, at times, create.

Background

The importance of research and the PhD to the sustainability of the national economy is of great significance to Governments that fund universities and students to undertake doctoral study. Discussion of the role of doctoral study and its value to society is not new. In the late 1960s a working group of the Committee for Manpower Resources for Science and Technology (CMRST) observed

> *This Committee's recommendations are that the scale of support for postgraduate training leading to academic research should be reviewed, that research grant support involving manpower should in general rise in step with the growth of university staff in the three fields, that industry and the schools should take all possible steps to attract graduates of high quality; that further attention should be*

given to meeting demand in industry and the schools, by redeployment, and the possibility should be examined of developing more long-term quantitative assessments of the balance of distribution of qualified manpower, in order to assist long-term plans for collaborative response of education and industry.

(CMRST 1996)

However education should take the initiative, e.g. examining the PhD and trying to orientate it towards the requirements of industry; while industry should vigorously recruit people qualified in science, engineering and technology.

(CMRST 1968)

In the early 1990s the desire to make research, and the Doctorate in particular, more relevant to the needs of the national economy intensified. Several national stakeholders began to question the nature and purpose of the PhD. Pressures for change were driven by three key concerns: (i) an apparent loss of international standing of the British PhD, (ii) lack of personal and professional skills, and (iii) disappointing time to completion and completion rates (although, as we show in Chapter 9, this latter reservation was probably ill founded at least for well-funded students).

The 1993 White Paper, *Realising our Potential*, formalized the debate about research and research training arguing that 'the Government welcomes the growth in postgraduate courses. It is concerned, however, that the traditional PhD does not always match up to the needs of a career outside research in academia or an industrial research laboratory' (DTI 1993: 57).

The White Paper highlighted the perceived nature of the concerns about the PhD when it stated that 'a period spent in PhD training represents a substantial investment of public funds and it is important to ensure that it represents good value for money for the taxpayer as well as the individual concerned' (DTI 1993: 57).

It went on to argue that there is a role for preparatory matters in research training when it suggested that 'for most students who have undertaken a first degree, the Master's qualification will provide an opportunity to acquire extra knowledge and skills, either in preparation for a period of research training leading to a PhD or for employment' (DTI 1993: 61).

Through the offices of the Office of Science and Technology (OST), Government steered a policy towards much more training in research methods and generic skills which led to a fundamental shift in the way in which PhDs are perceived and delivered. Specific details of these are discussed below. In 1994 the OST published a paper building on the proposals of the White Paper. It argued that those trained to postgraduate level should have skills better matched to the needs of potential employers, including those outside the academic world, and that this should include elements of non-science specific training including at the very least communication skills and human, material and financial resource management (OST 1994).

It outlined a recommended structure for a new one-year Research Masters (MRes) degree, which would include both taught and research components. This degree was intended as a foundation either for a Doctorate or for a research career in industry or the public sector. The OST proposed:

- a significant research component (60% of the 42-week postgraduate year);
- the provision of a grounding in research techniques relevant to a range of disciplines as well as the development of specialist knowledge;
- the inclusion of modules intended to broaden the students' experience and to equip them with transferable skills in management, communication, commercial understanding, the exploitation of research, and team working.

The Confederation of British Industry's response (CBI 1994) to the OST paper supported the implementation of pilot MRes programmes, provided that the Research Masters degree was seen as a valid terminal degree and not simply as a route to a PhD. The CBI also emphasized the importance of reviewing the structure of the pilot programmes and evaluating the extent to which they met the requirements of employers. The shift towards more generic training in the British Doctorate was then established.

This theme was picked up again in the Dearing report (1997) set up 'to make recommendations on how the purposes, shape, structure, size and funding of higher education, including support for students, should develop to meet the needs of the United Kingdom over the next 20 years'. The scope of the inquiry included teaching, learning, scholarship and research (Dearing 1997, Chairman's Foreword).

While there were a large number of recommendations in both Dearing and Garrick (Garrick 1996), the major thrust of the reports was towards the future funding of undergraduate education. Little was said explicitly about postgraduate research programmes other than, and therefore very significantly, a recommendation about postgraduate training:

> *We recommend to institutions of higher education that they should, over the next two years, review their postgraduate research training to ensure that they include, in addition to understanding of a range of research methods and training in appropriate technical skills, the development of professional skills, such as communication, self-management and planning.*
>
> (Dearing 1997, Recommendation 31)

Dearing therefore added to the growing body of opinion that training provision within the doctoral process was still less than perfect and did not provide students with the skills they would need in subsequent employment.

The need for training to satisfy the requirements of industry and the professions was well established by the end of the 1990s. The changes had gathered momentum during the 1990s to be accepted without question. There was, however, little if any research evidence to suggest that this shift was appropriate and little to support its efficacy. Nevertheless other agencies noted these shifts in policy and interpreted them in different ways – but with the same purpose in mind.

The Research Councils

Funded directly by the OST, the Research Councils have been active in interpreting Government policy and introducing initiatives that have reflected the views of Government and in so doing have influenced the way in which the Doctorate is managed. These might usefully be described as Policy Developments and Schemes.

Policy developments

Early in the process and responding to perceived need for training, the ESRC introduced its Postgraduate Training Guidelines (ESRC 1991), which identified the skills training that universities had to provide if they were to receive ESRC funding for doctoral study. The guidelines were of significance as they were specific in their identification of skills requirements of social science doctoral students in the different disciplines covered by the Council and provided a model for others to follow.

The latest guidelines from the ESRC (2001) indicate a one-year full-time masters course in research training as a necessary precursor to any recognized three-year doctoral programme, their (1+3) full-time model or (2+5) part-time model. Approved masters programmes are required to have substantial generic as well as subject-oriented research training elements followed by a research project.

The defined model has characteristics very similar to some of the models of the MRes, which the ESRC deliberately discarded, creating potential confusion among both students and potential employers about the nature of the programmes, both of which may be offered in the same university, faculty or department.

The MRes, on the other hand, has been adopted by many universities and supported by four research councils – the Biotechnology and Biological Sciences Research Council (BBSRC), the Engineering and Physical Sciences Research Council (EPSRC), the Medical Research Council (MRC) and the Natural Environment Research Council (NERC), who agreed to support proposals from universities for MRes programmes. By 1995/96 23 universities had responded to the Research Council initiative with a total of 35 courses. Four Research Councils were funding a total of 275 students (BBSRC 45, EPSRC 160, MRC 25, NERC 45). ESRC and PPARC did not participate in the MRes development. The UK Council for Graduate Education (UKCGE) reported 27 universities offering Research Council supported programmes with a further 18 offering programmes without such support in 2000 (UKCGE 2001).

In 1997 the OST issued an interim report on the first two years of the pilot MRes scheme. This document commented on statistics relating to the programmes, on monitoring visits to participating universities and on questionnaires completed by students at the beginning and end of their courses.

The broad conclusions reported by OST were:

- the high demand for MRes courses – three out of the four Research Councils have had 100% take-up on places offered;
- the high levels of student satisfaction with courses, and indications that student concerns over the worth of such a newly established qualification were diminishing as the reputation of the Research Masters was consolidated.

The report also indicated that the proportion of MRes students holding first-class degrees compares favourably with the proportion among students opting for traditional MSc programmes.

The OST report said little about the content of courses, the way in which they are delivered, the nature of the research outcomes expected and how they are assessed – all essential indicators of the success the courses have in responding to the requirement of Government. These characteristics are also important indicators of the way in which courses are adapting to the changing demands being made on researchers involving, for example, generic skills, report writing, presentation skills, team working, time management, interpersonal and dissemination skills.

An analysis of the nature of the evidence presented for assessment on MRes programmes suggests, for example, that programmes are addressing the changing needs of researchers and the requirements of employers and are positively encouraging students to experiment with ways of demonstrating research competencies and presenting their findings (Shaw and Green 1996). As we will show in the chapters on doctoral examination, there is little evidence that such innovation is being carried through into PhD outcomes and assessment.

Government, however, appears to have been satisfied at the achievement of the MRes. John Battle, Minister of State for Science, Energy and Industry, wrote in a response to a Parliamentary Question in February 1998,

> *overall the MRes continues to make good progress, with courses providing high quality research training. The MRes must remain a self standing degree and its design including a significant research component should be unchanged.*
>
> (UKCGE 2001a: 11)

Schemes

The EPSRC has developed a range of schemes that build on the Government's commitment to knowledge transfer and economic growth, bringing the research students and their supervisors into collaborations with industry. Even before the 1993 White Paper, they offered schemes such as:

- Collaborative Awards in Science and Engineering (CASE Awards)
- Total Technology Research Studentships
- Industrial Studentships
- Integrated Graduate Recruitment Scheme.

These schemes have been enhanced significantly so that the various Councils offer a wide range of industrially linked studentships (see EPSRC website www.epsrc.ac.uk).

A further response from the Research Councils was the introduction of the Graduate School Programme, a short residential programme concentrating on generic skills and team building which was managed by EPSRC on behalf of the Research Councils.

The Graduate School Programme, which concentrated on interpersonal and team skills, was designed and delivered by the Careers Research and Advisory Centre (CRAC) and the GPA Partnership. The programme consisted of five-day residential courses run at various locations across the UK. The schools had the broad aims of developing self-confidence and self-esteem in a multidisciplinary and support team environment. The schools were not compulsory and consequently attracted varying responses from students and supervisors, reflected at times in very low participation rates. For many they were seen as irrelevant or taking the students away from their research. Although the schools were open to students who are not funded by the Research Councils, lack of university funds meant that very few non-Research Council students attended, thus creating unequal opportunity among doctoral students even in the same department or research group. The programme was replaced in 2003 by the UK GRAD Programme.

Arts and Humanities Research Board

The Arts and Humanities Research Board (AHRB) has taken a different approach to research training. The AHRB has very recently added a specific training requirement to the PhD programmes that it funds, in the form of a framework.

> *The new framework is intended as a means of enabling institutions to reassure the AHRB that the doctoral students it funds receive appropriate and relevant preparation, training and support for their development, helping them both to complete a high-quality doctoral thesis and to develop a range of knowledge, understanding and skills necessary for their future employment.*

(AHRB 2004)

The framework adopts an alternative approach to that of the Research Councils and is needs-based, as advocated in the UKCGE report *Research Training in the Creative and Performing Arts and Design* (UKCGE 2001b). It is more sensitive to the distinctive and widely differing characteristics of research in the arts and humanities, without detailed prescription of what should be provided. In arguing for a needs-based approach, it offers a model that others might consider evaluating.

UK GRAD Programme

Since 2003 the 'UK GRAD Programme' has adopted many of the roles associated with research training as far as research council students are concerned. Its vision continues the relentless quest to ensure that the link between the postgraduate researcher and economic competitiveness is maintained and enhanced.

> *Our vision is for all postgraduate researchers to be fully equipped and encouraged to complete their studies successfully and then to make the successful transition from their PhD studies to their future careers.*
>
> (UK GRAD Programme 2004b)

> *Doctoral researchers are our most talented: they have the potential to make a significant difference to the economic competitiveness of the UK. The UK GRAD Programme has a key role in enabling them to realize their potential.*
>
> (UK GRAD Programe 2004b)

The UK GRAD Programme is deliberately regional in its approach, focusing its work around regional centres and in so doing has structures in place to address the increasing pressures for regional collaboration in the delivery of many aspects of research

Joint statement of the Research Councils and the AHRB

Building on these origins, the Research Councils and the AHRB came together and jointly agreed a set of requirements for research training in their funded programmes, the so-called *Joint Statement of the Research Councils'/ AHRB's Skills Requirements*. The statement is significant, not least because it brought together all the Councils and the AHRB and hence suggested that there was pressure to be seen to be acting in harmony on this potentially contentious issue. It gave an important steer to others, including universities, who could no longer argue that the skills requirement applied to 'other' disciplines or groups of students.

The purpose of the statement is 'to give a common view of the skills and experience of a typical research student, thereby providing universities with a clear and consistent message aimed at helping them to ensure that all research training was of the highest standard, across all disciplines' (Research Councils/AHRB 2001). Quite where this list of skills comes from is doubtful; certainly it did not involve HEIs nor is it based on any serious research about needs. The Councils and the AHRB emphasized that the statement should not be regarded as definitive, and they make it clear that it has less significance than the research work itself and should not be seen as a checklist for assessment. This suggests that the Councils are not really clear about the position of training within the doctoral process – an ambivalence that will do little to encourage students of its importance. It further diminishes what otherwise would be seen as a powerful statement. If the statements are to have any meaning beyond paying lip service to the demands of Government, it is essential that their achievement is acknowledged, recorded and ultimately assessed. We will return to this in considering the final assessment of research awards in Chapters 11 and 12. The seven groups of skills are set out in Table 2.1.

The Roberts review, *SET for Success* (Roberts 2002) added weight to the requirement, particularly for science and engineering students, that generic training programmes should be compulsory. Roberts recommended that each student should have a minimum of two weeks training per year and that this should be supported by additional money; this funding is popularly referred to as Roberts Money. It is unclear where the quantum of two weeks came from.

There remains some disquiet about the approach to research training and the link to employability skills in terms of content, approaches to delivery, certification, time spent away from 'the research', its compulsory nature and assessment. Indeed, the insistence on skills training has not always been received well by students and supervisors, many of whom suggest that it diverts from the research enterprise in itself.

The National Postgraduate Committee (NPC) notes with concern:

> . . . *however, it needs to be recognised that an increased emphasis on structured training as part of a research degree will significantly change the nature of the degree. Many students are concerned that they will have less time to carry out research; this means that either completion times for research theses will increase, or expectations of the content of theses will have to be lowered.*

(NPC 2001)

A recent report by the UKCGE notes

> *the result is that while there is widespread agreement – particularly among university managers – about the need for, and generic purposes of doctoral research training, thereby is also wide spread unease and scepticism – particularly among students and their supervisors – about the value of what is being provided.*

(UKCGE 2001c: 15)

Table 2.1 Skills training requirements for research students

A	Research Skills and Techniques
B	Research Environment
C	Research Management
D	Personal Effectiveness
E	Communication Skills
F	Networking and Team Working
G	Career Management

And, although the UKCGE report goes on to argue that research and scholarship in the humanities is distinctive, evidence from elsewhere suggests a similar disquiet about research training. Attendance at the Research Council funded 'Graduate Schools' which was free to all Research Council funded students struggled to attract 50% of eligible students.

More recently Mullins has explored this question in the Australian context, in a recent poster entitled 'Student perspectives on generic skills – Are we trying to sell pogo sticks to kangaroos?' (Mullins 2004b). Presenting data from several student surveys including the PREQ (Postgraduate Research Experience Questionnaire) he concludes that

> *we are in danger of devoting time, effort and valuable resources to skill development programs that students don't believe they need. Proponents of these programs will need to convince students that the programs add genuine value to students' existing research programs and that the extra time and effort is worthwhile.*

(Mullins 2004b, p. 1)

The Joint Statement is equally ambivalent about the acquisition of the skills it is recommending. It goes on to add the caveat 'that the development of wider employment-related skills should not detract from that core objective of making a substantial, original contribution to knowledge . . ., normally leading to published work' (Research Councils/AHRB 2001, www.grad. ac.uk/3_2_1.jsp).

The need for training was included in the first QAA Code of Practice for the Assurance of Academic Quality and Standards in Higher Education, Section 1: postgraduate research programmes (QAA 1999). Precept 13 states that: 'Research students should have access to training sufficient to gain the skills they need to design and complete their programmes effectively and to help prepare themselves for their subsequent career.'

The explanation beneath the precept outlines briefly how universities might implement the precept.

The 2004 revision of the Code is much more explicit about the need for training and devotes three precepts (18, 19 and 20) to the subject (Table 2.2). Each precept is followed by a full explanation of how institutions

Table 2.2 QAA Code of Practice: postgraduate research programmes

Precept 18	Institutions will provide research students with appropriate opportunities for personal and professional development.
Precept 19	Each student's development needs will be identified and agreed jointly by the student and appropriate academic staff, initially during the student's induction period; they will be regularly reviewed during the research programme and amended as appropriate.
Precept 20	Institutions will provide opportunities for research students to maintain a record of personal progress, which includes reference to the development of research and other skills.

may wish to implement it. Comparison between the two editions of the Code in the context of research training and employability highlights the growing emphasis on this aspect of doctoral work. However, the Code highlights one of the key problems associated with the increasing emphasis on training – that of explicitly giving credit to the work undertaken when it says 'Institutions may also wish to implement some form of recognition of the acquisition of transferable skills in parallel with, or as part of, the academic assessment of the student's progress' (QAA 2004: 22).

The Funding Councils

The Funding Councils (HEFCE, SHEFC, HEFCW) have increasingly been concerned about the quality of the doctoral student experience. The origins of these concerns go back some time, as the Harris report in 1996 recommended that:

> *each institution, where relevant to its mission, should consider, and keep under review, its organisational structure to ensure that this is the most appropriate to facilitate the work of postgraduate students, should monitor and manage graduate studies and should develop graduate recruitment and teaching policies, consonant with its research, teaching and learning objectives.*
>
> (Harris 1996: para. 4.55)

Subsequent comments by HEFCE in the Review of the Research Assessment Exercise (RAE) identified the need to examine the practice of research training in order to produce thresholds of provision and good practice guidelines (HEFCE 2000b).

> *Given the importance of this issue for the sustainability of the research base, and for a continued flow of highly trained individuals to meet the demands of industry and society more generally, we propose that the HE funding bodies, with the Research Councils, industry, charities and other interested bodies, should develop minimum criteria for postgraduate research training. These would apply equally to all institutions, and be applied as a condition for the receipt of funding for research students. Adherence to these criteria would be judged in future RAEs after 2001.*
>
> (HEFCE 2000b)

This was subsequently emphasized in the report on the consultation which stated that 'there was encouragement to the Council to implement the recommendations of the review by working with other bodies to establish minimum standards (and good practice) for research degree provision, and exploring means to help institutions to meet those standards, including assisting collaborations' (HEFCE 2001: Key points, 8). The joint Funding Councils subsequently commissioned consultants to develop a framework of standards and associated thresholds under the Chair of Roland Lewinsky. The report, *Improving Standards in Postgraduate Research Programmes* (HEFCE

2003a) laid the foundations for the development of the new QAA Code of Practice (QAA 2004).

The report identified a number of threshold standard that institutions would have to meet (Table 2.3). Following two phases of consultation – an initial informal consultation and subsequently a formal one – a revised proposal emerged, significantly modified and with fewer thresholds (Table 2.4). In the consultations, institutions were generally favourably disposed towards the proposal but were unhappy about four issues in particular. (see Table 2.5). As a consequence, the Funding Councils accepted the need to modify the proposals and produced their final document in late 2003 (HEFCE 2003b: 23).

The shift of emphasis that resulted from the consultations is a useful indication of the way in which universities have begun to assert their authority against what many see as growing interference by the Government. This is particularly reflected in this context where the Government of the day has attempted to steer the development of the Doctorate by mechanisms such as those noted above.

The Funding Councils took the advice of institutions, recognized that there was duplication between the Improving Standards agenda and the Quality Assurance Agency's (QAA) Code of Practice and asked the QAA to revise the section of its Code relating to Postgraduate Research Programmes.

Quality Assurance Agency

The QAA was established in 1997 following the Dearing and Garrick reports (Dearing 1997; Garrick 1996) to provide Government with reassurance about the quality of Higher Education in the UK. The Agency's role, as it affects doctoral education, is implemented through three aspects of its work: its Code of Practice, Institutional Audit and the Qualifications Framework.

The Code of Practice: Code of Practice for the assurance of academic quality and standards in higher education

Section 1: Postgraduate Research Programmes was the first section of the Code to be published (January 1999). Given the relatively small population of postgraduate research students it is noteworthy that it was 'first' in this way. We might ask whether this reflected a concern by the QAA of the need to improve the quality assurance of Postgraduate Research (PGR). It is also notable that while the remainder of the Code covers all aspects of taught provision, including postgraduate taught provision, it was felt necessary and appropriate to have a separate Code for all aspects of PGR.

The revised Code, launched in September 2004, is a longer and more

Table 2.3 Framework of quality standards for research degree programmes. Threshold standards: Informal consultation.

1	*Institutional arrangements*

1A Institution's code of practice for RDPs must meet, and preferably exceed, the standards in the framework.
1B Institution to monitor, review and act on the application of the standards in its code of practice, including the various standards set out in the framework.
1C Institutional and unit performance to be monitored [annually] on progress and attrition against agreed targets including gender and ethnic groupings:
  • submission rates [80% within 4 years]
  • average time to submission
  • completion rates [80% within 4.5 years]
  • level of appeals, complaints
  • student feedback.

2	*Research environment*

2A RDPs offered in units with a minimum RAE rating (consistent with QR funding).
2B Demonstrate, within the unit/cognate area, a way of providing effective interactions:
  • with a minimum of [5] research active staff/post-Doctorates
  • between a group of at least [10] students.
2C Sufficient facilities for the research project, including library and IT facilities, should be available at or above the level needed for research of a national standard.

3	*The selection, admission, enrolment and induction of students*

3A Institutional minimum level of academic entry standard [2.1, masters, or institutionally defined equivalent APL/APEL].
3B Selection process and admission decision to involve at least [2] experienced and research active academics, trained in admission processes.
3C Open access to all relevant material on web.
3D Formal offer letter should include:
  • fees and charges
  • period of study
  • direction of study
  • specific requirements
  • other requirements
  • direction to other relevant information and codes of practice (e.g. on the web)
  • student's responsibilities.
3E Student and institution to sign up to an agreement on the learning outcomes of the RDP.
3F Institution to provide a formal induction process with monitored attendance.

Table 2.4 Minimum threshold standards and good practice guidelines for RDPs.
Formal consultation

---

1   *Institutional arrangements*
    (a)   Implementation of a code of practice across the whole institution covering
          the eight headings in this framework

2   *Research environment*
    (a)   Unit/cognate area of research to facilitate effective interactions between
          the student and a mix of active researchers and students. For units
          with small numbers of active researchers and students, provision should
          be made for interaction with related units at the same or other
          institutions.
    (b)   70% of submissions made within four years for full-time students, or eight
          years for part-time students (calculated at institutional level).

3   *The selection, admission, enrolment and induction of students*
    (a)   Normal entry requirement to be either:
          • 2(i) degree in a relevant subject (or overseas equivalent).
          • Relevant Masters qualification (or overseas equivalent).
          • Institutionally defined equivalent accreditation of prior learning (APL)
            or experiential learning (APEL).

4   *Supervisory arrangements*
    (a)   All new supervisors to undertake mandatory institutionally specified
          training.
    (b)   Supervision to be provided by a supervisory team, preferably comprising at
          least two demonstrably active researchers with relevant knowledge and
          skills, one of whom should be designated as the main supervisor with
          overall responsibility for the student. Where this is not possible, one
          supervisor with relevant knowledge and skills is acceptable provided that
          an independent adviser is appointed to whom the student can refer
          general academic and pastoral issues.
    (c)   Main supervisor normally to have had experience of at least one successful
          supervision within a supervisory team (defined as taking a student all the
          way through to a research degree award). Where the main supervisor has
          not had such experience, supervision must be provided by a supervisory
          team comprising at least one demonstrably active researcher with
          experience of at least two successful supervisions.
    (d)   Main supervisor should normally take prime responsibility for a maximum
          of six students (head count). Where the main supervisor has responsibility
          for more than six students, the institution should demonstrate how it
          guarantees adequate contact between student and supervisor and avoids
          overburdening supervisors.
    (e)   There should be regular structured interactions between the student and
          the supervisor or supervisory team to report, discuss and agree academic
          and personal progress. Outcomes of all such interactions to be recorded.

5   *Initial review and subsequent progress*
    (b)   Progress of both full-time and part-time students to be formally reviewed
          annually by panels, including at least one person independent of the
          supervisory team.

(c) Final examination to be by a *viva* with an independent panel of at least two examiners who are demonstrably research active, at least one of whom is an external examiner.

6   *The development of research and other skills*
Institution to provide the student with access to a training programme to develop research and other skills, as outlined in the Research Councils' skills statement.

8   *Appeals and complaints*
(a) Institution to arrange and publicize separate, fair, transparent, robust and consistently applied complaints and appeals procedures, appropriate to all categories of students.

Table 2.5 Improving standards consultation: Key concerns in formal consultation.

Proposed targets on submission rates.
Maximum number of students per supervisor.
Numerical thresholds on critical mass.
Need for a separate set of standards from QAA code.

Source: HEFCE (2004)

thorough document which, prepared with the help of representatives from the sector, responds to the views of the Better Regulation Review Group (BRRG). The guidance sections of the first edition of the Code are replaced by explanatory text indicating why the individual precepts have been included. The QAA emphasizes that the Code should not be regarded as a document requiring compliance by institutions, but rather as one providing a reference to widely agreed approaches to good practice in the relevant areas.

Notwithstanding the reference to the BRRG, the Code remains heavily prescribed and, for some, unnecessarily so. The UKCGE response to the draft noted that

> *the current draft is considerably more prescriptive, longer and more complex than the previous version with a total of 30 precepts as opposed to 25 in the previous version. The general tone of the draft is also more imperative, with 'should' being replaced by 'will', suggesting that the precepts are standards for compliance rather than pointers to good practice.*
>
> (UKCGE 2004a: www.ukcge.ac.uk)

Underlying this discussion is a belief that the delivery of postgraduate research programmes requires special measures to ensure that it complies with the Government agenda. The discussion also highlights the sensitivities of academics towards the research degree process and that of senior managers towards regulation. In many cases both groups are blind to the difficulties that research students experience during their research studies and the need for a rigorous approach to the delivery of research awards. We have already made comment on the Code as it affects training in the section on Research Councils above; we will return to specific aspects of the Code in later chapters.

Institutional audit

The institutional audit is a second element of the QAA's work that can influence the doctoral process in institutions. The process of institutional audit was introduced in 2002/03 and developed out of the continuation audit process. In theory, and as far as doctoral work is concerned, both processes examine how institutions are responding to the Code of Practice. However, there is very little to suggest that the audits undertaken so far have paid serious attention to the research degree process (see, for example, Metcalfe *et al.* 2002). If continuation institutional audit is to have an impact on the improvement of doctoral research processes, considerably more time and effort will be required during audit by auditors with significant experience of the research degree process and the revised Code of Practice.

The Framework for Higher Education Qualifications

The FHEQ provides an overarching structure for levels and associated learning outcomes of programmes in Higher Education. The Framework's importance as far as doctoral education is concerned is its definitions of doctoral level (Table 2.6) and the doctoral descriptor (Table 2.7) as it attempts to better locate doctoral study in the context of all awards.

In theory at least the descriptors offer the opportunity to resolve many of the problems of comparability and level in doctoral work, as has been noted elsewhere (Shaw and Green 1996).

While the Framework is a major advance in thinking about the Doctorate

Table 2.6 Doctoral level

Doctorates are awarded for the creation and interpretation of knowledge, which extends the forefront of a discipline, usually through original research. Holders of Doctorates will be able to conceptualize, design and implement projects for the generation of significant new knowledge and/or understanding.

Holders of Doctorates will have the qualities needed for employment requiring the ability to make informed judgements on complex issues in specialist fields, and innovation in tackling and solving problems.

The titles PhD and DPhil are commonly used for Doctorates awarded on the basis of original research. Doctoral programmes, that may include a research component, but which have a substantial taught element lead usually to awards that include the name of the discipline in their title (e.g. EdD for Doctor of Education). A Doctorate normally requires the equivalent of three years' full-time study.

Table 2.7 Descriptor for qualifications at doctoral (D) level: doctoral degree

---

Doctorates are awarded to students who have demonstrated:

(a) the creation and interpretation of new knowledge, through original research or other advanced scholarship, of a quality to satisfy peer review, extend the forefront of the discipline, and merit publication;

(b) a systematic acquisition and understanding of a substantial body of knowledge which is at the forefront of an academic discipline or area of professional practice;

(c) the general ability to conceptualize, design and implement a project for the generation of new knowledge, applications or understanding at the forefront of the discipline, and to adjust the project design in the light of unforeseen problems;

(d) a detailed understanding of applicable techniques for research and advanced academic enquiry.

Typically, holders of the qualification will be able to:

(a) make informed judgements on complex issues in specialist fields, often in the absence of complete data, and be able to communicate their ideas and conclusions clearly and effectively to specialist and non-specialist audiences;

(b) continue to undertake pure and/or applied research and development at an advanced level, contributing substantially to the development of new techniques, ideas or approaches;

and will have:

(c) the qualities and transferable skills necessary for employment requiring the exercise of personal responsibility and largely autonomous initiative in complex and unpredictable situations, in professional or equivalent environments.

---

it remains vague in several aspects. Reference to outcomes associated with some of the higher-order skills of research are at best oblique or remain implicit. There is little direct reference, for example, to key skills such as analysis, synthesis, discrimination, criticality, evaluation, project management and creativity. Also there is virtually no direct reference to skills, qualities and attitudes normally associated with the affective domain.

In terms of the achievement of outcomes there are clear issues around:

• A requirement on students to achieve all performance criteria whether completely or partially.
• The relative importance of the different performance criteria – are some considered to be more important than others or even optional?
• Whether or not performance criteria should be weighted in some way.
• The means by which performances on a range of diverse criteria should be aggregated into an overall result at or beyond the threshold – e.g. averaging, profiling.

As far as outcomes are concerned the emphasis is firmly placed on the products of learning and research with little overt concern to promote the processes of learning and research. Any focus on process outcomes, such as time management, working to deadlines, interpersonal and group inter-action, motivation, tenacity, proactivity, independence and autonomy, are at best merely implied.

Doctorate and the workplace

Discussion so far has looked at the way in which the Doctorate has been influenced by Government and other agencies. The clear message coming from this discussion is the interpretation that doctoral candidates are a key resource in relation to the national economy and as such should receive appropriate training to ensure that they can maximize their contribution and deliver value for money to that economy. In this section we highlight the reasons why students undertake doctoral programmes and the jobs they take up subsequently.

Motivation for doctoral study

Evidence for this work is varied and at times a little fragile as there is little consistent data published on doctoral students and the labour market. The HESA data that are referred to below is based on the First Destination Statistics, in which all postgraduate students are lumped together. Other work, by NPC and the OST for example, is partial and hence may not reflect the behaviours of the majority of students (NPC 2002).

In their study of the reasons why students enter postgraduate study, the OST states that the most highly cited reason was 'interest in the particular subject' (32% of respondents) followed by 'thought it would help in getting a suitable or better job' (24%) and 'enjoy academic work research' (19%). If personal fulfilment (9%) and challenge (3%) are added into the equation, a category that we might call 'personal interest and challenge' is the broad reason for 63% of decisions. The OST report does note some variability according to the subject represented by the Research Council of the re-spondent. Interestingly, EPSRC students were the most highly job motivated (36%) with PPARC students the least (1%), perhaps reflecting the contrast between science and technology and particle physics in terms of job opportunities. Research students appeared to be less motivated by employ-ment prospects than those on taught programmes, while they were more likely to be studying out of enjoyment of academic work/research.

The survey by the NPC provides additional insights to the link between the Doctorate and the labour market (NPC 2002). Some 50% of the research students in the survey identified academic research or teaching in UK Higher Education as their career goal while an additional 12% identified academia, research or teaching elsewhere. In addition, 23% were intending to work outside higher education.

These surveys highlight the motivation of students for postgraduate and in particular doctoral work. They tend to suggest that there is a tension between student views and those of the funders – i.e. Government – which may explain some of the indifference to much of research training and skills development that is increasingly part of the doctoral 'offer'.

There does appear to be demand for PhDs irrespective of background and training. The recruitment consultant ECI Postgrad identifies that dedication, self-discipline and good organization are all skills that PhD candidates possess and are attractive to recruiters in a variety of fields, including investment banking, telecoms, defence and law (Miles Brignall, *The Guardian*, 2002). The Doctorate does not, however, automatically mean better employment. Many careers services note that while a PhD is now the established entry qualification for academic employment in HE and scientific research, other employers recruit on an applicant's personal skills, qualities and work experience, in addition to academic achievement. Some employers pay a PhD premium only if technically relevant. In some fields it may simply give a lead start in initial recruitment.

Destinations: what do graduates actually do?

As we have noted elsewhere in this discussion, data variability often limits our ability to discuss with complete authority the career paths of students having gained a Doctorate. Equally, systematic research on this topic is severely limited. Golde's work in the USA, for example, is one of the few large surveys of career destinations (Golde and Dore 2001) More recently a study commissioned by PPARC (DTZ Pieda Consulting 2003a, 2003b) has examined the career path of doctoral students who have received funding from PPARC. In addition, data is provided annually by the OST on First Destinations for the Research Councils, while individual learned societies undertake surveys of their own to establish career paths (see, for example, the Institute of Physics, 2004, and OST (undated)).

The OST data highlights the remarkable stability of the doctoral graduates who have received support from the Research Councils. While these represent only approximately 30% of PhDs, the data gives an indication of career prospects of a specific if privileged subset of the population (Table 2.8).

The data highlights the stability of the career paths over the period. Academic appointments (both permanent and fixed term) make up only approximately 30% of the total while the private sector and Government make a similar 30%. Given that many of the academic appointments, particularly the fixed-term contracts, relate to research-specific posts – postdoctoral work, research officers, fellowships – the numbers becoming lecturers, in the short term, is very small. Although the data does not allow us to be specific, it is suggested that those working in both the public and the private sectors will be employed because of their advanced research skills – generic and/or specific.

There are significant variations between the different research councils,

Table 2.8 First destination of Research Council funded PhD graduates

	1994	1996	1998	2000
Total number of leavers	3,166	3,201	3,735	3,262
Of which destination unknown	1,057	621	938	766
Known destinations	2,109	2,580	2,797	2,496
Of which:	%	%	%	%
Permanent academic appointment	5	5	5	5
Fixed-term academic appointment	29	21	26	25
Further training (excluding teaching)	5	4	4	4
School teaching or teacher training	3	2	2	2
Private sector, industry or commerce	22	33	29	24
Government or other public sector	5	5	6	5
Other employment	4	2	4	4
Not employed	19	18	15	18
Overseas	10	9	10	13

Source: OST: *Set Statistics,* Table 5:13

reflecting the different traditions of disciplines and the career opportunities that specific subjects open up. In 2000, for example, 3.3% of EPSRC graduates had permanent academic appointments compared to 18% for ESRC graduates. Respective figures for fixed-term appointments, private sector, and public sector, were 16.6%, 33.07% and 2.27% for EPSRC compared to 17.04%, 3.6% and 10.1% for ESRC (PPARC: Physics Students Career Paths for 1995).

The first destination data does not of course reflect the longer-term career destination of doctoral candidates, which gives a much better indication of the relationship between doctoral study and the labour market. Also as we noted above, research in this area is very limited. It is probable that many of the fixed-term academic appointments become permanent in the medium term for example.

The DTZ Pieda research for PPARC is particularly interesting because it is one of the very few analyses to look in detail at career paths in the UK. Unfortunately the data is not generalizable to the OST councils as a whole as PPARC students are not representative of the population at large, certainly at first destination stage with a much higher proportion of fixed-term academic appointments and private sector appointments, 44% and 33% respectively in 2000.

The research focused on two cohorts of students, the 1995 study on students whose PhD awards had finished 6–8 years earlier and the 2003 study on students whose award ended between 1995/96 and 1998/99. In both cases, adequate time had elapsed to ensure that a career path was reasonably well established. The studies noted some interesting changes in employment tracks during the period, particularly a significant increase in employment in the private sector (24% in 1995, 48% in 2003) and a decrease in both university and Government and other public organizations (47% and 24% in 1995 and 35% and 12% in 2003 respectively). The report notes that 'these findings might in part be a reflection of the fact that more of the students who undertook PhDs over this time *had to* look for employment opportunities in the private sector' (authors' italics) perhaps a somewhat biased view of the purpose of doctoral education. Of those employed in the university sector, only 17% had permanent faculty (academic) positions. Although the study concludes that the overall evidence suggests that the PPARC Doctorate is fulfilling its mission, it makes no comment on the changing demands on the Doctorate as revealed in the changing career destinations of candidates and implicitly assumes that the Doctorate is the most appropriate training for the careers described.

The recent UK GRAD report, *What do PhDs do?* (UK GRAD Programme 2004c) throws some additional light on the destination of recent successful PhD candidates. We should not be surprised that it reports that the majority of PhDs do not follow an academic or research career, nor that PhDs in arts and humanities and social sciences have little difficulty in obtaining posts. Perhaps this survey will finally open the eyes of those involved in doctoral education to the well-established but little acknowledged fact that doctoral education does not for the most part lead to academic or research-led employment in universities.

Similar patterns of post-Doctorate employment are found in other countries in Europe. Table 2.9 highlights the position for French doctoral completions.

There is a similar variation between the disciplines: 45% of biological sciences PhDs are in postdoctoral positions as opposed to less than 11% in the social sciences. There remains an ambivalence on the part of employers in the business sector to employ people with a Doctorate, '(The) Doctorate is often seen as an academic diploma and doctors are not considered interesting candidates in spite of (or because of) their high level of training' (Voisin-Demery and Poble 2004)

Table 2.9 Employment 18 months after completion

Employment	%
University tenured position	27
Business	25
Postdoctoral	26
Teaching in Lycée	6.7
Pubic sector administration	6.3
Unemployed	5

Source: Voisin-Demery and Poble 2004

Doctorates: fit for purpose

Government has attempted to influence the development and structure of the Doctorate, encouraging the greater emphasis on research and generic training – making the Doctorate fit for purpose. This, of course, begs the question: 'Fit for what purpose?' As we have seen, the demands and expectations of potential doctoral students vary significantly, as does the employment they will eventually follow. Our discussion in other chapters of this book highlight the growth of 'new' approached to doctoral work – adapting in different ways to the needs of different demands. Also, in the case of the New Route PhD for example, this has been, in terms of recruitment at least, remarkably successful with demand and funding rising significantly in response to its more paced approach to doctoral education. Some 34 UK universities now offer the New Route PhD in programmes covering 120 different subjects (*Research Fortnight* 2004).

It does seem appropriate to reflect on the approach taken by the New Route PhD and the other doctoral programmes and ask whether the current approach to development of fitness for purpose is simply tinkering at the edges, making changes without a full understanding of the evidence or implications of change. The time and effort spent on the implementation of generic training, much of which may have no relevance to large numbers of students, might have been better spent developing doctoral programmes that addressed the real issues.

Conclusion

Government has maintained an interest in doctoral education since the 1960s. The Thatcher years saw this interest expressed clearly in terms of 'value for money' as exemplified by the completion rate question discussed in Chapter 9. The concern about the link to the economy was emphasized in 1993 and this emphasis continues. In parallel with other aspects of Higher Education, regulation and the demands for higher quality delivery are reflected in the demands of the Funding Councils, Research Councils and the QAA. A review of these demands highlights the ever-tighter control that Government has attempted to place on institutions and the delivery of doctoral programmes.

The link between the Doctorate and the workplace is at the centre of much of this debate. How far does the Doctorate prepare students for the various employment opportunities open to them? We will see in later chapters how the Doctorate itself has developed and adapted over recent years. However, we might suggest that this has been in the absence of a fundamental understanding of the relevance of, or demand for, the Doctorate in all but a small segment of current provision. Fundamentally, is there a place for the candidate who simply wants to undertake doctoral research for enjoyment and personal satisfaction?

Summary issues

- What should be the role of Government in the doctoral process – funder, regulator, watchdog? Should Government be prescriptive in terms of quality, content and number?
- How far should institutions take an account of industry – or the labour market more generally – in the development of doctoral programmes?
- Should we recognize that the Doctorate may be an appropriate award that recognizes research skills, but also should we be developing programmes of Doctorate plus 1 for those successful Doctorate candidates who wish to teach in sectors of Higher Education?

Part 2

Range of Doctoral Awards in the UK

3

The PhD and the diversity of doctoral study

Introduction

The doctoral award as employed within the UK Higher Education sector is varied in its manifestations. Indeed this diversity and our understanding of diverse structures and their purpose represents one of the major current concerns for doctoral education in the UK. Students can work towards doctoral awards with different nomenclatures – involving different levels of entry qualification, modes and kinds of study. The broad categories of doctoral study in the UK can be summarized as follows:

- PhD
- Taught Doctorate
- Doctor of Medicine
- Higher Doctorates
- PhD by Published Work
- Professional Doctorate
- Practice-Based Doctorate.

The first four categories are explored in this chapter. The last three categories are separated out into later chapters. In this chapter we shall consider the origins of the doctoral award, its perceived purposes and the way in which the PhD is distinguished within the range of doctoral awards currently available in the UK. We shall also consider the changing nature of the doctoral submission, and the manner in which the evidence of doctoral work is presented. The overall impression is of increasing diversity and segmentation as different groups invent new approaches for specific purposes. In so doing the sector is increasingly at risk of confusion about the Doctorate, its structure, purpose and content.

Origins of the Doctoral Award

Early origins

Universities in the UK have been awarding Doctorates since the thirteenth century. Since that time the award has commonly been accepted as the highest level of academic achievement attained by university students. Initially, the broad outline of university awards was one in which (as outlined in Phillips and Pugh 2000):

- a bachelor's degree indicated a general education at university level (with specialization a more recent nineteenth-century phenomenon);
- a masters degree indicated that the bearer had a licence to practise within a specific domain (in the first place to practise theology as a member of the church);
- and the Doctorate indicated that the holder had a licence to teach within the university setting.

Initially, there was no separation of taught courses and research degree (independent) study. The level of learning was the marker rather than the mode in which that learning took place. Whatever changes have occurred since the origins of the university awards system, the doctoral degree has retained a notion – however loosely defined – that the holder is in command of the chosen field of study, can contribute to understanding within that field and is therefore worthy of being listened to as an equal within the particular faculty of scholars. These criteria tend to underpin the kinds of regulatory statements about attainment of PhD standard set down by many universities. Indeed, the notion of achieving peer status with relevant academicians permeates many of the different kinds of doctoral study described later in this book.

Despite this theme of acceptance by peers, the nature of doctoral study and the nomenclature attached to it have been subject to a variety of changes. Some of these are outlined in UKCGE (2002). In its earliest manifestations doctoral study was undertaken within specific disciplines and doctoral awards reflected that subject specificity with titles such as Doctor of Theology and Doctor of Law. In Germany the notion of a Doctor of Philosophy held sway and this was introduced into the UK system where, despite initial resistance, it became the standard with the title of PhD or DPhil. This resistance related in part to debates about the role of universities and more particularly the role of research in the mission of those institutions. In the second half of the twentieth century the view of universities as institutions necessarily engaging in research, and of academics as necessarily being researchers, became predominant. This view accommodated the notion of the PhD as a minimum requirement for academic tenure and, in one sense, the award became a type of qualification for academic employment within the university sector. (This notion of apprenticeship is revisited below.)

Late twentieth- and early twenty-first-century developments in the Doctorate

The pressure to move beyond the situation described above towards the kind of diversity that now exists came initially from the increasing intellectual demands of industrial and commercial contexts. As the complexity of the workplace increased and the need for highly qualified postgraduates developed, so the demand grew for more doctoral level work. However, the *raison d'être* of the PhD came under challenge. It was no longer the case that the Doctorate acted as a route into a career in academia; instead it became a qualification for work in diverse intellectual settings. The criticism was levelled that the PhD was too narrowly 'academic' and that the kinds of knowledge and skills displayed by successful PhD candidates were not readily usable in the contexts of the workplace they sought to enter. Pressure came from the areas such as engineering and chemistry for doctoral level study that was more applied and more relevant to the work expected of successful candidates as they entered the appropriate professions. These criticisms and pressures set the scene for the broadening of doctoral study from the PhD alone to the range of doctoral studies described in later chapters of this book.

Purposes of the Doctorate

Background

Questioning the purpose of the Doctorate is certainly not new and, as we have observed elsewhere in this book, recent Governments have increasingly attempted to steer an economic 'value for money' justification for Doctorate study and its funding. Notions of purpose vary among: (i) training for an academic career, (ii) training for a research career in academia, (iii) training for research in the economy at large, (iv) curiosity-driven work in its own right and for its own sake and (v) high level training within a professional context. As is noted in the chapters on examination, views differ on the extent to which a doctoral award signifies the training of researchers as opposed to the creation of new knowledge itself.

This section explores the issue of the purpose of the award in the context of the evolving structure of the Doctorate. Here we question whether the 'one-size-fits-all' approach is indeed appropriate to an award that is expected to fulfil so many purposes. In other chapters we reflect on the way in which the changing Doctorate that now includes the so-called 'New Route PhD', the Practice-Based PhD, and the Professional Doctorate is influenced by questions about the relevance of the PhD and fitness for purpose.

The Doctorate and the academic profession

The notion of the Doctorate as an apprenticeship for academia is predicated on two assumptions. First, that all academics need a Doctorate in order to practise their profession and, second, that the Doctorate provides the appropriate level of experiential learning to equip the individuals for academic life. It is noteworthy that in the USA, where the Doctorate is structured very differently to the UK, the Doctorate appears to be focused explicitly on the production of new faculty. Indeed, implicit in recent policy statements around the world is the assumption that the PhD is necessary to the training of the next generation of academics. The Canadians have estimated that they will need to replace between 2,500 and 3,000 lecturers in the period to 2006 and are developing PhD programmes to fill these posts. Nearer to home the recent British Academy report talks in similar terms (British Academy 2001) as does the Schartzenberg plan in France (*Research Europe* 2001) where it is suggested that there will be a need in France for 1,000 PhD graduates between 2001 and 2010 to fill academic posts.

The Doctorate as an apprenticeship for academia

In assessing the appropriateness of the Doctorate for those wishing to enter academia, it may be useful to examine roles that academics are required to fulfil. Not necessarily in order of importance, these may be identified as: research, teaching and 'other' (where 'other' will include administration, management, consultancy, exploitation of IPR, counselling, etc.). The proportion of each of these activities will vary across institutions and through the career of any individual academic.

Let us consider the research role. If we assume that research is a dominant activity in some relationship to the submission of staff to the Research Assessment Exercise (RAE), then in 2001 research was a key activity for 48,022 members of staff in UK universities (HEFCE 2001) which represents 41.25% of the 116,405 academic staff recorded by HESA in 2000/01 (HESA 2002). This level of activity is however skewed towards particular groups of institutions for which research is a key driver. Equally, if one relates the importance of the Doctorate to the level of research funding derived from the RAE in the block grant following the 2001 RAE, then research is of very minor importance for over 30 UK institutions where this represents less than 5% of total turnover. It can be suggested therefore that, for a considerable number of institutions where research is not a key driver, the possession of a Doctorate is not a necessary prerequisite for academic staff.

Turning to the second activity – that of teaching – the relationship between research and teaching is one that has challenged many writers in recent years. Although it is not the purpose of this book to explore this relationship (Jenkins *et al.* 2003), it is however valuable to explore it in terms of the portfolio of activities demanded of an academic and hence, by extension, the demand for PhDs, before assessing the appropriateness of the PhD to this need. We might identify two major benefits: (i) exposure to the cutting edge development of the knowledge base of the subject and the development of an approach to enquiry and the use of data to test theory, and (ii) the transferable skills of critical analysis and presentation of findings based on evidence. It is questionable whether either of these depends on high levels of research activity, and in the case of the Doctorate we would suggest that the current debates around generic skills training suggests that successfully gained transferable skills are lacking in many doctoral programmes. Indeed, when identifying the potential positive and negative impacts of research on teaching, Jenkins notes that 'unfortunately, the list of potential negative effects of lecturer research on student motivation is not much shorter than the positive' (Jenkins *et al.* 2003: 37).

In terms of the other activities within the broad definition of teaching, we might include curriculum design, creation of effective learning environments, modes of assessment, student support and guidance and quality management and enhancement of learning. In all of these it is arguable that the Doctorate itself makes only a tangential and small contribution, unless of course the research is in the field of pedagogy itself.

The limitation of the PhD as an apprenticeship for academic teaching has been recognized in recent years through the initiatives of organizations such as the Institute of Learning and Teaching, now part of the Higher Education Academy. Many HEIs require new staff to undertake a formal programme of training in teaching and learning, and many have a probationary period of as much as three years to ensure that they are effective teachers. Most recently, the QAA Code for Postgraduate Research Programmes emphasizes the limitations of the Doctorate process as a training ground for supervisors, recommending that all new supervisors, presumably some of whom at least will have Doctorates, will undergo appropriate training: 'New supervisors will participate in specified development activities, arranged through their institutions, to assure their competence in the role' (QAA, 2004: 14).

Other activities expected of an academic member of staff include a range of academic activity commonly identified as comprising the 'third leg' of an academic career as noted above, for example: consultancy and services to industry, development and exploitation of IPR and outreach and work within the community. In these cases, it is questionable whether the Doctorate is of particular relevance other than perhaps in individual branding, esteem and confidence.

In short, while those who appoint staff to university posts interpret the Doctorate as a signifier of qualification for the job, there does seem to be a gulf between what the Doctorate is and what is required of many academic staff once they are in post. This suggests that the Doctorate itself has not evolved with the changing demands on such academic staff.

Taking as a starting point the market position of the Doctorate in university recruitment, an analysis of the jobs page of the *Times Higher* and Jobs.ac.uk in the week of 8 June 2004 highlighted the fact that the majority of the lecturer and senior lecturer posts identified possession of a PhD as essential, while the remainder indicated a strong desirability for such a background with phrases such as 'significant progress towards . . ., near completion of . . ., be about to complete . . .'. There appeared to be no significant difference between institutions in terms of their research or teaching intensity. We can therefore make the tentative assumption that the majority of institutions identify the Doctorate as a prerequisite for success in academia though clearly there may be some variation between disciplines (where, in some cases, doctoral study has not been a typical feature of advancement).

However, the division between research only, mixed portfolio and teaching only in higher education appears to be changing with a possible knock-on effect on the training needs of academic staff. The most recent HESA data on the UK HE sector reporting on the period 2002/03 has highlighted a shift in the growth of staff with research-only contracts. According to these data, 31% of the 147,000 university staff employed in this period are now on research-only contracts, an increase of 41% from 32,518 to 455,835 since 1993/94. The majority of these researchers are also on fixed-term contacts. Numbers of staff on teaching-only contracts remain quite small although the rate of increase of 27% (from 11,734 to nearly 15,000 over the same period) is greater than the 22% for staff on mixed contracts (HESA 2004a).

The Doctorate as an apprenticeship for industry

Significant numbers of successful doctoral candidates follow careers in industry and the professions in a range of capacities. The demands may relate specifically to research. Although the UK's performance in research and development is not at the top of the international league, UK industry still takes large numbers of Doctorates into research posts. The pharmaceutical and petrochemical industries are good examples. Here the benefits of the Doctorate may relate to specific technical knowledge or laboratory competences. It was from these types of employers, however, that concerns about Doctorate capability arose in the 1990s. Such concerns have led to greater emphasis on a broad range of skills in addition to those associated with research itself. In short, some employers were complaining that successful doctoral candidates knew 'an awful lot about an awful little' and were lacking in skills of, for example, communication and team working. These concerns formed a key element in the development of the MRes (OST 1994) and the funding initially of the OST Graduate Schools and subsequently the development of the UK GRAD Programme.

The Doctorate and the professions

Data are not available within the UK on the number of employees in the professions with Doctorates and hence it is not possible to identify clearly the importance of the Doctorate to those professions. We can, however, make certain inferences from the data on the number of Doctorates awarded in a number of subjects that are predominantly professional in nature, as illustrated in Table 3.1. In terms of the number of awards made, the Doctorate appears to be of limited importance to many of the professionally related disciplines. For many, the postgraduate diploma or masters is the passport to the profession. This does perhaps highlight the need for innovation and the importance of the Professional Doctorates discussed elsewhere in this book.

These data suggests that for many professionally related subjects, the traditional Doctorate is of little significance. It is perhaps for this reason that the recent developments in Practice-Based Doctorates and the Professional Doctorate have arisen. In this case the Professional Doctorate has responded to, and found purpose in, a number of changes in the professions. As the UKCGE noted in 2002 (UKCGE 2002: 17) 'the complexities of employment in the modern world require a high level of intellectual sophistication, and this has generated pressure for higher qualification'. The Professional

Table 3.1 Number of awards awarded in 2002/03

Subject	Doctorates	First degrees	All awards
Medicine and dentistry	1,360	6,175	9,875
Subject allied to medicine	885	23,665	63,145
Biological sciences	2,375	23,725	32,730
Veterinary science	70	560	760
Agriculture and related subjects	230	2,150	4,560
Physical sciences	2,180	12,480	19,225
Mathematical sciences	370	5,100	6,895
Computer science	375	18,240	33,560
Engineering and technology	2,020	19,455	33,420
Architecture, building and planning	175	6,555	12,470
Social studies	1,245	25,315	47,285
Law	255	11,745	24,515
Business and administrative studies	555	40,310	85,345
Mass communications and documentation	65	7,415	11,870
Languages	900	20,025	28,305
Historical and philosophical studies	855	13,285	19,355
Creative arts and design	310	26,465	36,295
Education	620	9,730	53,760
Combined	25	9,990	34,415

Source: HESA (2004a)

Doctorate has filled a gap that the traditional PhD was unable to fill, linking to the competency philosophy of some professions. In the health field, for example, this was associated with the move to bring an increasing amount of professional training into the HEI environment. It might be added that in this particular field, where credentials are often seen as vital, the title of 'doctor' is of particular importance.

For many Professional Doctorates, the underlying purpose has been fundamentally re-examined and programmes reflect the explicit demands of changing professional environments. Such purposes and demands are considered more fully in the chapter on Professional Doctorates.

Supply of Doctorates

There has for some time been a concern about the supply of doctoral candidates with questions being asked about whether or not enough doctoral candidates are being 'produced' and indeed how 'enough' can be defined with any accuracy in an ever-changing world. These questions have a resonance world wide but frequently only in the context of a supply to replenish the academy. Thus, in Canada in the late 1980s, Gerson (1989) was speaking of a shortage while Zur-Muehlem (1987) believed that a shortage was less likely; Maslen (1991a) reported that a shortage was imminent. In the USA shortages were predicted for the 1990s and the need for 500,000 new academics (and hence Doctorates) by 2010 suggested (Bowen and Schuster 1986). Yet in the earlier 1970s concern both in Australia and the USA was of oversupply (Davies 1992; Kerr 1975).

UK Government thinking about the concentration of doctoral programmes and research degree-awarding powers in university designation essentially comes from the perspective of a research environment and infrastructure viewpoint. Funding of doctoral programmes influences indirectly the production of doctoral students from a total cost perspective; a finite amount of money is given to the Research Councils and Funding Councils and, depending on the price, this will 'buy' a given number of students. If price changes, the number of Doctorates that can thus be bought will rise or fall. If funding comes from universities or other sources, the supply is again influenced by the amount put into the system. In all these cases no consideration appears to be given to the total level of production that may be seen as free a market.

As far as some universities are concerned, there are incentives to recruit students. This is particularly the case where the Research Assessment Exercise (RAE) and subsequent funding model has increased the incentive to recruit (Sastry 2004). Institutions have no reason to consider the total production of Doctorates as long as they are profitable.

There is then good reason to consider the supply of Doctorates in a more systematic manner and ask why the UK Government does not adopt such an approach. There seems no systematic search for evidence as to whether the

UK has too many or too few. The only thing we may say is that the destination data suggests that the employment prospects of doctoral graduates are good and consequently it may be that supply and demand is in balance. In January 2004 only 3.2% of the 2003 graduating cohort of PhDs described themselves as unemployed, 14.8% of whom were about to start a job within a month. Of course what we do not know is whether they require the PhD for the jobs they are doing and hence whether the PhD is an asset for those entering the labour market.

There are several examples of attempts to link supply to demand in the USA and critiques of the production of Doctorates (e.g. Goldman and Massey 2000). These studies tend to confirm the view that 'these continual increases in programme enrolment are ordinarily driven by employment demands or, most importantly, the educational needs of graduate students' (Triggle and Miller 2002: 287).

The PhD as a distinctive doctoral award

Criteria for the PhD

The PhD is generally accepted as a research-based qualification centred on an extended piece of research. The intention is that the research will lead to an original contribution to knowledge. Institutions vary in the way in which they describe that contribution: for example, as *significant* or *substantial* or simply as a *contribution.* But what is common is the view that to gain a PhD a candidate must demonstrate, by contributing to understanding in the relevant disciplinary field, that he/she has the requisite skills and knowledge to be able to make such contributions and thus to continue to make them. It is also usual for the candidate to be required to demonstrate that he/she has command of the knowledge that is extant in the relevant field and be able to demonstrate mastery of the research skills that will enable him/her to continue to contribute in an independent way to the advancement of knowledge within that field.

A further criterion often cited is the notion that the work has the potential to be published; clearly, this links in to ideas of mastery of the subject and being at a level with peers noted above. Finally another, often unwritten, marker for level of Doctorate is what a good student can achieve in three years of full-time research-based study. The stipulation of three or four years of research only, marks out the PhD from the Higher Doctorates described below.

QAA identifies the key features of doctoral level in its descriptors within the Framework for Higher Education Qualifications (FHEQ) and what is noted above in this section can be found there. These topics are revisited later in this book in the chapters on final examination of doctoral candidates.

Dissertation or thesis

The terms 'dissertation' and 'thesis' are sometimes used synonymously in UK higher education in that both may be taken to mean the submission made by a doctoral candidate. We would argue, however, that there is a distinction between the two terms that is more than merely pedantic. In our view, a thesis is an intellectual position adopted by the candidate and then defended in a written submission and subsequently in an oral examination. The written submission is then a disquisition (which might be referred to as a dissertation) – an elaborate treatise or discourse in which that intellectual position is defended. To use the terms 'thesis' and 'dissertation' synonymously is therefore to conflate two quite distinct meanings. This might not matter except for the danger that students and examiners may lose sight of the facts that (a) doctoral level work requires the adoption of an intellectual position (a thesis) and (b) what is presented for examination (which in our interpretation should be referred to as a dissertation) is a defence of that position and will contain an explanation of what the candidate has achieved, why the work was done, the manner in which it was done and its implications for further work in the field. We feel that the understanding of this crucial aspect of a doctoral submission (i.e. that it should contain a thesis as we define it above) may be lost and therefore the import of the doctoral submission is diminished. We should also note that across the disciplines there is a range of what counts as a legitimate doctoral level 'intellectual position' – thesis to be defended – in some sciences the product of doctoral study may represent simply the exposition of an experiment or series of experiments that have not been previously attempted.

Having set out our own view above, we have to acknowledge that custom and practice in many UK universities has led to the word 'thesis' being commonly accepted as both the intellectual position *and* its defence – in short, to encapsulate the entire submission. Dictionary definitions do not help us much here, with dissertation sometimes (according to the dictionary used) being given as a definition of thesis and vice versa. Nor is there consistency across Europe in the use of the terms. For the purposes of this book, therefore, we will make use of the term 'thesis' for what is submitted, on the grounds that common usage has rendered this appropriate. In so doing we are not ignoring the arguments set out above.

The use of credit rating in PhD programmes

Systems of credit rating work within higher education make use of notions of both level and volume. Both these prove problematic within PhD study. In the first instance (level) it is difficult to separate the amount of time a PhD student spends within one overall unified programme of research study operating at masters level, and the amount spent at doctoral level. Most supervisors would recognize that a PhD student begins at a level of apprenticeship and graduates to a level of intellectual equal; indeed supervisors need to recognize that their students have to exceed their own levels of expertise, within the limits of particular projects at least, if those students can be said to have become contributors to knowledge and able to continue to make independent contributions in the future. So, there may be some period operating at masters level even though the ultimate award is a PhD. On the other hand, it is often the case that students enter PhD programmes with masters qualifications and with well-formed PhD programmes agreed. In this case it may be that such students are operating almost wholly within a doctoral level from the beginning of their research studies. Second, it is difficult to allocate a volume measure to 'contribution to knowledge'. Given that a PhD award is typically made on the basis of the presentation and subsequent defence of an intellectual position set out in the thesis, dividing this out into areas in which volume might be variously allocated is problematic. Most UK HEIs eschew the use of credit rating within their conceptions of PhD study though not necessarily in the case of Professional Doctorate study (see Chapter 5).

For their part, QAA in the Framework of Higher Education Qualifications allocate 540 credits at level HE5 for a Doctorate.

Supervision

Students undertaking a PhD in the UK will be supervised by one or more academics. Issues surrounding supervision are returned to and explored in more detail later in this book. Here it is worth noting that the relationship between student, supervisor and project varies between disciplines. While in some laboratory-based science subjects students may work as part of a team on funded projects initiated by others, where their work is one part of a whole and where they may meet with their supervisor(s) on a daily basis – in other disciplines, such as Humanities, a student may enter a PhD programme to pursue a project very much of his/her own initiation and where the expectation of meetings with supervisor(s) will be very different. In short, while supervision is a constant in PhD study – its nature varies between disciplines.

The Master of Philosophy degree

It is necessary here to mention the degree of Master of Philosophy (MPhil) because, although it is not a doctoral award, it is often used within UK universities as a precursor to the PhD or as a contained award. Indeed, in many universities candidates cannot register for the award of PhD directly but have to register for an MPhil in the first instance or, more commonly, for an MPhil 'with possible transfer' to PhD. Other universities operate the latter of these systems but offer a direct route to PhD for those candidates who already have a Masters qualification in an area related to the proposed PhD study. Again, in some universities examiners have the option of awarding an MPhil degree for work that was submitted for PhD but was judged to be of MPhil rather than PhD standard. In all of the above, the MPhil functions as a degree that is of the same kind as the PhD – that is, gained by research work culminating in a dissertation that is examined by viva – but deemed to be at a lower level. This latter issue of level has proved problematic. Phillips and Pugh, for example, describe the MPhil as being 'limited in scope and degree of original-ity' (2000: 24). It is hard to envisage degrees of originality; clearly work is original or it is not. In any case, one would expect engagement in research of a two-year duration (the typical minimum time period for the MPhil degree) to produce results that are original. Indeed, if work was solely duplication of existing studies then it seems unreasonable to expect any kind of postgradu-ate award for its production. We should note here that Phillips and Pugh (2000) argue that originality is a complex concept (p. 28) and explore it in some detail (pp. 63–4) giving 15 different definitions.

Phillips and Pugh also argue that, to gain an MPhil degree, a candidate would be expected to produce a full summary of the literature, yet 'it does not have to be an evaluative review as in the PhD' (2000: 24). In our view, it is difficult to imagine how a non-evaluative review could be deemed satisfac-tory at any postgraduate research degree level. To distinguish between the two awards under consideration here, it is necessary to distinguish the amount of work completed (i.e. work commensurate with two years of full-time study for the MPhil and three years for the PhD) and the level of evaluation, analysis and implication. Judging level in these terms where there is no clear cut-off point may be seen as similar to judging classification of undergraduate degrees on sliding scales of these same kinds of qualities. The MPhil continues to cause some difficulties in the typology of awards with lack of clarity and consistency between institutions and commentators – exacer-bated by the fact that some institutions award MPhil for predominantly taught programmes at masters level.

Taught Doctorate

By definition a Taught Doctorate contains a significant element of taught work. This work is set out in agreed curriculum statements with specified learning outcomes that are subject to formal assessment. To distinguish a Taught Doctorate from a conventional PhD, the taught content would need to include more than just research methodology, and here the boundaries between the two forms of doctoral study are blurred. Many universities in the UK now offer taught elements in their PhD programmes even though they would not describe those overall programmes as 'taught'.

The issue here is perhaps in the nature of the process of teaching that is implied by the phrase 'Taught Doctorate'. At undergraduate level and, to a lesser extent, at taught masters level the 'teacher' would typically be conceived of as someone in charge of an intellectual area able to impart set knowledge and skills to students. At doctoral level there is a general consensus that what is required of such a teacher is guidance of the student in appropriate questioning and methodologies. Because the research student is required to contribute to knowledge, then necessarily the teacher's own knowledge will be overtaken. The teacher cannot impart what is not known and therefore the nature of the pedagogy changes. We return to this topic in the chapter in this book on the 'Nature of Doctoral Supervision'.

Typically the curriculum of a Taught Doctorate will include the production of a substantial research project and this will be examined by *viva voce.* Students in a Taught Doctorate would typically be taught in cohorts but their examination would be individual and similar to that in the conventional PhD.

The so-called 'New Route PhD' may be seen as an example of a Taught Doctorate, though here again there is fuzziness around the relationship between taught elements and the overall research programme. This New Route was originally known as the 'Enhanced PhD' and this title gives the flavour of the intentions of its originators. It revolves around a consortium of UK universities. It arose along with the concerns about the PhD being too narrowly focused and sought to address some of the perceived needs of the international market for doctoral study. In its partial emphasis on front-loaded, taught, enhancing elements it leans towards a North American model. However, it differs from that model in distributing taught elements throughout the course rather than focusing them entirely in the early stages of the programme. It may be that another distinguishing feature of the New Route PhD is the emphasis on subject content. There is an implication that undergraduate courses may not always have given adequate subject-specific coverage and that, therefore, some compensation is required if a candidate is to go on to the highest academic award.

Doctor of Medicine

The Doctor of Medicine is distinct within doctoral qualifications in that it is awarded by a thesis written by qualified medical practitioner. Again, criteria for the award are variable across universities, as are the kinds of supervision involved. According to Phillips and Pugh (2000) the title of doctor as used by general medical practitioners is an honorary one. Such 'doctors' do not in fact have a Doctorate from their universities but rather are credited with two bachelor's degrees that jointly encompass the (Masters) notion of being licensed to practice [medicine]. Because this book is intended to focus on the Doctorate as a research degree award, we have therefore elected not to consider the Doctor of Medicine award specifically, though we should note that, again, there is some blurring of the boundaries with the possibilities for those working in the health-related professions to gain a Doctorate (either in the form of a PhD or as a Professional Doctorate) that is not a Doctor of Medicine yet is focused on health issues.

Higher Doctorate

The notion of Higher Doctorates, again, differs across the sector in the UK. Where the PhD has come to indicate mastery of a narrow field (narrow in the sense of representing three years of research study only) the Higher Doctorates are typically seen as indicating command over a field of study and a sustained contribution to understanding within that field. Historically, the fields of study were, for example, DD (Divinity), MD (Medicine), LLD (Law), DMus (Music) (Phillips and Pugh 2000). More recently these titles have been joined by DSc (Science), DLitt (Letters, i.e. Arts), DSocSc (Social Sciences) (Phillips and Pugh 2000).

Powell (2004) noted that Higher Doctorates – where they are made available in the UK – are typically awarded partially or wholly on the basis of published work, and in many institutions the kinds of restrictions on eligibility would be similar to those for the PhD by Published Work noted in the relevant chapter in this book. He also noted that some of the respondents to the UKCGE survey reported that the PhD by Published Work was managed within their universities by 'Higher Degrees Committees'. This latter use of the term 'Higher Degrees' introduces a further confusion as far as the Doctorate is concerned as most universities offer a 'Higher Doctorate' as a more advanced award to the Doctorate. It is not entirely clear, for these institutions and possibly for others, where the Higher Doctorates sit in relation to the PhD by Published Work and, indeed, the 'traditional' PhD.

Doctoral submissions

Submissions in relation to variation in kinds of doctoral award

The ever-widening range of doctoral awards is challenging the ways in which doctoral evidence is presented. While the traditional thesis is still the dominant form of submission in the UK, other methods are emerging. It is worth noting here that the doctoral submission, as is typically conceived in the UK, stands apart from the kinds of submission prevalent in several other parts of Europe. In much of northern mainland Europe and Scandinavia a doctoral submission typically comprises, in part or in whole, previously published papers. Indeed, where European partners tend to be more flexible in approach the UK may be seen to demarcate more rigorously in terms of traditional thesis versus PhD by Published Work (see Chapter 4 and Powell 2004). While some universities in the UK are beginning to break down the barriers in how to treat, within any submission, previously published work as opposed to traditional thesis material, and are beginning to adopt more flexible approaches. Such flexibility was called for by UKCGE (1996b) and in our own view may well be an important feature of future developments with regard to doctoral submissions in the UK.

The submission within Professional and Practice-Based Doctorates

In the Professional Doctorates, while in many cases the thesis mode is retained, there is an increasing move to a portfolio model, similar to that adopted by the more innovative MRes programmes (Green *et al.* 2001). It is perhaps in the practice-based fields of the performing arts, art and design and fine art that the concept of the written thesis is most commonly challenged. Within these fields several universities allow alternative methods of submission. For example, the University of Wales regulations specify that other media can be included as full or part submission. These may include:

- artefacts, score, portfolio of original workshop performance or exhibition accompanied by 5,000 word commentary;
- audio or video tapes, diagrams and maps.

Where such submissions are allowed, many universities would insist (as does the University of Wales) that such items must all be enclosed in a container suitable for storage on a library shelf, its title readily readable in its stored position. In this case, although alternative formats are permissible, the intention is that they replicate the nature and style of the traditional thesis as they have to be similarly storable in a library. Here the Doctorate is awarded on the basis of evidence presented which demonstrates that the criteria determining the standard of the art and its relationship to the criteria for the award have been met. The container holds the evidence that is then available to others to both verify and make use of the furtherance of their own studies.

This requirement for written components is seen in submission requirement for the creative and performing arts. At the University of East Anglia, for example, a PhD can be awarded for musical composition. The submission is

> *a substantial portfolio of original compositions written specifically for the degree, together with an appropriate written commentary. The compositions shall show coherence and originality in invention as well as in the treatment of musical techniques. The written commentary shall discuss the structure of each of the compositions and provide an exposition of the creative process. In the written commentary, and in the examination, the candidate is required to show a critical understanding of the relationship of the submitted compositions to contemporary music thought.*
>
> (UKCGE 1997: 32)

In the case of fine art or performance, a written commentary – often referred to as an exegesis, particularly in the Australian context – is still required, as at the University of Roehampton.

> *A candidate for either degree whose course of study is in the visual or performing arts may submit a portfolio of original works that he or she has undertaken while registered for the Degree in lieu of a thesis. The portfolio may be presented for examination in the form of an exhibition or live performance. The works shall be*

accompanied by notes on each item in the portfolio and with an extended analysis of one item or a dissertation on a related theme.

(UKCGE 1997: 37; authors' emphasis)

While not specifying the nature or length of the extended analysis or dissertation, there is nevertheless a requirement to resort to the written word and replicate, in part at least, the traditional thesis. As in the case of the Professional Doctorate, it is arguable that candidates in these cases are being asked to jump through two hoops rather than one and produce significantly more evidence than the scientist and engineer. (For a fuller discussion of the different forms of submission see UKCGE 1997.)

One of the major limitations in doctoral submission in many areas of research has been associated with the presentational media and the maintenance of a durable record of the presentation. The development of multimedia introduces the possibility of more imaginative or appropriate forms of submission for subjects as diverse as chemistry and performing arts. There must be significant opportunity, for example, for the chemist to present real-time modelling of experimentation during an examination; equally for the performing artist, multimedia must offer much greater scope for the presentation of visual research outcomes.

Size of submission

It may seem that size is not everything in a doctoral submission and, of course, it is the case that length of thesis does not necessarily bear any positive correlation to quality of work. Table 3.2 sets out the typical requirements for Doctorate and professional research Doctorate in the UK. It is worth noting that several institutions do not have upper or lower word limits.

There is considerable variation between institutions in the words that

Table 3.2 The thesis

Normally the thesis is not expected to exceed the following (excluding ancillary data):

PhD	Science and Engineering	40,000 words
	Other areas	80,000 words
Professional Research Doctorate		60,000 words
MPhil	Science and Engineering	20,000 words
	Other areas	40,000 words

(Based on an analysis of the regulations of ten institutions)

count towards the total and the rigidity with which length is interpreted. The Faculty of Social Science at Southampton University, for example, has 'a maximum word length of 75,000 words including references and appendices *unless prior permission to exceed this has been given by the Faculty Board*' (University of Southampton 2001: 15; (authors' italics). The University of Nottingham, on the other hand, notes that the thesis should not normally exceed 100,000 words or 300 pages inclusive of appendices, footnotes, tables and bibliography. It observes that 'the word and page numbers are limits not targets . . . Academic Board concerned has power to withhold a thesis from examination that exceeds the word and page limits . . .' (University of Nottingham undated: 27). One wonders how frequently this power is invoked.

For most disciplines the outcomes are in written form and are defined by length rather than any other criteria. We may note that sciences generally require fewer words than social sciences and humanities; presumably numbers or formulae are not deemed to count as words. Up to the present little has been conceded to electronic production in which numbers of characters rather than words relate better to content or weight. It is also interesting to note that the MPhil, frequently awarded after two years full-time study, is often regarded as half a PhD in terms of words. More interesting are the Professional Doctorates that typically retain a significant written component, in addition to the other project and taught elements (see the chapter on the Professional Doctorate). This reflects what is, in our view, an ill-conceived notion that the Professional Doctorate must demonstrate equivalence in the research element, not withstanding the other elements delivered at doctoral level.

Electronic submission of theses

More recently there has been growing interest in the submission of theses in electronic format with the ultimate objective of creating a repository of theses at national or sub-national level that will be accessible on-line. Although many students have been producing their theses electronically for several years, the UK has been lagging behind other countries such at the USA, Australia, New Zealand and Germany in building on this as an opportunity for better dissemination. (See, for example, http://www.ndltd.org and http://www.scholar.lib.vt.edu/theses). In the USA the company Pro-Quest (http://www.umi.com/) has built up considerable capability and experience in this field. Data from Virginia Polytechnic Institute and State University suggests a dramatic increase in the accessing of research information from doctoral theses since their introduction of electronic theses. In addition to greater accessibility of research outcomes, electronic submission offers advantages such as improving IT skills and greater creativity and flexibility in the content of the submission.

This kind of approach to submission is as yet embryonic across universities in the UK although some are already well on the way to an established system. In Scotland, for example, the University of Glasgow, Robert Gordon University and Edinburgh University have electronic submissions systems as does Cranfield University in England. As is often the case in the UK, developments are sporadic although a recent JISC initiative has given much greater prominence to the opportunities in its JISC FAIR (Focus on Access to Institutional Resources) Project.[1]

There are significant opportunities to be gained from electronic submission of theses that benefit both the research community and the individual student. As we noted above, electronic storage and accessibility give a much greater exposure to the research itself and hence can raise the profile of the researcher. The immediacy of access dramatically increases the propensity of the research community to access and read current work. This also has the added benefit of ensuring that work is not duplicated where this may be the case when there are long lead periods between thesis submission and publication in journals.

There are, in addition, more operational benefits from electronic submission and storage. Some UK universities produce over 600 theses each year and therefore the magnitude of the difficulties of storage, retrieval and access becomes readily apparent. The associated printing of multiple copies is also financially and environmentally costly. This is not to argue that electronic submission and storage is without its problems, which can encompass the technical, academic and cultural.

On the technical side the challenges will relate to the need for agreed and standard software. In the ever-changing world of IT, a final agreement on common systems and standards may be more difficult to achieve than the standard A4 bound paper copy. Equally, standardization of search tools may be difficult to achieve. And, of course, all this will require a different type of support from that currently involved in the doctoral submission process and will require technical training.

Academically, the key issues relate to the examination process, threats of plagiarism, bogus submissions and intellectual property. Until a technical solution is available which provides electronic paper and solves the difficulty of reading large amounts of text on screen, electronic submission will still require paper copy for examination. Who produces this, and who pays for it remain questions that are treated differently at different universities.

It might be suggested that because of greater accessibility to thesis texts, it would be easier to plagiarize, in particular from previously obscure material. However, these perceived threats of plagiarism are probably exaggerated. Currently, with far reduced accessibility to material, this is less likely to be the case. The concerns over plagiarism are, however, mediated by the use of plagiarism identification software, which with electronic submission could now become a standard process at submission and one that could be far more rigorous than at present where the supervisor spots plagiarism in a less than systematic way.

[1]   http://www.jisc.ac.uk/index.cfm?name=programme_fairef.

Linked to plagiarism is the possibility of bogus submission or straight-forward fraud or theft, as in the case of the so-called 'Degree Mills' in the USA. While the submission of bogus theses may be possible and in some sense encouraged by electronic submission and storage, it should be pre-vented, in the UK system at least, by rigorous management processes as outlined in universities' procedures. Universities will be protected from the potential scares of bogus candidates submitting stolen theses in this way. Particular attention will be necessary for those programmes that are delivered and examined at a distance and for which home university monitoring processes are less effective.

The issue of intellectual property (IP) is perhaps more significant. We deal with the broader issue of IP and the Doctorate elsewhere in the following section. For now, we identify the issues as they apply to electronic submission. Legally a thesis is an unpublished work (accepting differences here in rela-tion to certain PhDs by Published Work). Electronic storage may change this status to one of a publication, locally accessible, searchable and ultimately remotely available for hard copy production, which is a far cry from a thesis retained by an academic library, retained for reference only, and subject to restriction as far as duplication and photocopying is concerned. There are other secondary issues that are generated relating to embedded material which itself is protected by copyright if published. Such material might include maps, diagrams, representation of works of art, text and photo-graphs. Although this does not normally constitute a copyright problem for the unpublished thesis, it may do so in the case of the electronic thesis.

The cultural challenge is perhaps the major obstacle in the introduction of electronic theses. As we have noted above, the nature of the PhD submission has changed little during the last 50 years and the written submission of a particular word length has been the vehicle for assessment during this time. Although information technology has allowed students to enhance the pre-sentation of the product, it has as yet had little impact on the product itself. To move to an electronic submission with all the potential for innovative presentation and influence on content will come as a significant cultural challenge if not shock.

The introduction of electronic submission does present some obstacles including changing institutional cultures, attitudes towards the Doctorate, issues of access, the location of electronic theses, security protocols and of course the funding of the exercise. Perhaps partly because of these obstacles and certainly in respect of the potential gains to be made from electronic submission, we suggest that the implementation of any initiative in relation to it should not be left to the idiosyncrasies of individual universities. The dissemination of appropriately protected research findings is too important to the UK research base. In our view then, it is a development in which the funders of research, the national treasuries and the holders of national research archives and the national libraries should have a direct involvement. What is needed is a robust national system that all can access.

Intellectual property rights, confidentiality and doctoral submissions

The relationship between intellectual property rights (IPR) and doctoral work are not straightforward and, like many other aspects of the Doctorate discussed in this book, vary significantly between universities. Intellectual property rights cover a range of intellectual products, all of which are potentially applicable to the Doctorate process or doctoral outcomes. These include:

- *copyright:* essays, reports, creative writing, computer programs, music, drawings, images, independent studies and any other credible work undertaken for assessment;
- *design rights and registered designs:* patterns and shapes;
- *trade marks:* logos and signs;
- *patents:* invented products and processes that may be patented.

UK universities are becoming increasingly aware of the importance of IPR and, in particular, its potential for generating commercial income. As a consequence they are increasingly explicit about ownership and IPR management. Interestingly, there are two diametrically opposed approaches to the ownership of IPR. In the first, IPR is retained by the student, whereas in the second it is held by the university. An intermediate approach is taken by some universities in which a student may agree to share the IPR or transfer it to a third party. This latter case is often where a third party sponsor is involved.

The student ownership of IPR becomes more complex in joint or collaborative projects in which more than one party is involved and may well involve written agreement about sharing among the parties. The candidate will normally be asked to empower a university librarian to allow a thesis to be copied in whole or in part, without further reference, on the understanding that only single copies are made for study purposes and are subject to normal acknowledgement.

It is notable that IPR is one of the few areas in which doctoral students are regarded as any other student, undergraduate or postgraduate, and yet, in terms of the potential benefits to either party, the Doctorate is a very different product from that typically achieved by undergraduates and taught postgraduates. Normally theses are available for consultation once a final definitive copy has been lodged in the university library or 'thesis store'. In certain cases, theses many remain confidential for an additional period of time. Typically, confidentiality is granted for reasons of commercial sensitivity, protection of IPR for patents, protection of sources or individuals involved or finally overall sensitivity of the subject matter. There is again variability across the sector concerning the length of time a thesis can remain confidential. While the usual model is two years, periods of up to five years are not uncommon. The University of Kent allows the candidate to stipulate the period, which is usually in the range of 5–10 years, while at Leeds University the thesis may remain confidential for an indefinite period subject to regular review by the librarian and Head of School (UKCGE 2004b). Other universities (e.g. Hertfordshire) give importance to the public availability of the thesis on the grounds that (i) part of the essential ethic of undertaking research is to disseminate findings so that knowledge can be furthered and (ii) standards are publicly on show and can be readily verified by the academic community. Such a stance leads to confidentiality only in exceptional circumstances and for very limited periods.

Finally, in this consideration of what is essentially ownership of ideas, it is appropriate to note the various traditions in publication that involve supervisors or other members of a research group. This typically is more a concern in the sciences in which groupwork or teamwork is more common. It is, however, relevant to all disciplines in which a supervisor may have or may aspire to have ownership of some or all of the ideas that underpin a PhD. The fundamental concern is often the order of names on a publication and the manner in which such ordering can indicate, or not, the lead author, originating researcher and others less closely involved in the work. While there has been a tradition for the supervisor or research group leader to head the author listings, there is rightly increasing pressure for the research student to be named first in the listing, with the supervisor identified as the corresponding author. Some universities are now embedding such approaches in their regulations in order to ensure that the student is not disadvantaged.

The University of Southampton sums up the approach which many universities are now adopting when they say

> Your supervisor will encourage you to publish parts of your thesis in appropriate academic journals. . . . In some cases it may be appropriate for you to publish co-authored papers with your supervisor. The Faculty does not support any attempt to require co-authorship as a right for all supervisors . . . no presumption should exist about authorship and in every case a decision should be made on a genuine assessment of the contribution of both the research student and supervisor.
>
> (University of Southampton 2001: 9)

Conclusion

The list of doctoral awards on offer in the UK and the number of variations within them may seem uncomfortably complex. It may be that there is little common ground that is certain enough and universal enough to establish an agreed standard let alone the kind of degree that can be described as doctoral. Yet there are some themes in all of the kinds of doctoral study considered in this book that are constant. The doctoral award indicates that the holder is in command of his/her subject, is able to make a contribution to understanding within the relevant discipline or field of enquiry and is therefore worthy of being listened to by peers. The holder of a Doctorate should, in turn, be able to make sound, respected judgements about the research work and findings of peers. These tenets hold true for all the kinds of doctoral award described in this chapter and in the three that follow. Subsumed within these tenets is the notion that the holder of a Doctorate is licensed (in the informal sense of the word) to practise at the highest level within his/her chosen domain. This notion persists whether in the case of the DClinPsy, where the successful candidate can practise as a clinical psychologist, or in the PhD which still retains its usage, possibly erroneously, as a basic qualifier for work in the university sector or in the PhD by Published Work where the holder has indicated that he/she has contributed to the relevant field and can demonstrate and defend the contribution to knowledge made in this context.

Summary issues

- How can we resolve the confusion that the ever-increasing range of titles under the Doctorate banner creates for both potential student and employer?
- How far has the nature of the doctoral submission reflected the changing nature of the doctoral process and the increasingly diverse community of stakeholders and their needs?

4

The PhD by Published Work

Introduction

In the UK higher education sector the use of publications in doctoral submissions has been a practice marked by lack of consistency and ill-defined borders. Many institutions offer the award but only to members of staff, and some extend the privilege to alumni. There are different notions of what counts as a publication and different notions of how a submission containing publications can be constructed and assessed. The evidence for this can be found in the two national surveys of this award undertaken by the UK Council for Graduate Education (UKCGE 1996b and Powell 2004) and which indicate a persisting trend of variation. These issues and others are explored in the light of current practice both in the UK and abroad.

This chapter focuses in the main on the PhD by Published Work as a distinct award separate from the PhD – that is, as an award with its own regulatory structure and with distinctive mechanisms for submitting work and its subsequent assessment. Mention is also made however of the place of publications within the traditional PhD submission.

Background

Context of the award

A central tenet of doctoral research is that the work achieved should have an impact on the knowledge base in the relevant field and that the candidate should be able to understand that impact (including how the impact within the immediate field interfaces with other related areas), present it clearly in a thesis and defend it against peer critique. In this sense, making findings public and testing them in a public arena are necessary parts of doctoral study and assessment. Clearly, a caveat needs to be applied here in relation to work that is deemed to require confidentiality for reasons of commercial exploitation and most, though not all, UK institutions would accommodate that requirement in their regulations. Whatever the case with regard to confidentiality, most UK universities would expect the PhDs that they award to contain material that is of 'publishable quality'. Publication is, then, one of the criteria by which PhDs are judged, though the extent to which this is made explicit by institutions in regulatory statements varies considerably.

Where publication, or the potential for publication, is seen as integral to doctoral level achievement in this way in the UK, it has not, typically, been seen as the sole route to a doctoral award. Doctoral theses are made public in the due course of events, but such publication has often succeeded rather than preceded the doctoral examination. In many institutions publications may be included in a doctoral submission or appended to the submission as additional evidence, but the distinction is still drawn between a *PhD* and a *PhD by Published Work* – these two awards are seen by most UK universities, but not all, as separate though related (see Powell 2004).

Differences in the composition of a candidate's submission via the two routes may call into question the relevance of a traditional thesis to the candidate's future career as a trained researcher where the recognized symbol of success is commonly, though not universally, high-quality, refereed publications. The rapid advancement of knowledge and the pragmatic concerns of national research assessment exercises mean that priority is attached to publications; therefore training in the preparation of research publications would seem to demand recognition as an essential component of PhD training programmes. Such recognition would need to be reflected in the assessment process for the traditional PhD submission (i.e. success in publication or the potential for success).

The origins of the PhD by Published Work are summarized by the UK Council for Graduate Education (UKCGE) in its first report into the award (UKCGE 1996b). It is noted that the concept of having a PhD submission wholly or largely based on published works originated in nineteenth-century Germany where it was a requirement of doctoral theses that they be printed, and copies lodged in all national university libraries. The genesis of the notion of 'publishability' and of 'going public' can therefore be traced to this requirement (see Simpson 1983 for a fuller description). Subsequently the concept of publishing doctoral theses was adopted across other European countries, and the USA, in the early part of the twentieth century.

The next phase of development seems to have been driven at least in part by pragmatic concerns. In both mainland Europe and the USA the expense of printing the whole doctoral thesis increasingly became a limiting factor in the award of the degree. As a reaction to this constraint the practice of making the award on the basis of published journal articles, book chapters or whole books emerged. The practice of having a PhD submission based on published works became well established in some European countries, notably Belgium, Holland and Sweden, though in these countries it is not necessarily the sole content of a doctoral submission.

In the UK there was anxiety that the award of PhD itself would undermine the established Higher Doctorates and in some cases the Masters degrees based on two years' supervised research. This anxiety and the subsequent resistance to the 'new' award meant that the argument about published work as part of a doctoral submission was delayed. It was not until the United Kingdom Universities Conference of May 1917 recommended the award of the PhD that the degree was first awarded by Oxford, albeit as DPhil (Simpson 1983). As for the relationship between published work and a doctoral thesis, the issue appears to have been taken up first by the University of Cambridge, which set up a committee to report on the award of the degree of PhD in the early 1960s and took the decision to introduce the published work route in 1966 (UKCGE 1996b). According to Simpson (1983), the original Cambridge regulations opened the degree to the alumni but excluded failed PhDs and prevented candidates from transferring from the conventional route. They required a compulsory oral examination and no college residence time.

European context

Academic institutions in many other European countries perceive merit in encouraging doctoral candidates to include published works as an integral part of their doctoral theses (UKCGE 1998b). Indeed,

> *in a minority of faculties/universities, the regulations explicitly require the candidate to have published before submitting their thesis. The evidence from the survey indicates that this enthusiasm for encouraging candidates to pre-publish at least some of the results of their research in advance of their examination, has been led by scientists, particularly in universities in Northern and Eastern Europe. It is equally evident, however, that this enthusiasm is not confined to science as many replies from non-science faculties emphasised the importance attached to published work and expressed the intention to attach greater priority to it in the future.*
>
> (UKCGE 1998b: 14–15)

It seems clear that many parts of Europe have adopted regulatory structures that are typified by flexibility in terms of the way in which a candidate's programme of study is pursued and the nature and content of his/her doctoral submission (UKCGE 1998; Kouptsov 1994). This flexibility is in contrast to the situation in many UK institutions where the two models of PhD exist as separate entities – one based on an individual programme of research training leading to the submission of a doctoral thesis which is defended at an oral examination, and the other based on submitted published works (Powell 2004). This separation between the two sets of regulations appears to distinguish, for the most part, the PhD and the PhD by Published Work in the UK from models of doctoral study prevalent in much of the rest of Europe. It should be noted, however, that some institutions in the UK do allow the possibility of publications being included in a traditional

PhD submission in addition to having a separate route known as a PhD by Published Work. Such institutions are closer to the European model. Indeed, there is also a small minority of UK universities where no separate route exists but where nevertheless publications are permissible within a traditional PhD submission, and indeed may form the major part of the evidence submitted (Powell 2004).

Prevalence of the award in the UK

Changes in the number of institutions offering the award

The UKCGE surveyed UK universities with regard to their use of publications in doctoral submissions over an eight-year period (in 1996 and again in 2004). Over these two census points there was an increase in the number of institutions offering the award. In 1996, 51% of the institutions that responded offered the award while in 2004 that percentage had increased to 80%. Caution needs to be used when interpreting these figures because of some differences between the two surveys (e.g. in terms of respondents). Nevertheless, there were indications that in the eight-year period leading up to 2004 the award was becoming more common across the sector. Taking this with the indication of the number of institutions that allowed published work to be part of a PhD submission that is not defined as 'by Published Work' (see Powell 2004: 13), it seems that published work in a general sense was figuring more largely in research degree submissions by 2004. Certainly there had been no movement indicated in the UKCGE data from offering to not offering the award. Further, a number of institutions appeared, at the time of the UKCGE survey in 2004, to be in the process of changing their regulations in the direction of encouraging the use of publications in doctoral awards (see Powell 2004: 10).

Number of PhDs by Published Work awarded

Despite the increase in use of publications in the regulations regarding PhD by Published Work, the actual number of awards made by this route remains small in comparison to the PhD itself and indeed in comparison to the Professional Doctorate awards. Of the 80 UK universities surveyed by UKCGE in 2004, 49 offered the award of PhD by Published Work and made, in total, 116 awards over a preceding two-year period. The mean number of awards by this route then was 2.4 for this sample over a two-year period. Of the universities sampled, 57% made between one and five awards over the two-year period. In 2004, fewer institutions than in 1996 made no awards of PhD by Published Work despite having it available.

In summary, while there had been no marked change over the eight-year period of the two surveys in the situation with regard to the awarding of PhDs by Published Work, if there was any trend at all it was towards the awarding of more of these degrees by a larger number of institutions.

Fees

Fee levels

Fee levels for the award of PhD by Published Work become an issue because where an institution has a regulation that allows the award to be gained on the basis of previously published work and where, therefore, the candidate may not require much, if any, supervision in the traditional sense of the term. The topic of supervision is considered later in this chapter.

Many universities operate a differential fee for the degree: with university staff either paying no fee or a substantially reduced one relative to the fee paid by other eligible candidates. This is, of course, the case with other university awards. Institutions operating a two-stage submission (*prima facie* and final) might also reimburse a substantial part of the fee if the candidate's submission failed at the *prima facie* stage. The range of fee charged for making registering/submitting for the award is wide. Powell (2004) reported a range within the 'pre-1992' sector from £260 to £1,640 with a mean of £722 while in the 'post-1992' sector the range was from £235 to £2,940 with a mean of £1,192.

The basis for fee levels

This wide range of fees does call into doubt the rational basis on which the fee has been set (UKCGE 1996b: 8). However, it may seem that the way in which institutions levy a fee for the award indicates something about the way in which they perceive it in terms of what it requires from candidates and, indeed, from academic staff with the responsibility for assessing any *prima facie* stage, supervising or advising on any written critical appraisal of the publications and finally for examining the submission. Clearly, such academic input is in addition to the administrative costs of managing the award. The range of fees charged probably reflects a wide range of interpretations of what the degree demands of candidates and of academic staff. This, in turn, reflects the kinds of varying interpretations of what the degree is being awarded for, that are discussed below.

The PhD by Published Work in relation to the PhD

Place of publications in PhD submissions generally

As noted earlier in this chapter, some UK universities that offer the specific, separate route of PhD by Published Work also allow publications as part of a non-specific research degree submission, and a further small number of universities that do not offer a separate route nevertheless allow publications to be included in submissions in this way (Powell 2004). In our own view, allowing or encouraging publications within a submission makes sense in as much as a doctoral level of award requires evidence that research outcomes have been judged by peers who have made a contribution to the field; clearly publication in a peer-reviewed journal indicates such a contribution. Publications used in this way become just one means of providing evidence in support of the candidate's thesis. In short, we think that a doctoral candidate ought to be required to develop an intellectual position that he/she then defends in argument, using evidence as appropriate. Publications become part of that evidence, used in argument to support the intellectual position taken. This issue is returned to later in the chapter (see page 78) where the merging of the two routes is considered.

The historical overview given earlier highlights one of the key tensions in terms of the relationship between publication and the award of a PhD. There is a measure of universal agreement in UK Higher Education Institutions (HEIs) that a PhD should be awarded on the basis that the candidate has contributed to knowledge in an area of intellectual endeavour. There is variation in the wording, with some requiring the contribution to be 'significant' and others using 'understanding' rather than, or as well as, 'knowledge' but the underpinning value judgement being made is that the doctoral award of PhD means that the successful candidate can demonstrate that he/she has contributed to knowledge and is capable of continuing to do so in an independent, original way. For a body of work to be realized as a contribution in any real sense, it has to be available to others in the field and has to be published in one form or another. For this reason, most institutions are wary of allowing theses to be held as confidential for other than a short period of time. Lengthy confidentiality runs counter to a main ethic of research, which is about the necessary dissemination of findings (again, recognizing here the need for confidentiality in respect of some intellectual property rights where patents are pending). Yet within this overall tension there is considerable variation: some institutions do not allow publication of material to be submitted prior to examination for PhD; some allow published material to be referred to in the text of the PhD thesis; some allow such material to be appended to the thesis; while others allow published work to be included in the main body of the text.

There is, then, some agreement about the importance of PhD level work being published, or at least being of 'publishable quality', but there is a lack of consistency about the place of published work in a PhD submission. Examiners may well be confused about the status of any published work in a PhD submission though relatively clear about the value of publication or publication potential.

The nature of study within the two kinds of PhD award (traditional and 'by Published Work')

There is a difference at one level between the two kinds of PhD in terms of relationship to research training. Many in the UK would define the PhD, in part at least, as a training in research methods and methodology. Such training may be readily defined and identified within PhD programmes of study whereas in the PhD by Published Work any training in research skills and knowledge may have been undertaken in a range of professional situations and may not necessarily have been clearly identified as such. Therefore, there is not necessarily any direct parity between the PhD by Published Work and the PhD at the level of those degrees being awarded for the pursuance of a programme of research training. However, it may be argued that in the PhD by Published Work the evidence of training can be determined by the quality of the publications and, in this sense, it is the products that are being judged regardless of the processes by which they were attained. Further, it is the case that what has been learnt by the candidate in his/her research training is not, typically, assessed directly in PhD examination. The difference between the two awards in relation to training is at the level of definition and identification of training undertaken rather than in its assessment.

If the PhD by Published Work is to be understood as a separate and distinctive award, then its relationship to the PhD that is awarded for something other than publications needs to be addressed. If both kinds of award are closely tied to the notion that publication is an essential part of doctoral level work, then it is important to understand why any distinction between the two awards is necessary at all. For many, the answer to this question is in the nature of the period of study rather than the nature of the assessment that follows that period. In the 'traditional' PhD there is a supervised programme of research – typically equivalent to three or four years of full-time study. However, in the PhD by Published Work this notion of supervision differs. In some cases it does not exist at all – the candidate binds together his/her published works and submits them for examination. In others, the candidate is supervised in the writing of a document that summarizes or critically appraises the publications. The nature of this document differs across institutions. For example, according to Powell (2004) the length of the document varies from 3,000 to 25,000 words and it is referred to variously as: commentary, summary, report, synthesis, supporting statement, doctoral statement, critique, critical essay, review, appraisal and analysis. As well as differing in name, the document seems to be seen to serve different purposes. Most commonly it is seen as a critical review of the collected publications.

For the most part, HEIs in the UK seek to ensure that the award of PhD by Published Work meets the same criteria as the PhD – that is, the successful candidate is judged to have made a [substantial] contribution to knowledge. The distinction between these two forms of Doctorate can be argued to be one of process. In the former the contribution will have been arrived at by research endeavours resulting in publications that may have taken place over a number of years prior to enrolment, whereas in the latter it will be by a supervised research programme resulting in a thesis. In this sense, the PhD by Published Work offers a different route to the same end as the 'traditional' PhD.

Institutions awarding the PhD by Published Work require that the contribution to knowledge be summarized and subjected to a critical analysis. The regulatory wording used by many institutions seems to imply that the candidate has to state the intellectual position that the publications lay claim to, and then defend, that position by argument. This is, of course, close to a working definition of what thesis means. Candidates for the PhD by Published Work are being asked in these latter cases to justify their implicit claim that their publications do contribute to knowledge within the particular sphere and that they can summarize that contribution and defend it in the written document and subsequently, perhaps, in an oral examination.

Locating the contribution to knowledge in the PhD by Published Work

Most universities in the UK with regulations enabling the submission of a PhD by Published Work require that the candidate critically appraise the contribution that his/her publications make. The length of this critical appraisal varies between institutions, as does its importance in the process of examination. A continuum of status is afforded to the critical appraisal – at one end it is either deemed unnecessary (the publications should 'speak' for themselves) while at the other it is what is judged (the publications are in support of the argument put forward in the appraisal). In this sense, in the former the contribution to knowledge is in the published works and in the latter it is in the appraisal. Clearly, somewhere in the middle of this continuum is the view that the contribution is made within the publications and, drawn together, made overt and critiqued in the appraisal.

The above section leads to the question of whether an examination for the award of PhD by Published Work should focus on the published works themselves or on the supporting document or, of course, on both.

The question relates essentially to where the contribution to knowledge is made, in the supporting document or in the publications. For most universities this is a simple matter; the contribution is in the publications and is summarized in the document. But for those institutions with a requirement of a substantial supporting document that critically analyses the significance of the publications and places the work in the context of other research, the matter may be less straightforward.

Institutions that have adopted a system in which candidates for the award of PhD by Published Work are supervised in the writing of this kind of critical supporting document, are implicitly accepting that those candidates need to construct and defend an intellectual position and that what is examined is the strength of that position and the candidate's ability to present and defend it. Such institutions are closely relating the two types of doctoral award – the PhD on the one hand and the PhD by Published Work on the other. Indeed, for these institutions the only real difference is that in the traditional model the programme of research is negotiated, at the outset of the registration, between candidate and supervisor and carried out under the guidance of that supervisor, whereas in the PhD by Published Work the research work will already have been, in the main, carried out and what is being supervised is the development of an intellectual position built upon those works and the production of a written document that seeks to explain and defend that position. There is then common acceptance that in the traditional PhD the contribution to knowledge is made manifest in the thesis. However, in the PhD by Published Work it may be that the contribution is to be found, if at all, in the findings of the research as reported in the publications, and the supporting document becomes a mere summarizing of those findings. An alternative view is that the contribution is to be found, as in the traditional model, in the critical account of the intellectual position presented by the candidate – and here the publications themselves contribute supporting evidence. Critics of the latter approach may suggest that such a construction is necessarily somewhat *post hoc* and hence compares unfavourably with a planned programme of research leading to a coherent contribution.

Summary of similarities and differences between the two routes

There are then similarities and differences between the two routes to a doctoral qualification – the PhD and the PhD by Published Work. There is similarity in that both emphasize appropriate research methodology and the requirement that the candidate should make a contribution to the advancement of the research field. There are differences in that while the PhD is based typically on a supervised programme of research and the submission of a traditional thesis, the PhD by Published Work is based upon research leading to a number of coherent publications, each of which has been subjected to peer review. Of course, the researching and the publishing in this latter case may or may not be supervised – according to an individual institution's regulations and practices – and in conventional registrations the appointed supervisor(s) takes responsibility for training the candidate in research methodology and for ensuring that the candidate develops appropriate personal and interpersonal skills. In the published work route such training is recognized and evaluated in retrospect and in this respect may be interpreted as analogous to the acceptability of accrediting prior learning in taught undergraduate and postgraduate programmes.

Merging the two routes to a PhD

It was argued in the UKCGE (1996b) report that there is merit in allowing the two routes (PhD and PhD by Published Work) to merge by encouraging all theses to include published work and for unpublished data to be written in the style of published work (UKCGE 1996b: 17). While there is no direct evidence that such a merger would be beneficial, it would mirror the situation that is prevalent in other northern European universities (UKCGE 1998b). While there is no indication in Powell (2004) that this notion has been taken up in UK institutions, from our perspective we consider the merging of the two routes, or at least a more flexible approach to the inclusion of publications in doctoral submissions, to be worthy of consideration – given the prevalence of publications as part of a doctoral submission in much of the rest of Europe and given the importance of publication as a key part of doctoral level work.

Certainly, there seems to be a strong argument for harmonization on the grounds of the need for parity to be transparent between the traditional and the 'by Published Work' route. UKCGE (1996b) noted, 'greater harmonization of policy and guidelines on these key regulatory issues between awarding institutions would help to allay anxieties about the academic merits of the publication route to PhD' (p. 19). It does seem that on some of the issues noted here, perhaps in particular the issue of restrictions on eligibility for candidature (considered below), the differences in practice are underpinned by very different views about the nature of the award of PhD by Published Work and more specifically its relationship to other forms of doctoral study. Differences of view at such fundamental levels may be problematic if the sector as a whole seeks to develop the range of doctoral study with some sense of coherence.

Eligibility of candidates and of publications

Eligibility of candidates

Many UK universities restrict registration for the award of PhD by Published Work to current members of staff. Sometimes this is extended to former members of staff and again to alumni. The variations on eligibility criteria are considerable. In the two UKCGE surveys of the PhD by Published Work in the UK (UKCGE 1996b; Powell 2004) it was apparent that quite a number of institutions operated a qualifying period for eligibility ranging from one to five years' employment in the institution. Some included technical and research staff and others did not. Yet again, in others, former members of staff were required (as a condition of eligibility) to submit within one to two years' of leaving the institution. There were numerous, and sometimes complex, references to eligibility requirements for those working in what may be summarized as 'collaborating establishments' or having connections with the university of one kind or another.

Powell (2004) indicated that the trend over the period 1996 to 2004, with regard to eligibility, was towards extension rather than further restriction. This was in part due to some of those institutions that had begun to offer the award since 1996 doing so with broad eligibility criteria and to the fact that some of those who have offered the award in both 1996 and 2004 had extended their eligibility criteria. The only category where eligibility has not increased, as a proportion of the number of institutions offering the award over the two surveys, was staff 'other than' academics. The biggest increase in eligibility related to the category of alumni. Powell (2004) also noted that there were indications of an increasing proportion of institutions making the award available to any applicant who was appropriately qualified, whether or not he/she had worked at, or been a graduate of, the institution.

Restrictions with regard to eligibility – effectively only awarding the degree to 'those on the inside' may create the impression that this route to a doctoral award is a privileged one. It is a short step from the notion of privilege to an impression that it may be less demanding in academic terms than the traditional PhD. There is no evidence that this is the case – we refer here to impression only. Individual institutions will have a view of the reasoning behind the restriction of the award to those on the 'inside' – yet if the award is deemed worth while for its own members, then a justification perhaps needs to be made for such restriction. Of course, the justification may relate quite reasonably to the issue of research training and the individual candidate's contributions to collaborative projects. On the other hand, it may reflect an uncertainty about the nature of the award and a hesitancy to open it up as an alternative mode of learning about research and gaining a research degree award subsequently. In the same vein, those institutions that have opened up the award to all suitably qualified applicants, whether or not they have an existing or previous connection with the institution, clearly have taken a stance with regard to the relationship between the award itself and evidence of research training. Similarly, the minority of institutions (Powell 2004) that require all or the majority of the research to be carried out within the candidate's current appointment in the institution will perhaps have a view regarding why research in a previous appointment should be discounted.

It does seem that if the critical review component of the submission is developed – so that it mirrors more closely the stating and defence of an intellectual position as in a traditional thesis – then some issues of doubt about the candidate's training in research methodology or contribution to collaborative projects may be allayed. Powell (2004) noted that those institutions that open the degree up to all comers tend to expect a substantial supporting document to accompany the publications.

It is clear from the above that many institutions in the UK restrict enrolment for the award to members of staff (often including ex-members) and to alumni. The justification for this is not always apparent in university regulations and may well relate as much to funding as to propriety in relation to the quality of the degree. Looking to the future, this is one area where the PhD by Published Work may need to develop. It seems that, for many institutions, the award is deemed good enough and inherently respectable enough for members of staff and alumni but is not available to those outside the institution. In our own view, this indicates, at the very least, a lack of equality of opportunity and, at worst, a closed system of 'rewarding one's own'. We would argue that there should be institutional rigour in ensuring the standard of the award and therefore it might be argued that it is invidious that the opportunity to submit for a PhD via the publication route should be dependent upon where a candidate studied for his/her first degree or where he/she is currently employed.

Time period for eligibility of publications

Powell (2004) noted that the majority of UK universities responding to the UKCGE survey recorded no restrictions at all with regard to time period for eligibility of publications. In contrast, small minorities recorded either (a) that only those publications produced during a candidate's appointment at the institution could be included in a submission for the award or (b) that a significant proportion of the publications needed to be published within the term of appointment. Some institutions recorded that publications needed to fall within a ten-year period, others a five-year period and another within a time frame of between three and six years. One institution recorded that it required candidates to have published within the two-year period prior to submission; another that it required candidates to have published for at least a two-year period prior to submission; and another that there was no formal statement and practice varied between disciplines. In short, the variations of practice in this matter across UK universities are considerable.

Restrictions on publications as related to a candidate's employment

Powell (2004) also noted that, for a minority of institutions, restriction with regard to time frame of publication follows on from restriction on eligibility of candidate. The candidate must be a member of staff and must undertake the research and publish it within his/her period of tenure. In one sense at least this may be seen to enable the institution to have some sense of quality control over the processes that enabled the research to be undertaken and the publications to be produced. One institution noted that, while it had no restriction in its regulations, this did mean that 'examiners need to be able to assess if the work was a contribution to new knowledge at the time of publication' (Powell 2004: 24). This kind of judgement may be interpreted as easier to make when the work falls within a limited time frame.

However, it seems that the majority of UK institutions set down no limitation of time. In these institutions it may be assumed that the responsibility for judging contribution to knowledge and impact on the field is given to the examiners and, further, that they will look for evidence to support a judgement in the critical appraisal that accompanies the publications. It may be argued that an institution's regulatory practice in respect of time periods for publication should reflect its considered view on just what is being assessed and on the kind of judgements that need to be made to enable that assessment to be effective.

Number of publications to be submitted

Notions of how many publications can or should be submitted for the award of PhD by Published Work vary across the UK sector. The majority of institutions make no statement about number in this sense (Powell 2004). A minority, however, are quite specific – for example, 'a submission must consist of either one or two books, or at least six refereed journal articles or research papers already in the public domain' (p. 24). Some referred to discipline specificity and others emphasized quality or kind (i.e. location in the public domain) rather than number.

The question of 'how many publications are needed' may be one that, typically, is asked by potential applicants for the degree. But, more importantly, any answer to the question indicates perhaps what is being judged in the submission. Where a selection from a candidate's published work is taken and is used by the candidate to illustrate or defend an intellectual position – embodied in a thesis – then what is being judged may be seen to be that thesis. On the other hand, where all of the works are expected to be submitted – or at least an indication of the candidate's bibliography – then it is the collected works that are the focus of the judgement as to whether or not the candidate is worthy or not worthy of a research award.

UKCGE (1996b) noted that, 'in spite of the requirement that the award of a PhD by published work and by a conventional thesis should achieve comparability of standards [the question of how many publications] probably leads to an overestimate of the number of publications required for the published work route' (p. 10). There is no evidence in Powell (2004) to suggest that this over-estimation in any way diminished or indeed increased over time. It does seem, however, that the way in which institutions have begun to treat the critical appraisal as an increasingly significant part of the submission for a PhD by Published Work does fit in with the view of the fundamental importance of such an appraisal to the 'establishment of the coherence and quality of the submission and hence of the case for the award of the degree' (UKCGE 1996b: 11). Clearly, the actual number of publications will vary necessarily between disciplines and between projects just as the number of actual or potential publications differs in the sense of being contained within traditional PhD theses. What should matter is the contribution to knowledge that the publications have made and the impact on other work in the area, as well as the appropriateness of the methodology to the project and the evidence that the candidate is an independent master of the relevant methodologies.

The question that may arise, in the light of the above, is the cohesion of the works submitted and the need to exclude publications that weaken the cohesion, however meritorious they may be in their own right.

Kinds of 'publication'

Many UK universities would include explicitly in their (regulatory) notion of 'published' areas such as art and design where output may not consist solely of printed works. For example, within submissions many would accept 3D artefacts with written contextualization, or unpublished papers or other medium formats. There is little evidence readily available concerning the different ways in which institutions may interpret whether or not any particular work(s) is in a form that is 'constant' enough and accessible enough to peer review to permit it to be judged as 'published'. It may well be that institutions make interpretations in this respect that are similar to those that they make in the context of work(s) submitted for a traditional PhD (albeit in some kind of category such as 'non-traditional' or 'non-literal' submissions) or for a Practice-Based Doctorate where such exists. Whatever the case, it is arguable that the issue of what counts as accessible within the public domain takes on a greater significance in the realm of a PhD by Published Work than is necessarily the case in a traditional PhD submission – though for many it remains important that every doctoral thesis is in a form that is constant enough to be accessible to others working in the field.

Supervision

Extent of supervision in the PhD by Published Work route

Whether or not an institution appoints a supervisor is indicative, to at least some extent, of its understanding of the relationship between the candidate's claim to have established an intellectual position which contributes to knowledge and the award of a PhD by Published Work. A majority of institutions in the UK appoint at least one supervisor, a minority appoint an adviser or mentor rather than a supervisor (Powell 2004). Assuming here that supervision implies a closer kind of intellectual intervention than merely advising or mentoring, then it seems reasonable to suggest from the data presented in Powell (2004) that there is a discernible trend towards the need for a more clearly defined kind of (supervisory) intellectual support from academic staff for the candidate for the PhD by Published Work.

In some institutions a candidate for the award of PhD by Published Work will be allocated a supervisor or mentor who is an identified, specific post-holder such as a Head of Department. Again, if the institution regards the degree of PhD by Published Work as one in which publications are used to support a unifying, critical statement about an intellectual position, then supervision is appropriate. If, on the other hand, the institution regards the degree as one to be awarded for the contribution to a field as made by a collection of publications and merely summarized in a sense of annotation rather than critique, the supervision becomes a matter of guiding the candidate through the institution's regulations and procedures or is non-existent. Similarly, the person identified as supervisor or adviser is perhaps indicative of the perceived nature of the task. In the institutions where the supervisor is named as the Head of Department or School (or nominee) or a member of a Research Degrees Committee – then presumably this person does not necessarily have subject expertise relevant to the specific area of the submission. In others, and more commonly, there is a supervisor (rather than adviser) who is experienced in the specific area and in supervision of doctoral candidates generally. Indeed, many institutions may apply the same requirements for supervision as are typically required for the 'non-published work' route.

Roles and responsibilities of supervisors

Powell (2004) reported a trend towards an increased importance being given to interpreting the degree as awarded for a contribution to knowledge that is set out in order to demonstrate its coherence in an analytical and critical way. In this sense, the submission would be constructed around, and would include, previously published work. The work may have been in the public domain for some time but the trend seems to be towards seeing the degree as being awarded on the basis of the case that is made (i.e. based on the publications but not consisting of them alone – their cohesiveness need to be overtly demonstrated and critiqued). Clearly, such a case would necessarily require intellectual effort and learning and therefore demands access to advice and guidance – in short, to supervision.

The survey reported in Powell (2004) does not pursue questions of how the roles of the supervisors of the PhD by Published Work are defined – beyond their existence and their title. Nevertheless, it may be reasonable to suggest that there are marked differences across the UK sector in terms of what is expected of the supervisor in the case of a PhD by Published Work that are in line with the range of differences that are reported in that publication. If this speculation is correct, then questions arise. For example, the training that is given to supervisors in many institutions is based on the notion of supervising the traditional PhD candidate. Yet, inasmuch as we have described earlier qualitatively different kinds of process underlying the traditional versus the 'by Published Work' routes, then there is an argument for suggesting that the training needs a differentiation that mirrors those differences, or at least recognizes them. In short, to supervise a candidate in designing and carrying out a programme of research study over a three- or four-year time span is a different task to supervising the writing of 25,000 words of critical exploration of the context and the impact of an existing body of work and, in turn, this is different from advising a candidate on how to assemble a set of existing publications and submit them for examination.

While there are differences there are also commonalities in what counts as supervision. Indeed, UKCGE (1996b: 13) suggested that the commonalities should be written into institutional regulations and thus become one device in efforts to 'harmonize' the regulations for the two degrees. We suggest here that it may be possible to conceptualize supervision as involving, *inter alia*, guidance on (i) the selection, coherence and quality of the candidate's work whether it be published or not, (ii) the preparation of the critical summarizing that accompanies any set of findings whether they be published or not, and (iii) preparation for the oral examination.

Assessment of the PhD by Published Work

Issues of assessment of the PhD by Published Work are dealt with in later chapters on monitoring and final examination. Among other things consideration is given to where the contribution to knowledge is located (in the works themselves or in the submitted summarizing text), how the award can relate to training in generic skills, the sense of parity with other forms of Doctorate and the tasks facing examiners in both assessing the submission and in undertaking an oral examination of the candidate.

Use of MPhil and MA/MSc by Research awards in the Published Work route

While the focus of this book is on doctoral study, it is perhaps worth noting briefly the place of the MPhil and MA/MSc by Research degrees in terms of academic awards gained for published works. In Powell (2004) it was noted that 15 institutions (from an overall sample of 80) offered the MPhil by Published Work in addition to the PhD by Published Work and two institutions offered, in the context of published works, a Masters (MA or MSc by Research) as well as an MPhil. Powell (2004) does not cite data relating the relationship within institutions between the MPhil (and Masters by

Research) in the traditional and in the 'by Published Work' routes. Nevertheless, given the prevalence of the MPhil across the sector it does seem reasonable to raise as an issue the offering of the degree (and indeed of the MA and MSc by Research) in the traditional but not in the Published Work route. If an institution operates some criteria for awarding the MPhil degree within the traditional route then it may be presumed that those could be considered in terms of whether or not they are achievable by the production of a submission, including predominantly previously published work. Of course, different institutions may treat the award of MPhil differently and therefore the issue may not be as straightforward.

Conclusion

The UK Higher Education system is at odds with many of its European neighbours in treating publications within doctoral submissions with some suspicion. While this is not universal or overt, within UK institutions, a reading of institutional regulations leads inescapably to this understanding. In our own view the way to resolve many of the issues that institutions face is to treat publications with more flexibility and openness. If a doctoral award is made for a contribution to knowledge, then whether or not that contribution is published or part published is of less importance than the way in which that contribution is elucidated and its import and impact. A fundamental rethink is required in respect of the relationship between the criteria for doctoral awards, ways of meeting them and publication.

Summary issues

- Does the PhD by Published Work offer the opportunity to bridge the divide between the different doctoral traditions in the UK and mainland Europe?
- Should the published papers' approach to submission become an accepted form of submission for the British PhD rather a discrete form of Doctorate?

5

Professional Doctorates

Introduction

We observed at the outset of this book that the last ten years has seen a significant diversification in doctoral awards offered, with a range of different practices and requirements. Perhaps the most clearly differentiated is the Professional Doctorate (UKCGE 2002), characterized by a significant taught element and delivered in cohorts. Indeed, the Professional Doctorate may be described as a development of the notion of a Taught Doctorate. It is one where the field of study is a professional discipline and where the student is supervised within a professional context or supervised within a university setting, but in relation to that context.

Number and range of professional doctoral programmes

Table 5.1 indicates the number of professional doctoral programmes available in the years 1998, 1999 and 2000, and Table 5.2 highlights the diversity of subjects covered by these programmes. Although we do not have data on the number of students engaged in these programmes, their existence draws attention to the range of studies that fall within the notion of doctoral education. If Professional Doctorates are to be valued and encouraged and seen as a viable and equitable part of doctoral education, then clearly they need to be treated with parity when it comes to quality issues.

Origins of the Professional Doctorates

A doctoral level of professional qualification

The Professional Doctorate has its origins in dissatisfaction with the PhD as a qualification appropriate for advanced professional work outside of

Table 5.1 Professional Doctorate programmes in UK universities – 1998 to 2000

Year	PD programmes
1998	109
1999	128
2000	153

Source: UKCGE (2002)

Table 5.2 Professional Doctorates in the different disciplines – 1998

Doctor of Education
Doctor of Engineering
Doctor of Clinical Psychology
Doctor of Psychology
Doctor of Educational Psychology
Doctor of Counselling Psychology
Doctor of Occupational Psychology
Doctor of Clinical Science-Psychotherapy
Doctor of Psychoanalytic Psychotherapy
Doctor of Business Administration
Doctor of Administration
Doctor of Finance

Source: UKCGE (2002)

academia. It is also the case that a doctoral level of study is seen as needed by those operating within the professions. First, professions tend to be marked by an increasing complexity and an increasing interrelatedness with other linked professions. Professional workers are increasingly in need of the kinds of research-based, analytical approach to problem solving that are the hallmarks of doctoral level study. Second, and more pragmatically, holding a first degree no longer gives a professional worker an advantage over colleagues. Many professions are 'degree only' and many entry level qualifications incorporate Masters level work: thus the need for an additional, advanced qualification is apparent.

International origins of the Professional Doctorate

The genesis described above first took place in North America and subsequently in Australia. According to Allen *et al.* (2002) the EdD developed in Canada in the late nineteenth century as a response to a perceived need for teachers and lecturers to further their professional education at the highest level. An EdD programme was established at the University of Toronto in 1894. However, Allen *et al.* (2002) also note that the Professional Doctorates have never established a firm popularity in Canada, and the end of the twentieth century has seen a decline in the number of programmes, with more faculties redesigning the PhD award rather than developing separate professional doctoral awards.

In 1921 the first Professional Doctorate award was developed at Harvard University in the USA. Again the award in question was the EdD. The development of Professional Doctorates in the USA is distinctive inasmuch as here they have been used as pre-service (high-level) qualifications rather than as awards gained by experienced professionals 'in-service', and they have been developed in professional schools (e.g. in schools of psychology) as well as in universities. Professional Doctorates in this context have typically involved more taught coursework than the PhD (which in the USA usually involves substantial coursework) along with shorter dissertations and periods of supervised professional practice.

Scott *et al.* (2004) note that the situation in Australia more closely resembles that in the UK with the first award being established in 1984 (Doctor of Creative Arts at the University of Wollongong) and the EdD appearing around the same time as in the UK (University of Melbourne in 1990). The findings of Bourner *et al.* (2001a) and of Poole and Spear (1997) suggest that in Australia and the UK the 1990s were the decade in which the Professional Doctorates became established in subjects such as education, business, law, psychology, health sciences, humanities, design and architecture. While the roots of the Professional Doctorates may approximate between the two countries, subsequent development can be distinguished in as much as there has been a stronger focus in Australia on a so-called 'second generation' of such doctorates (Maxwell 2003) in which there is increased flexibility of delivery, more integration with the professional workplace and more widespread use of a portfolio model of assessment rather than 'coursework plus dissertation'. This second generation then serves to reduce the dominance of the university sector (the 'academy') and its tendency to give academic knowledge precedence over professional knowledge.

Growth of the Professional Doctorates

One of the features of the Professional Doctorates programmes has been a rapid growth in numbers over a relatively short period of time. From beginnings around the end of the 1980s, UKCGE (2002) quote figures for such programmes as noted in Table 5.1 (that is, 109 in 1998, 128 in 1999 and 153 in 2000). Bourner *et al.* (2001b) (cited in UKCGE 2002) quote an approximate 20% increase per year over recent years.

The UKCGE report (UKCGE 2002) noted that the Professional Doctorates were initiated predominantly within the pre-1992 sector: by 1998, 26 of the 35 universities in this category 'offered at least one professional doctorate compared with only 12 of the new universities' (p. 24). Drawing on a source (Bourner *et al.* 2001b) the report also noted that subsequent growth has been largely in the post-1992 universities. Reasons for the slow beginnings of professional doctoral awards in the post-1992 sector and the subsequent rapid growth may be speculated upon – but certainly the need to staff cohorts of students at doctoral level may have militated against the adoption of these degrees in the new university sector initially. Subsequently, as expertise and experience has grown, so has the development of new Professional Doctorate awards. These awards may well seem to be well suited to many of the post-1992 sector – where applied courses firmly rooted in the world of work are often central to mission statements.

In terms of growth in the respective professional areas the UKCGE (2002) report also noted that 'the whole professional doctorate market is significantly skewed towards the public sector' (p. 39). The EdD is here reported as having the largest share of the market with the 'various psychology related professions occupying a further big tranche' (p. 39). Thus the public sectors of education and health make up substantial parts of the Professional Doctorate scene. Interestingly, growth in terms of the professions seems to correspond negatively to the payment by employers of tuition fees. UKCGE (2002), in their survey, note that in the business and technical areas (e.g. the DBA and the EngD) employers typically pay fees and expenses whereas in the higher growth area of education (e.g. the EdD) the student typically either pays or contributes whereas, in the second key growth area of the psychology disciplines, the student is usually self-funding (UKCGE 2002: 40).

Entry criteria

One significant difference between the PhD and the Professional Doctorate is the way in which the criteria are determined for entry to the programme. Entry to PhD programmes is usually determined on the basis of academic qualifications, whereas Professional Doctorate candidates may need to have professional qualifications in addition to those of an academic kind – that is, particular kinds and levels of professional experience may also be required.

Level of award

UKCGE (2002) indicated that there was a general consensus across the sector that the Professional Doctorate should be equivalent in terms of quality to the PhD. As the latter preceded the former, it is perhaps natural that the new award should be measured against the older. And clearly, to have two awards that carry the title of 'doctor' implies that there is equivalence of level of achievement. Yet it is also the case that the criteria for the two awards differ, and so at least in claiming equivalence there is the danger of not comparing like with like. It may also be suggested that the Professional Doctorates require more of their students: if they are to be successful such students need to demonstrate the achievement of various learning outcomes as well as match up to the more implicit requirements of the PhD. Indeed, pressures to give the 'final thesis' element of the assessed work of the Professional Doctorate some sense of parity with the submitted thesis of the PhD, by indicating a similar word length, is in effect to skew the weight of the study towards the Professional Doctorate because that kind of doctorate will almost inevitably have involved the assessment of other pieces of work prior to the final stage.

Relation to professional discipline

In a Professional Doctorate the field of study is a professional discipline which may, of course, subsume different academic disciplines. The Professional Doctorate will be closely related to the development of practice within the profession and may indeed be accredited by a professional body and result in a professional qualification. It follows that, typically, the professions concerned are those where there is a strong practice element that, in turn, is mediated by intellectual understanding and reflection. UKCGE (2002) noted that the main disciplines that had developed Professional Doctorate programmes were:

- Engineering where the EngD was seen as a way of fast tracking talented engineers – deemed to be in need of training in high level problem solving skills allied with sophisticated technical expertise and the ability to collaborate effectively in team-based industrial situations (Science and Engineering Research Council 1991).
- Education where a dissatisfaction with a contribution to the field by researchers that was felt by many to be too remote from the actual needs of teachers practising at the 'chalkface'. The EdD typically seeks to constantly bring evidence based research tools to bear on practical issues within teaching and learning and within the management of the educational system.
- Clinical Psychology where the kinds of masters level courses, accredited by the British Psychological Society, for those with a first degree in psychology wishing to specialize in clinical work have been extended to take in doctoral level study. The DClinPsych is now accepted as the entry-level qualification to engage in clinical practice.

The Professional Doctorate may have begun within the three areas noted above but other fields of disciplinary study such as nursing and business administration have also developed doctoral awards (e.g. the DNurse and the DBA). It is perhaps also important to note here that increasingly the professions are marked by a need for interdisciplinary working and hence professional workers at the highest level are required to be able to operate effectively at the interface between disciplines. Again, to know a lot about a very little is often not sufficient for doctoral level professionals – the kind of education they require reflects the need for this interdisciplinary, intellectual activity (Powell 1999a).

Nomenclature

Clearly, one major distinction of the Professional Doctorates is the use of the professional area as part of the nomenclature. This stands in contrast to the PhD where no qualifier is used. Yet the nomenclature of the professional doctoral awards is not wholly standardized. For example, Professional Doctorates in engineering can be described as the EngD or the DEng, in education as the EdD or DEd. Some institutions collect all the Professional Doctorates that they offer under the award title of DProf. The title of DBA to denote a Doctorate in Business Administration proves problematic where the Diploma in Business Administration (again DBA) already exists. HEIs may seek other titles to differentiate the doctorate from the diploma. This lack of standardization is not, of course, restricted to Professional Doctorates. UK Higher Education Institutions jealousy guard their right to develop, describe and award their degrees.

The UKCGE report on Professional Doctorates (UKCGE 2002) identified the trend of increasing detail in the way in which these degrees are named. For example, the report noted that in 1998 the following named Professional Doctorates existed within the professional area of psychology: Doctor of Clinical Psychology, Doctor of Psychology, Doctor of Educational Psychology, Doctor of Counselling Psychology, Doctor of Occupational Psychology, Doctor of Clinical Science-Psychotherapy and Doctor of Psychoanalytic Psychology. Similarly, in Business Administration degrees such as Doctor of Management, Doctor of Administration and Doctor of Finance have appeared to differentiate the main field more precisely. Clearly, there is a tension here between useful increased specificity and confusing proliferation of titles – and particularly perhaps of the abbreviations of those titles – that is, the letters after the name that candidates are entitled to use in their professional work. Arguably, if a title is not widely recognized in the profession then its usefulness is diminished.

It may seem that having moved away from the use of a single title (e.g. PhD or DPhil) for all doctoral awards, including those gained by work within a defined area of professional knowledge and expertise, the HE sector in the UK has inevitably moved towards ever-increasing fineness of definition within titles. If the professions become ever more subdivided in terms of specialisms within disciplines then one may presume that a corresponding amount of increased differentiation will occur in professional doctoral titles. Where specific skills and/or knowledge are required for a particular level of professional responsibility then the marketplace may well require that the professional worker be seen to be equipped with them – that he/she is suitably qualified. However, the increased differentiation also brings with it a lessening of the notion that someone operating at doctoral level is not necessarily constrained by the specifics of any one situation but can apply their skill and knowledge to new and challenging problems as they arise and can understand how their knowledge and skill interfaces with and impacts upon other areas. The world of the professions requires interdisciplinary abilities of its doctoral workers. Marking out defined areas of knowledge and skill within existing professional disciplines in professional doctoral titles is therefore more than just a matter of the 'naming of parts', it reflects on understandings of the nature of professional knowledge and the roles of the most highly qualified professional workers.

Career development

All of these professions require initial and 'in-service' training and therefore, Professional Doctorates form the highest pinnacle of professional engagement. They tend to attract high-achieving individuals, many of whom see the Professional Doctorate as a dimension of their career development.

Mode and kind of study

Mode of study

Most Professional Doctorate students will be working full-time in their profession and therefore registered as part-time students. Yet they may also be working on their doctoral qualification as part of their continuing professional practice. The distinction between part time and full time is therefore of a particular kind in the realm of the Professional Doctorate.

Kind of study

Where Professional Doctorates are described as containing 'taught' elements, these may well not conform to a traditional notion of a didactic delivery of a curriculum. Various forms of directed or guided study are used to deliver particular kinds of learning outcomes. Many Professional Doctorate programmes may involve the student in no, or very little, class contact though clearly in others such contact will exist. It is unlikely that any more than one-third of a student's time would be spent in taught elements. The notion here of describing specific learning outcomes for doctoral study again marks out the Professional Doctorates from the PhD where, in the latter, outcomes are typically couched in more general terms.

The kind of study involved in a Professional Doctorate has implications for the kind of teaching involved. It is likely that there will be some elements where a didactic mode is deemed appropriate for the delivery of certain key skills of, for example, research methodology and professional practice. But it is also the case that there will be substantial parts of a programme of study requiring supervision of the student. Here again there is a difference between the notion of supervision of a PhD as opposed to a Professional Doctorate student. In the former a student is likely to be allocated a supervisor or team of supervisors who remain constant throughout the programme of study, whereas in the latter the student may have different supervisors for different phases of the programme. For PhD students it is likely that the supervisor who is allocated to them (or indeed who they 'choose' for themselves) is an expert in the particular research programme to be pursued, whereas Professional Doctorate students may find themselves being supervised by someone who is an expert in the professional discipline but not necessarily in the particular work-based projects that the students undertake. Indeed, while PhD students typically define their projects within the early stages of registration, Professional Doctorate students may not define their 'final' projects until the latter stages of the overall programme, at which time supervision then becomes a matter of matching up as best as one can student project with supervisor expertise. (Clearly, this is commonplace at taught Masters level – but there the emphasis is not on knowledge creating.) Further, Professional Doctorate students may need supervision at the local level within their professional working environment. In this scenario issues arise of (i) conflict of interest (a local supervisor may have to act as both mentor and judge) and of (ii) the ability of the local supervisor, especially if he/she is outside of academia, to make judgements that take account of the range of abilities and achievements within a cohort of students.

Kind of knowledge

The Professional Doctorate typically demands not only a profound understanding of professional issues and the current state of professional knowledge but also an understanding of how research methods impact on the professional world. Such understanding is clearly necessary but not sufficient. Most institutions offering Professional Doctorate awards would require that successful candidates for such an award should have sufficient understanding and skills to enable them to continue to use researching in an independent and creative way within their professional work. It is clearly not enough for someone at doctoral level to know about the research that impacts on the field in which one operates; such a professional would need to be able actively to employ research as part of his/her professional work. Restriction to a reactive mode of operation would not be sufficient to meet most HEIs' criteria for the award. The criteria, as discussed below, would involve contributing to professional knowledge and practice, and being able to contribute in this way requires both understanding of extant knowledge and the ability to add to it or change it. In the context of the Professional Doctorate, the knowledge at issue may well be of the 'applied' kind but it is still knowledge – open to expansion and change through processes of investigation, evaluation and so on. It is notable that where the kind of academic knowledge typically referred to in PhD regulations may be general, the kind within the context of a professional doctorate may be specific to a professional context, albeit with implications for a broader understanding of the world. In both cases, we suggest that contributions can be made that can be deemed 'original'.

Criteria for the award of a Professional Doctorate

Most HEIs would claim that the Professional Doctorate should be awarded for the same level of work as the PhD – however, there is an acceptance that the routes to the two awards will differ and the kinds of experience of learning for the students will differ. It is much a matter of emphasis: where the PhD typically demands a substantial and original contribution to knowledge, the Professional Doctorate will demand a similarly substantial and original contribution but to professional practice. Of course there is scope here for considerable overlap. A successful PhD thesis submitted by a teacher and involving pedagogy and children with dyslexia will necessarily make an original contribution – but only to professional practice in relation to such children rather than to 'knowledge' more generally. The boundaries here are fuzzy. Similarly, it can be argued that the successful EdD student in contributing to an understanding of, for example, the impact of dyslexia on the process of education is contributing to knowledge. Again, the distinction here is one of emphasis and intention rather than epistemology. The criteria for the award of a Professional Doctorate would necessarily need to encompass an original contribution to the knowledge and practice of the relevant profession.

Typically the PhD is awarded on the basis of a substantial written piece of work described as a thesis that is examined by *viva voce* (where held). In the case of the Professional Doctorate the situation is similar though the submission may be more of a portfolio type and the *viva voce* may need to take into account the candidate's progress through a whole programme of study.

Assessment

Assessment criteria

Assessment of the Professional Doctorate is typically by a mixture of course work and *viva voce*. In terms of the criteria for assessment, where the PhD is typically referenced to a 'norm' – however ill-defined – and where the previously stated criteria for the award are usually related to a contribution to knowledge, the award of the Professional Doctorate may well be related to set learning outcomes encompassing professional skills and knowledge. It would be too bold to claim that the PhD is norm referenced whereas the Professional Doctorate is criterion referenced, but certainly the former relates to a notion of doctorateness whereas the latter will relate, in part at least, to defined criteria (aspects of professional knowledge and skills). The edges of this distinction are blurred because the Professional Doctorate tends to have predetermined learning outcomes as part of a learning programme that leads to, or supports, a contribution to professional knowledge and understanding. In essence the Professional Doctorate combines the notions of the predetermined curriculum that pervades taught course programmes with the individually designed programmes of research study typified by research degrees.

The kind of combining that is mentioned above does carry inherent dangers, particularly perhaps in respect of the amount of assessing that may occur in the Professional Doctorate programme in contrast to that occurring within the traditional PhD route. Where a candidate has to complete components of a Professional Doctorate programme that involve directed learning and specified assessments in addition to a substantial individual piece of research that contributes to knowledge about the profession and its practice, then clearly there is a possibility that the total amount of work will exceed that in the traditional route. Scott *et al.* (2004) note that all the programmes in their sample included such assessed 'taught' components in addition to the production of a thesis and that all the components and the thesis contributed to the final award. Certainly a cursory look at advertised Professional Doctorate programmes indicates that, in terms of the crude number of words alone, the typical expectation far exceeds that within the traditional context. This is not to argue that the number of words produced equates to quality achieved but rather that, if the Professional Doctorate is a different route to the same level of doctoral achievement, then there needs to be acceptance that it might well involve different kinds of output, assessed in different ways, albeit at the same level. Final theses do not need to be of the same volume where the thesis is a greater or lesser part of the overall work. In short, we suggest that what is necessary across types of doctorate is parity of level, and that this is not achieved by parity of word length and substance of final submission.

Critical reflection

Both PhD and Professional Doctorate require reflection; however, it is likely that the kind of intellectual reflection required in the latter is more clearly defined than in the former and will often relate to reflection on practice specifically. The Professional Doctorate candidate is likely to have to focus on his/her own practice in a structured and overt way, whereas the PhD candidate is likely to be required to give evidence of his/her reflective capacities within the way the research is conducted and reported. In a related sense, the kinds of problems that candidates for the two differing awards try to address may differ. PhD candidates are able to choose from a range of issues and problems, some of which may be long term and some of which may be 'pure' as opposed to applied. The candidate for a Professional

Doctorate is more likely to have to address problems in the short term as well as take, for example, strategic long-term views.

Final examination

The final examination phase of Professional Doctorate study is referred to in Chapters 11 and 12. It is important to note the contrast with the situation of a PhD examination. In this latter scenario the candidate is examined, typically, on the basis of one submitted piece of work – the thesis – while a Professional Doctorate may be awarded on the basis of a number of disparate pieces of work and on the basis of recognized skills acquired.

Group-based work

Cohort-based course structures

Here again a clear distinction between the PhD and the Professional Doctorates is hard to make. In the past it might have been possible to define the PhD as not cohort based in contrast to Professional Doctorate programmes which invariably were. Even here such a definition would have been overly simplistic and not universally applicable where many science-based individual research projects were strongly linked to other student projects within the same laboratory. But, setting aside such collaborative research environments, the increased number of research training courses that are integral to PhD programmes of study, and so-called 'New Route' PhDs that include significant taught elements, has reduced this distinction further. It is no longer clear that Professional Doctorate programmes can be readily distinguished from PhD programmes by being cohort-based, though clearly cohorts in the formal sense are more likely to be a feature of the former rather than the latter.

Collaborative work

Following on from the discussion above about working within cohorts, it is noteworthy that many professional situations require teamwork (Powell 1999a) and that, as a consequence, Professional Doctorate programmes may to a greater or lesser extent make collaborative working the focus of study. Students on such programmes are likely to be required to gain understanding of the dynamics of working with others and give evidence that they have the requisite skills to make them initiators in professional situations where group working plays a significant role. Again, assessment of these skills may be problematic, particularly where they can only really be evidenced in specific, often fast-moving, professional situations where the interplay of variables not only serve as signifiers of the complexity that is required of the participants but also confound comparability of assessment.

The distinction between the PhD and the Professional Doctorate

The perception of tensions in doctoral study that gave rise to the notion of Professional Doctorates as distinct from the PhD related to (i) the need for a high level of professionally related skills in programmes of study and (ii) a focus on practice rather than theory. Yet in both these instances the boundaries are not clear. The Framework for Higher Education Qualifications in the UK indicates a need for employment-related skills to be part of the doctoral qualification. This rather obscures the first of these points of differentiation between the PhD and the Professional Doctorates. Similarly, that same framework does not separate out practice from theory and, in any case, such a separation is hard to sustain in the increasingly complex professional worlds where knowledge about theory that underpins practice is not readily distinguishable from knowledge about practice, and where professional skill and knowledge are seen as mutually dependent (the professional worker needs to know why as well as how to apply a skill in any particular context, and the successful application of a skill is necessarily dependent on that understanding).

Throughout this section it has become clear that the distinctions between Professional Doctorates and the PhD are fuzzy and have become increasingly so over recent years. The question arises, therefore, as to the need for the distinction. It is possible to conceive of students following different pathways to the same kinds and levels of academic achievement and all receiving a singular doctoral award – the PhD. Indeed it could be argued that the HE sector in the UK is in danger of proliferating the kinds of nomenclature available for this level of doctoral study. This becomes an issue of recognition in national and international contexts. A university can choose to award a doctor of management and call it a DMan; the 'D' then becomes the signifier for a whole range of possible awards. This may or may not be satisfactory to those in the world outside of academia who need to be able to recognize and respond to levels of award. The roots of this proliferation are in the need to give students a recognition for the particular type of professional disciplinary study in which they have engaged. In short, engineers need to be able to indicate in their high achievement that it has been about engineering.

Some UK universities offer a DProf. Such an award is typically either (i) a set of Professional Doctorates collected together and delineated from the PhD or (ii) a generic notion of doctoral study within professional domains in which individual candidates negotiate a programme of study that is at doctoral level, makes use of core modules on methodology, etc., and is within his/her particular profession. This is seen as a solution of sorts but in fact merely draws a line around a kind of study that is based on professional practice, as opposed to a kind that is not (or rather may not be).

The use of credit

The use of transferable credit for defined learning outcomes permeates the postgraduate scene within universities in the UK. Yet the position of doctoral study in relation to credit is not straightforward, as has been noted elsewhere in this book. Many Professional Doctorate programmes make use of modules from other postgraduate programmes, notably at Masters level. Where such modules are credit rated, an issue clearly arises concerning the usability of those credits within any doctoral award. UKCGE (2002: 31) notes that it would not be appropriate to award credit for a significant contribution to knowledge. A tension arises then at this interface between the traditional notion of a non-credit-rated PhD and a Professional Doctorate that makes use of existing credit-rated courses. A similar tension arises where a Professional Doctorate that does not make use of such existing courses is offered nevertheless in a modular format that defines learning outcomes that are, in turn, amenable to credit rating. The tension relates specifically to the value that can be put upon proportions of the overall achievement, and UKCGE (2002: 32) suggests that 'an appropriate credit requirement for a professional Doctorate would be in the range of 120 to 270 credits, depending on the proportion of total time devoted to the taught elements'. That report also notes that the national credit consortia (CQFW, NICATS, NUCCAT, SEEC – see list of abbreviations for full descriptors) proposed a contrasting notion: 'The model proposed for Professional Doctorates is 540 credits in total of which up to 180 can be at level 7 (equivalent to masters degree level), while the remaining is at level 8 (defined as doctoral level)' (cited in UKCGE 2002: 33).

There are, then, differences of approach to trying to interpret the doctoral part of a programme of professionally focused study in terms of learning outcomes that can be allocated credit. On the one hand, there is doctoral achievement (e.g. the 'contribution to knowledge') and on the other are the professionally focused research skills that are the learned outcomes of study. It may be possible to define the level of credit that would be operable within doctoral study (though even here it is arguable how much of an overall programme is at masters rather than doctoral level) but it is harder to allocate a volume measure to what is effectively a judgement about proven ability to contribute to, as well as make use of, knowledge.

There are two purposes to credit rating: to enable the transfer and the accumulation of credits. While individual institutions may respond differently to the issue of credit rating parts or the whole of doctoral study, in the main they seem to be reluctant to engage in the transfer of credit at doctoral level. Where it is used at all, credit is therefore seen as a device to enable the identification of a student's accumulation of discrete parts of a learning process in the form of learned outcomes.

Conclusion

With its origins in both dissatisfaction with the structure and demands of the PhD award and a perceived requirement for the need to recognize at doctoral level contributions to professional knowledge and practice, the professional doctorate offers a new way of looking at the doctoral qualification. In so doing it challenges notions of the learning processes that might lead to a doctoral award and it causes a rethinking of the relationship between teaching, learning and the creation of new kinds of knowledge. Perhaps the challenge for the professional doctorate is in maintaining the confidence of academia on the one hand and of the professions on the other that the Professional Doctorate is at the same level as the PhD, and is in essence a different way to achieving the same advanced level of study and 'contribution'. It seems to us that those institutions that conflate the notion of 'taught doctorate' with 'professional doctorate' make this challenge more complex. The Professional Doctorates need to be seen and treated as research degrees that produce doctoral thinkers and doers, albeit in specified areas of professional practice and by different means. What is common is 'doctorateness' and that is a standard, or an elevation, that is attainable by different routes.

Summary issues

- Does the Professional Doctorate fundamentally challenge the concept of doctorateness as a level of academic achievement by focusing on intellectual content rather than originality of findings or outcomes?
- Should the tendency towards portfolio evidence challenge the conventional PhD thesis?
- Does the concept of professionally oriented research, as opposed to academic research, give rise to a false dichotomy?

6

Practice-Based Doctorates

Introduction

This chapter examines some of the features of the 'Practice-Based Doctorate' and explores issues that surround it. These revolve around how readily a separate category of Doctorate can be defined in a way that is sustainable and what the basis for such an award might be. There is discussion of the relationship between (i) designing and creating products, (ii) researching and (iii) the criteria of research degree awards. What is submitted and how it is examined are discussed.

Context of the development of the Practice-Based Doctorate

The concept of the Practice-Based Doctorate has become an issue in the UK and subsequently in some other parts of Europe since the early 1990s (Durling *et al.* 2002; Frayling 1993) though the award, and in particular the PhD by musical composition as an example of it, predates this. Since 1990 there has been a trend in the UK towards integrating independent art and design schools into universities. This process brought with it an increasing emphasis on research training in areas where previously studio skills were valued 'rather than analytical or intellectual skills' (Durling *et al.* 2002: 8). Those working in areas of art and design within the university system of the UK, and who were interested in engaging in research, began to take PhD degrees in order to gain the necessary skills to become researchers. The situation in North America was slightly different in this respect with the Master of Fine Art (MFA) being seen as a terminal award and as having equivalence with the PhD in as much as it indicates a contribution to the profession. In the UK the situation described above was the context of, and to some extent the stimulus for, a debate about the relationship between art and design, research and pedagogy. For example, Frayling (1993) discussed concepts of research *into* design, research *by* design and research *for* design; later Durling *et al.* (2002) noted eight different models of kinds of Doctorate related to the art and design field.

A separate category of doctoral study

A particular orientation to the process of researching

There is a view in many parts of UK academia that doctoral level study may be accommodated within all intellectual domains and further that a PhD award can be made in any such domain. This view suggests that the PhD is a generic award made for contribution to knowledge, whatever the nature of that knowledge. The Professional Doctorates discussed elsewhere in this book are delineated because the contribution is to the particular profession and to knowledge and skill within that profession. In that case, nomenclature follows the distinctiveness of the profession. There is, however, another sub-group of areas within which distinction from the PhD is drawn – that is, areas that are based in 'practice' and where contributing to knowledge is done, arguably, through the practice itself. So, while many professions involve practice and various levels of application of distinctive knowledge and skill, the areas being referred to here typically involve a 'creative product' of some kind and a different orientation to the process of researching. Also, the outcomes may be presented for examination in forms of submission that differ from the 'standard' PhD (sometimes referred to in institutional regulations as 'non-standard' submissions). Out of these beginnings arises the notion of a category of doctoral study that relates specifically to disciplines that involve a creative, recordable outcome; this category is commonly labelled as the 'Practice-Based Doctorate'.

It is perhaps worth stressing that this kind of Doctorate is not, therefore, merely a Doctorate awarded in an area that includes an element of practice. After all, areas that involve practice such as medicine, teaching or engineering can lead to forms of study that may operate at doctoral level. In such areas knowledge may be advanced about practice and within a practice environment. The distinction, which needs to be considered here, is between these kinds of doctoral study in practical areas and a kind of study where knowledge is advanced by means of the practice itself.

For the purposes of this book, 'practice-based' is being interpreted as practice linked to the creative arts and involving a contribution to knowledge through practice. This is not to deny the view expressed above that all areas of practice might be included in the concept. Here most other 'practices', which are not usually encompassed within the creative arts, are encompassed within Chapter 5.

Prevalence of the award

It is difficult to identify how many institutions in the UK offer awards at research degree level that are specifically demarcated in their regulations as 'practice-based'. This difficulty reflects the artificiality of the distinction. However, the evidence from the report by the UK Council for Graduate Education (UKCGE 1997) was that 45 of the 90 institutions that responded to the Council's national survey offered such awards – that is, these institutions had regulations in this respect that were specific enough to require separate, distinct regulatory practice. This is not to say, of course, that other institutions did not encompass creative outcomes within their research degree regulations in non-specific ways.

Nomenclature

This chapter deals for the most part with the award of the PhD for practice-based work. However, it should be noted that some institutions offer different doctoral titles for practice-based work, notably the Doctor of Music (DMus) and the Doctor of Art (DArt). The DMus degree was recorded as being awarded by 13 institutions in the UKCGE (1997) survey; however, it was also used to denote a 'Higher Doctorate' award (a topic that is dealt with elsewhere in this book). According to the UKCGE report (UKCGE 1997: 24), a distinction can be drawn between the practice-based PhD and a doctoral award relating to a specific named practice-based area (again, such as the DArt and the DMus). The distinction drawn in the report is between the former category (the PhD) that requires 'research orientation' and the latter (*inter alia*, the DArt and the DMus) that do not. In the report it is suggested that the latter category '*allows individual excellence to be recognized and celebrated . . . but does not imply or require research orientation*' (p. 24). For our part it seems that this distinction is not sustainable across the sector. There is undoubtedly confusion over titles but trying to categorize kind in relation to nature of title is likely to mislead in some cases. Indeed, in the UKCGE report referred to above, at least one institution was recorded as offering an 'AMusD' signifying a Doctor of Musical Arts. The diversity across the sector in this matter militates against useful categorization of titles in relation to level of award (Doctorate or Higher Doctorate) and to content of submissions.

It should also be noted here that we are leaving the Doctor of Medicine (MD) out of this particular discussion because it seems to us to represent a different kind of award in that, while it does involve practice, it is not necessarily of the sort that ends with creative outputs and it is, in any case, primarily a licence to practise. The MD has been discussed earlier in this book.

Basis for the award of a Practice-Based Doctorate

The production of creative works

Perhaps the most common view (see UKCGE 1997), though not universally accepted, is that the Practice-Based Doctorate is distinguishable from both the PhD and the Professional Doctorates in that, typically, it involves production of creative works as a direct way of contributing to knowledge. There are clearly some problematic issues arising from this view. Primary among these is the question of whether or not a Practice-Based Doctorate can be awarded solely on the basis of the production of a creative work(s) – assessed by knowledgeable peers who are experienced in the field and who can therefore pass judgement on whether or not the work(s) is worthy of note as excellent in respect of the criteria operating in that field and as contributing to knowledge in itself. An alternative is to suggest that however much critical acclaim can be agreed upon in these respects, the work(s) requires an intellectual contextualization and critical interpretation if it is to be deemed worthy of a doctoral award. Both of these views are manifest in particular institutional regulations in the UK – there is no national consensus.

Explicit and implicit indications of processes

Underpinning the second of these views is a two-fold notion relating to the purpose of the PhD as a doctoral award. First, many across the sector would concur that the PhD is closely tied to training in how to do research. While a creative output may indicate that the creator *has* engaged in such training – for example, has investigated, designed and made use of research techniques – such an indication will remain implicit unless the candidate sets down a discursive account of how the research goals were achieved. The second, related, issue concerns the dissemination of findings as a necessary requirement of doing research and, therefore, of being awarded a higher degree for doing it. Research at doctoral level ought, by common consent, to result in a contribution to knowledge if it is to be counted as 'successful' in terms of an award. And this contribution can, *de facto*, only come about when it is communicated to others in the field. Similarly, if an oral examination is deemed necessary for a doctoral award (which is the case in most UK universities) then that examination needs to be *of* something and typically it would be an examination of the argument set out and defended in the thesis. There seems then to be a clear distinction between a creative work that is presented (or indeed not presented but in some way made available) but is devoid of explanation or critique, and one that is presented with an attendant critical analysis that seeks to expound its origins, the skills and knowledge that contributed to its genesis and its impact on other works in the field. Both, of course, are legitimate in their own right. The former conveys meaning to, and carries potential emotional impact on, its audience. The latter conveys critical explanation and analysis about that meaning and that impact. Many would argue, however, that it is the latter rather than the former that can be deemed an academic exercise that may be rewarded by an academic award. This is not, of course, to deny the intellectual effort required in a creative act. There is a contrary view that we should note here and which suggests that the intellectual position and its defence *can* be embodied in the creative output. This view is perhaps most prevalent in the area of musical composition.

The relationships between creative works, design and research

Creative activity as research

Having tried to separate out the creating of a work from the development of a thesis about that work (and recognizing that some would argue that the creative output can embody the thesis and that therefore this separation is a false distinction), it is necessary to try to distinguish different relationships between creative works and research. Clearly, there is research into creative works and those who create them. This kind of research may be seen as traditional and accepted – certainly in the areas of humanities and arts research. For example, a doctoral thesis may be developed that relates to Picasso as a creator (his impact on society and culture, etc.) and/or that relates to the works that he created or similarly to the creative genre(s) of which he was a part or his use of particular materials in particular ways.

It is also possible to conceive of creative work as part of a wider research enterprise – where, for example, an artist plays a part in the researching of a new technical product, thus bringing artistic skills and knowledge to bear on an intellectual problem. But it is also possible to conceive of creative activity *per se* as research. Here the intellectual processing is an integral part of the outcome. It is this final view that has led some in the university sector in the UK to call for a specific title such as Doctor of Art (DArt). The same arguments about just what is to be examined – as set out in the preceding paragraph – apply, and many would agree with the UKCGE 1997 report on *Practice-Based Doctorates in the Creative and Performing Arts and Design* where it is suggested that for the instigator of a creative work(s) to lay claim to a doctoral award then he/she would have to accompany that work by what is effectively an exegesis – a critical account of the work in its intellectual context. He or she would have to record for peers the processes that took place in the conception and production of the creative work in order that those peers might learn more about the processes for their own future reference – and here the link back to a contribution to knowledge is clear. It should be noted at this point that those suspicious of the arguments set out above would suggest that there is a danger in giving words primacy over objects – referred to by Wollheim (1980) as the 'heresy of paraphrase'. Whatever the right and wrong of that argument it seems reasonable to suggest that what will differ, in art and design submissions, from the more scientific PhD submissions is in the nature of the knowledge to be extended as well as in the tools and procedures used to set up and expound the intellectual argument.

Process and product

One way of interpreting the argument above is to conceive of a creative work in terms of both process and product. The creator in any creative endeavour goes through a process(es) that leads to a product (however transitory or non-product like that may seem – i.e. using the term product here to indicate simply the outcome of the process, accepting that an outcome may be a continuing part of the process). There is then a difference in the way in which that creator would go about presenting his/her work for an exhibition on the one hand and as part of a doctoral submission on the other. In the first instance, it may be enough to prepare the product to give access to the work in a way that the creator thinks is appropriate to that work. But in the second, the creator needs to include some communication about the process because processes cannot satisfactorily be determined from the product alone. Further, what is required in the second is evidence that supports an intellectual argument of which the product is an integral but not a sole part.

As Frayling (1998) points out, this is not so far removed from the medieval notion of a 'masterpiece' – where an apprentice would produce an example of his/her craft, and be able to expound on the skills employed in its making. The apprentice would then, if successful as judged by other Masters, be able to join the 'society' of Masters. The origins of the Masters and of the Higher Doctoral degrees is clear and there is, then, a sense in which the Practice-Based Doctorate harks back to those origins.

The relationship between artefact, argument and communication

The section above leads to questions about how an artefact is conceived in relation to how any conception is communicated. Many would argue (following Foucault [e.g. 1974a, 1974b]) that an artefact does not in itself embody knowledge – any understanding of it only comes about through its contextualization. Such contextualization will involve, among other things, the physical, temporal and social. According to this argument, artefacts can never have a single, unalterable meaning. Indeed, meaning is generated by context. In this sense, an artefact in itself cannot be said to contribute to knowledge except in the individual, parochial sense (one person at one time in one place might learn something from it, but that knowledge would remain personal and open to different interpretation by any other person). If it is to be possible to claim that the artefact impacts upon knowledge beyond the personal, there must be some communication about it. Biggs (2002) argues that it is the 'particular combination of artefacts and words/ text that gives efficacy to the communication' (2002: 23). He goes on to suggest that the criterion of a contribution to knowledge necessarily requires more than either artefacts or text alone. In his terms what is required is a 'combination of artefact and a critical exegesis that describes *how* it advances knowledge, understanding and insight' (2002: 23).

While it is possible to conceive of research being done in isolation, it is arguable that a central ethic of doing research involves communicating with others about it – without such communication knowledge cannot be advanced (again, in any sense beyond the personal). Certainly, to gain an academic award through research necessarily involves communicating methods and findings in a persuasive way to examiners at the very least. Biggs (2002) takes various examples from literature and the arts to illustrate that objects cannot be relied upon to communicate in isolation (see Hooper-Greenhill 1992 for an earlier discussion of this point). It follows that artefacts alone cannot communicate in a way that is sufficient for the criteria of an academic research degree award to be met. What is necessary for this to be possible is a critical account of the artefact – an examination of the way in which the artefact operates in relation to the world. It is conceivable, of course, that such an account may not require words though, for our part, we find it difficult to imagine an effective account devoid of text. What is important is that the critical account must involve reflection on the processes of research and an explication of the way in which processes and products impact on knowledge and understanding – the medium through which that is achieved remains debatable.

Design projects and transferability of knowledge

The point is made above that research and communication about that research are necessarily interdependent. This argument takes on a particular significance when the research in question involves technology and design. Here there is, typically if not wholly, an intention to generate artefacts in order to change aspects of the world in a positive way. Scrivener (2002: 26) describes ten features that would be required of a viable research project in technology and design. These include: an artefact is the product of the research; the artefact is either new or is an enhanced version of earlier artefacts; the artefact resolves a known and identified problem; the knowledge embodied in the artefact can be described in a way that is separated from it and is therefore both 'sharable and reusable'; the knowledge embodied in the artefact is applicable to other contexts; this transferable knowledge is 'of greater value than the artefact itself' – the latter being 'merely a demonstration of its existence'. This last feature may be difficult to prove, but Scrivener's intention is clear – it is the transferability of the knowledge that is of prime interest rather than the artefact itself.

Scrivener then makes the point that even if all of the features he describes are present in a technology research project, that would not be enough to enable an academic research degree award to be made. For such an award to be made the candidate would have to show that he/she had 'arrived at the problem and its solution in a self-conscious and reasoned way' (Scrivener 2002: 27). This returns us full-circle to the point that is made in various ways throughout this book – that a Doctorate necessarily involves reasoned argument. In the context of design and technology a doctoral candidate would need to provide satisfactory evidence in his/her submission of reflective and systematic problem setting and solving. This evidence would need to be in the form of argument defended at oral examination.

Creative-production and research

What is described in the paragraph above may fit reasonably well with projects that fall within the area of design. It is less clear that the features noted above would apply so straightforwardly in a project where the intentions of the instigator are to explore issues in a more open way and where particular 'problems' are not defined let alone particular 'solutions' sought. Whereas in the design project the artefact itself may be discarded because the solutions it embodies are the real focus of the work, in an example (from the authors' own experience) in which the student explores issues that arise for those with leprosy in sub-Saharan Africa through the medium of sculpture, then the sculptures themselves become the focus of the work – they are less readily discarded. Indeed, as Scrivener points out, the features he describes as applicable to design projects can be written in the converse for the kind of 'creative-production' (Scrivener 2002: 30) that is engaged in by the sculptor in this example.

Certainly, there would be no necessary requirement for the sculptor to describe her methods accurately enough for someone else to repeat her study and produce similar artefacts. The sculptures are more than merely a demonstration of their own existence, for the candidate they become part of her own identification as a creator. The purpose here is not to evaluate the way in which the medium of sculpture might contribute to our understanding of leprosy but rather to find ways of producing sculpture that create a human experience of that topic. Some of the actions may be the same, but the underlying purpose, and hence the focus, is different.

Creative-production as an original contribution to knowledge

It might be argued that if such a project had never been completed before, then any outcomes would necessarily contribute to an understanding of the topic – but the question of being the first person to undertake such a project is not the issue for the candidate. Indeed, the candidate's starting point is his/her own interest regardless of anything that had gone before. If a project along similar lines had been completed, the candidate would not necessarily see the need to discuss strengths and failings in that work – or to analyse its impact. In short, his/her work cannot be reduced to the resolution of specific or indeed non-specific problems, it persists in being individually instigated and pursued. The methods used are not the focus of the work – means to an end, not ends in themselves – and the candidate sees no need to report on them to enable others to replicate them because such replication would seem to serve no purpose. Essentially, the sculptures are seen not as exemplars of what the candidate intends but as the intended outcomes. Whereas in the kind of design project noted earlier artefacts may eventually be discarded without any loss to the project (because the outcomes are in the understanding of the methods and principles of embodied in those artefacts), here the sculptures cannot be discarded without losing the essence of the project.

Research as the creation of new kinds of subjective response

The question that arises from the example given above is the extent to which the project of making sculptures on the theme as described can be said to be 'research' and specifically such that is amenable to assessment for a research degree. Typically, as discussed elsewhere in this book, research degrees involve original investigation in a defined topic resulting in contributions to knowledge and understanding. It is possible to engage in a semantic argument about whether the sculpture project involves investigation. However, in the broadest sense of the term it may be acceptable to argue that it does involve investigation – and creativity too. The 'contribution to knowledge and understanding' is more difficult to argue. There is a sense in which knowledge and, to a lesser extent, understanding are things to be discovered. Unknowns become knowns and can then be applied in other contexts to other problems or issues – things not understood become understood and those understandings can be brought to bear on 'new' problems. In contrast, the student in our example brings the sculptures into being – he/she creates them and any audience has then to try to know about them and understand them. They may bring about a new subjectivity in the audience but not an objective knowledge of this aspect of the world.

While the successful design project will add to knowledge and enable others to understand more effectively, the creative-production project may cause others to reflect on what they already know and understand about – in our exemplar – leprosy and its impact on individuals and sub-Saharan cultures. In this latter sense, to accept the creative-production project as research, one would need to define research as involving the creation of new kinds of subjective response to stimuli rather than as involving the contribution to existing knowledge and understanding. In the former the subjective processes of the audience's knowing, understanding and appreciating of the issue is the target of the work, whereas in the latter the target relates to the knowledge and understanding itself, i.e. in an objective way that is not personally circumscribed.

Definitions of research in the arts with common currency

It may, of course, be that the definition of 'research' given above renders the term meaningless, or at least redefines it in such a way as to change the internal logic of the term irrevocably. Certainly, the kinds of definition of research set out within the Higher Education Funding Council of England (HEFCE) research assessment exercise (HEFCE 1999) and by the UK Arts and Humanities Research Board (AHRB 2001) would seem to deny such a redefinition. To qualify as research, both require that artistic projects should specify and be located within a 'research context'. Further, HEFCE (1999) requires that the work should be open to critical review and that it should be possible to judge its impact and influence on the work of peers. Again, AHRB requires that the work should specify and justify the particular research methods chosen. Of course, research context, methods and impact are often not defined or are ill-defined, nevertheless the implication is clear – for artistic endeavour to be 'counted' as research (and therefore be available for assessment within the domain of research degrees) it would need to involve critical reflection on both processes and products.

Creative-production, reflective practice and research

Scrivener (2002) argues that while creative-production projects, typified here by the example of the sculpture project, might not meet the criteria of a problem-solving project within the design field, they are subject to identifiable norms that are testable as criteria of reflective practice (following Schon 1983). That is, the candidate may demonstrate that he/she has described the origins and drivers of the work, indicated how the work reflects cultural concerns and responds to stimuli in ways that are culturally original, further indicated the relationships between stimuli, concerns, responses and artefacts. In presenting an artefact that provokes novel subjective responses from its audience, the candidate may also need to communicate knowledge and understanding gained during the work and thus be seen to be a 'self-conscious, systematic and reflective practitioner' (Scrivener 2002: 34).

The notion of reflective practitioner – in the case of our example, of the practice of sculpting – is underpinned by the notion that experiment in practice is different from research in the traditional sense. It involves an implicit understanding that the practitioner intends to act upon the medium and/or the context to (in some sense) improve it or give meaning to it. The sculptor takes the raw block of clay or stone and creates shape, hence enabling a new meaning to be understood. In Scrivener's terms the actions of the practitioner involve experimentation that is 'at once exploratory, move-testing and hypothesis testing' (Scrivener 2002: 35). He also claims that hypothesis testing is of an 'imperative' kind – that is, the practitioner reworks the material to make the hypothesis fit it rather than reworking the hypothesis to fit the demands of the material. This reworking is necessarily a trans-actional process – the practitioner will affect his/her material but will also, in turn, be affected by the results of his/her work – which in course will affect the practitioner's future work. The experimentation is therefore both cyclical and transactional – a non-linear contrast to research paradigms in which experimental context and variables are objectively controlled and, typically, set out in advance of any acts of experimentation.

Schon's work (e.g. Schon 1983) may be helpful in interpreting artistic, creative-production as a reflective process that can be discussed in the context of research paradigms. If it can be agreed that the student engaged effectively in creative production reflects on his/her own knowledge and ways of working, then it seems reasonable to suggest that there would be benefits for that student in recording and reporting on the process of reflection overtly and systematically – though clearly there may be some issues surrounding the way in which, by making the implicit processes explicit, one might affect the automaticity of aspects of the creative process. There is also an issue inasmuch as what is reflected upon is a description of the creative-production and the description is clearly not necessarily the same as the act itself; it is one step removed. Communicating this description to others is clearly another step. This is perhaps not the place to explore aspects of reflexivity in research design (it is done elsewhere, e.g. Hughes 2001; Bolton 2001). For our purposes here it is enough to suggest that creative-production may be interpreted as falling within the parameters of qualitative research where it involves defined cycles of reflexivity reported systematically.

Relating creative-production to the notion of a thesis

Clearly, a debate is required about the way in which creative-production may be interpreted as research, or indeed the conditions under which it can justifiably be described as such. There is a further argument about how amenable this kind of research is to being assessed for a research degree. For our part, we would argue that while in our example the sculptor would not merit a doctoral award for the products of his/her project on leprosy, i.e. for the sculptures alone – he/she would be in contention for such an award if the project involved the development of an intellectual position and the production of a thesis in defence of that position. The sculptor's thesis might relate to the way in which his/her project was conceived and carried out and to the relationship between, for example, subjects, context, medium, artefacts, audience and his/her own learning and development. The sculptor's thesis would need to be a rigorous analysis of the reflexive process involving these relationships. The development of an intellectual argument and the attendant thesis would then mark out the project as being of doctoral study rather than 'everyday' art making. The demarcation then becomes a matter of intention and emphasis.

Criteria for Practice-Based Doctorates

Commonality of doctoral criteria

It seems reasonable to suggest that, if they are to have parity with other doctoral degrees, Practice-Based Doctorates should stand scrutiny under the same standards of assessment as any other kind of Doctorate. The criteria used to attain the standard might differ in kind but it should be possible to relate them to other doctoral criteria in terms of level. Successful candidates will be expected to demonstrate that they have learned to place their work within the arena of other related work and to judge its impact on related areas of creative endeavour. They will be able to demonstrate that they have understood how they have applied particular methods (both conceptual and practical) in the production of their creative works and justify why choices of those methods were made. They will be able to communicate both their methodologies and their resulting works in an explanatory and analytical way to an audience of critical peers. They will also be able to develop, set down in a written text and defend an intellectual position relating to their creative works by sustained argument. As with all other forms of doctoral education, students need to move from a position in which they are instructed in forms of knowledge and relevant skills to a position in which they are in command of knowledge and skill in such a way as to enable them to contribute to the knowledge as well as just to understand it. Further, the doctoral qualification demands that they be able to continue that contribution in an independent and self-critical way.

Criteria for the work itself and the analysis of the work

What may mark out the Practice-Based Doctorates from the more traditional form of PhD is that the criteria for success are, to some extent, as much related to the creative works as to their critique. From its survey of regulations at the time, UKCGE (1997) suggests that the written exegesis will have equal, or 'near equal', weight in the assessment process. They note exceptionally that this may not apply to musical composition. Clearly, that weighting will relate to an institution's interpretation of what the doctoral award is being given for: the work or the analysis of the work. The arguments above would indicate, to us, that both should be treated as necessarily interdependent facets of the overall submission (a point that is revisited below).

The submission for a Practice-Based Doctorate

Regulations about the submission

In the survey of UK Higher Education Institutions reported by UKCGE in 1997 there is evidence of a consensus on just what is required in a submission for a Practice-Based Doctorate. Ninety UK institutions responded to the survey. Of these, 45 had specific regulations relating to the Practice-Based Doctorate. All of the institutions that had such regulations included the following requirements for a final submission for this specific Doctorate (there was not total unanimity, however, in relation to musical composition, and in this latter case the requirements are presented separately below – UKCGE 1997).

Consensus on general requirements of a submission for a Practice-Based Doctorate. Paraphrased from UKCGE (1997).

General
- Work undertaken must have been part of a registered research programme.
- A permanent record of the creative works must accompany the submission.
- The creative work must be set in its relevant theoretical, historical, critical or visual context.
- There must be a written thesis.
- The length of the 'accompanying thesis' will usually be 30,000–40,000 words. In the case of musical composition the length of the 'accompanying commentary' (the word thesis does not appear in the responses reported) is implied to be brief (in the order of 3,000 to 5,000 words).
- The work will constitute an independent and original contribution to knowledge.
- The submission will demonstrate an understanding of appropriate research methods.
- There will be an oral examination.
- The written thesis and the creative work are of equal, or near equal, importance. In the case of musical composition, there is mention of a 'portfolio' forming the predominant part of the submission.

Musical composition

In addition, the varied responses to the question of regulations in respect of musical composition included (again paraphrased here) the following indications.

• Typically, the size of the portfolio of compositions was described as 'substantial' and at least one composition should be for 'large forces', e.g. a large orchestra.
• The submission should indicate 'technical proficiency'.
• Compositions should be worthy of public performance (and in this sense publication).
• The composition should be 'an exposition of the creative process'.

Stable and permanent evidence

We have argued elsewhere in this book that doctoral awards require that candidates set out an argument in support of a particular intellectual position and then defend it using evidence as appropriate. The issue in the context of Practice-Based Doctorates may, then, become one of how that evidence can be arranged in such a way as to be stable enough to be examined by assessors (and by stability here we mean a state that remains static long enough for a judgement to be made) and permanent enough for others to be able to reflect upon the judgement made by the examiners (transparency of assessment) and upon the impact of the submission on their own work (contribution to the field). The need for accessibility and permanency mirrors the situation with regard to electronic submissions where again questions are asked about how the submission can be made accessible to all at the time it is made, and into a future where electronic systems are prone to change. In short, what is required in both scenarios is that a submission must address the universal need (in a doctoral sense) of permanent access for current examiners and future researchers.

The naming and weighing of parts

Some of the arguments that underlie the separation of the area of musical composition from the rest of the Practice-Based Doctorates, and some of the issues raised but often not resolved by respondents to the UKCGE report in general (UKCGE 1997), can be likened to the issues surrounding the submission for the PhD by Published Work as noted elsewhere in this book. The tension lies between the judging of the quality of the 'works' and the judging of the quality of the thesis or exegesis that is submitted with those works. There is considerable difference between a situation in which it is seen as possible to divide out these two elements for the purpose of allocating value to them (and to subsequently judge them to be of equal or near equal importance or again to give preponderance to the works over the 'accompanying' text or *vice versa*) and one in which the two are interpreted for the purpose of assessment as an indivisible whole in assessment terms – with neither signifying anything in the absence of the other. Of course, the works will always exist and a critique of them can always be written – but it may be argued that a submission should comprise a coherent exposition of an intellectual position. As a submission for assessment, then, the works and the exegesis are not reducible to their separate entities. It is not a matter of weighing one entity against another, it is a matter of conceiving of them as a whole, as an intellectual position and its defence, and of assessing that whole against the agreed criteria.

Having asserted that it is not a matter of weighing parts of a submission, we do nevertheless need to address the disparity between common understandings in the field about expected word lengths for submissions in most areas of Practice-Based Doctoral work on the one hand, and in the area of musical composition on the other. It does seem (UKCGE 1997: 23) that there is a long tradition and a subsequent consensus among academics in the area of musical composition that here the creative output itself *does* embody the research process and hence is indicative of it. In this consensus, therefore, musical composition is equated with text-based musicology.

We should also note at this point that the difficulty of weighing parts of a submission is not unique to the practice-based submission. Examiners of a 'standard' PhD may be faced with a submission that contains physical results of research work such as computer programs or scientific procedures and critical accounts of how those results were achieved. In such cases the examiner is necessarily weighing the value of the result itself (in terms of its contribution to knowledge) alongside the elucidation of the research processes that led to the result (the candidate's achievement in understanding and communicating how the contribution was made, its impact and its implications for further study).

Scholarly requirements and practice-based submissions

Clearly, one agreed criterion might be that the submission should meet relevant scholarly requirements. The difficulty here comes in deciding which of such requirements might be deemed relevant to any specific submission. In short, does the relevance relate to the disciplinary area in question or more generically to some notion of universal standards of doctoral, scholarly behaviour. Given that there are marked differences in the way in which research work is conceived, undertaken and reported across traditional PhD areas, then it seems hard to pin down such 'universal standards' that would receive general acceptance. It may be that statements can be made that would be widely accepted but there is a danger that they may become general and tend to leave open different ways and levels of interpretation.

For example, it might be possible to argue for a need for overt critical appraisal of research processes as well as results as a *sine qua non* of a scholarly approach to doctoral study. But what counts as a research process itself varies necessarily (indeed the concept of 'data' varies from one discipline to another). Similarly, in terms of communication of findings it might be possible to agree that all doctoral study should necessarily involve the presentation of outcomes in such a way as to inform others working in the same, or in a contingent, area. But conventions of, for example, referencing vary between disciplines, as do the value of different forms of communication (e.g. understandings of the usefulness of research posters varies greatly).

One aspect of the scholarly requirements of a submission – which relates to what was noted earlier about process and product – is that, typically, the practice of arts-related subjects does not begin with a predetermined set of questions or hypotheses and proceed according to set procedures within defined parameters. In arts-related endeavour there is more likely to be an emphasis on 'emergent' themes, where the direction of the project may be influenced by developments within the project itself (or the interaction of others with it) and, as mentioned above, an emphasis on reflexive practice. One key scholarly requirement then would be to map those processes in such a way as to produce a critically reflective account, which includes depth of analysis and evaluation and enables others to gain a greater understanding of the genesis and development of the creative, design processes that have been undergone. Clearly, we have separated out process and product here in an effort to describe the submission, but, in the chronology of the work, this critically reflective account may be an indissoluble part of the process itself.

Subsequent to the above, institutions tend to fall back on the notion that the scholarly requirements that are acceptable when judging a submission are those that are acceptable within the discipline – as judged by experts (experienced peers) within that discipline. The problem that arises of course is that, in new or emerging areas, acceptability in these terms may be a developing concept – and indeed examiners may be coming to one special area from others, and their experience may thus be firmly rooted in a particular tradition that no longer applies. Another approach may be to tie the scholarly requirements back to criteria for the award that are couched as learning outcomes that the candidate must demonstrate (e.g. the candidate must demonstrate that he/she can contribute to knowledge and is able to continue to do this in an independent way). If those criteria are clear enough then the candidate has to strive to meet them and the examiners have to judge whether or not the candidate has met them (the candidate has to demonstrate that he/she has made a contribution to knowledge and understands what he/she has done well enough to be able to see ways of progressing the work to a new stage, and so on). In this sense the criteria are all that are needed by way of scholarly requirements.

Examination of the Practice-Based Doctorate

The examination panel

The constitution of the examination panel of the Practice-Based Doctorate in the UK tends to follow the pattern of other kinds of doctoral study in that the typical requirement is for at least two examiners, one of whom is external to the university concerned. The panel would be expected to be experienced in the particular area of research and in examining at doctoral level. It would need to include both academic and artistic expertise in the relevant subject area if it is to be able to judge effectively the creative standard of the works against some kind of marker for excellence in the field. With this in mind perhaps, UKCGE (1997) noted that, for the Practice-Based Doctorate, examiners might be drawn from outside academia. While many institutions would allow such individuals to examine across the doctoral spectrum – not just within this one kind of Doctorate – it does seem that the like- lihood of going outside the university sector is increased where part of the judgement making relates to creative practice.

The oral examination

Where the submission consisted in part of an exhibition, then there would be a need to ensure that the way the exhibition functions does not run counter to the kinds of regulations that institutions have in place with regard to the PhD examination. It may be that the examination panel visits the exhibition before or during the *viva voce* – with or without the candidate. Clearly, if this is the case then there is a need to define the status of such a visit in relation to any subsequent questioning and to any representations of the work that may have been included in a submitted thesis. Most would agree that photographs, video, drawings or other representations of an artistic work are necessarily not the same as the work itself. Examiners would need to be clear at the outset of the examination process about where the event/object begins and ends in relation to representations of it and in relation to points of judgment making. UKCGE (1997) noted that some institutions require that examiners should not arrive at, or record, any decision on the merit of the submission until they have 'experienced the creative work' (p. 36).

Typically, the oral examination is seen as either important or crucial in the UK system across the range of kinds of doctoral study. It may take on a particular significance however in the Practice-Based Doctorate where it offers a unique opportunity for the candidate to demonstrate the relation- ships between his/her research programme and its practical outcomes. In this context it becomes a way in which the effects of research on practice – and the way in which particular aspects of researching are contained within the artefact – can be made explicit by the candidate and can be explored by the examiners. While the candidate should have made every effort to make plain these things in the textual commentary, it is nevertheless arguable that they can only be fully demonstrated and explored in the presence of the works themselves.

The examination outcomes for the Practice-Based Doctorate will tend to mirror those for other forms of doctoral examination. However, special consideration may need to be made in the case where work is to be 'resubmitted'. It may be inappropriate in the context of some kinds of creative artefacts for them to be reproduced in the same form as originally submitted – though clearly representations of them in, for example, photographic form may be amenable to such resubmission.

Supervision of a Practice-Based Doctorate

The nature of supervision of a candidate for a Practice-Based Doctorate will relate to the way an individual institution conceives of the degree and organizes programmes of work that may lead to its assessment at doctoral level. In the UKCGE (1997) report, no institutions were recorded as denoting supervision of Practice-Based Doctorates as in any way different from supervision of traditional PhDs. Yet it does seem that if the award is separated out in any way as distinctive, then the kind of supervision on offer ought to reflect that distinctiveness. At the very least the supervisor should have a clear understanding of the institution's view of the submission in terms of the relationship between the creative works and the critical appraisal of those works. It also seems reasonable to suggest that the supervisor ought to be able to act as 'critical friend' during the development of the works themselves in a way that is perhaps distinctive from that of the similar role in the context of the traditional PhD. The distinctiveness may relate primarily to the nature of the creative act within arts-based areas as opposed to the act of intellectual enquiry in non arts-based areas. Certainly, both may require originality in thinking, but in the case of practice-based doctoral work this may well involve different levels of personal exploration of meanings and materials and of interpretative account making. In this sense the very act of supervising may be distinctive.

Conclusion

It can be argued that in as much as the award of a Doctorate signifies admission to a community of scholars, then no area of intellectual endeavour, such as the creative arts, should be excluded from this process on the grounds that assessment is difficult to conceptualize and organize and because the outcomes of creative research may require judgements of a subjective kind.

There is a need to establish some sense of parity of level between the 'traditional' PhD and the Practice-Based Doctorate. To do this a consensus on what can legitimately count as doctoral qualities is desirable. Further, parity may be achieved where the criteria against which a doctoral submission is judged to accommodate creative works.

The issue of nomenclature with some practice-based areas – such as music, in making use of subject-specific titles such as DMus – is likely to remain unresolved where there is a lack of clarity about relative levels of esteem. Titles at least indicate the focus of the candidate – as someone interested in pushing forward the boundaries of his/her subject (e.g. music) or of knowledge itself (e.g. which may happen to be knowledge about music).

Summary issues

- Is the Practice-Based Doctorate a distinct award, or a subset of the Doctorate distinguished by its outcomes rather than it conceptual or intellectually underpinnings?
- Does the Practice-Based Doctorate, and particularly the potential for creative approached to the submission itself, challenge the conventional submission particularly in terms of appropriateness in demonstrating research capability and outcomes?
- How far is the 'practice' community putting at risk its own creativity by attempting to emulate a science model of doctoral research?

Part 3

Issues Surrounding the Development
of Doctoral Study

Part 3

7

Funding of doctoral programmes

Introduction

The funding of doctoral programmes has been the subject of considerable debate for several years. At a national level this has related to the stipend, its adequacy in relation to, and impact on, the supply and demand for doctoral students and the manner in which the models of funding of the Funding Councils reflect Research Assessment Exercise (RAE) performance rather than the costs of training doctoral students. This appears to encourage universities to attempt, in many cases very successfully, to manipulate the funding model to their financial advantage. At the university level discussion has concerned the adequacy of doctoral funding and its adequacy for quality programmes. More recently the HEFCE has undertaken a study of the cost of research students that has further raised the issues associated with funding. The current chapter examines the funding regimes both for universities and students and examines the impact that the interplay of funding factors has on doctoral provision. In so doing, it highlights the current byzantine funding models and the need to step back and look fundamentally at how doctoral programmes, and the PhD in particular, should be funded.

The current funding debates

Dual support

The current arrangements (December 2004) for the funding of universities for research students are complex and, as with all funding regimes, is open to manipulation. It is bound up in the structure of the dual support system of research funding which itself has been the subject of review in the recent past. Following Gareth Roberts's review of the RAE (Roberts 2002) some changes will be made in the next RAE in 2008, but in principle the current arrangements hold true. Put simply, the dual support system provides universities that reach a particular level according to the RAE funding stream often referred to as QR, reflecting the quality of the research. The precise level of funding is determined by:

- The quality rating. This rating is a scale of 1–5 plus 5*. In principle on only departments with a rating of 4 or above receive QR funding.
- The number of staff rated in each department, the volume measure. The more staff the greater the funding. Research students, as we will see, contribute to this volume.
- The academic subject under consideration (see below).

The basic philosophy of this side of the model is to provide universities with a level of funds to maintain staff and infrastructure at an adequate level to undertake research.

The other funding stream of the dual funding model comes from those agencies that fund specific projects. These agencies include the research councils, the research charities, government departments and commercial organizations and companies. And although universities are moving to a full cost recovery approach to research funding, the principle of the dual support approach will for the present be retained for research.

The costs to universities for the delivery of doctoral programmes are funded through a dual support structure similar to that for research projects and scholarship. In the case of doctoral programmes, the Funding Councils provide one element, and students (frequently through a sponsor) provide the other through their payment of fees. Following the Roberts Review an additional element of £850 on average for the period 2004/05 has been added to support the delivery of research training for Research Council funded students only (Loeffler 2004). A similar approach has been adopted for 2004/05 by the AHRB, which currently contributes £450 per year for its research students. The AHRB will join the 'Roberts' allocation from 2005/06.

Funding Council support comes to universities through three different streams. In year one of study (pro rata for part-time students) universities receive funds through the block grant for teaching in the same way that they receive funding for undergraduate study. The amount of money received will relate to the Academic Cost Centre (ACS) in which they are working and the figure will hence vary across three price groups (see Table 7.1). There is an implicit understanding in this part of the model that the majority of work in the first year is more akin to 'being taught' than engaging in independent

Table 7.1 Funding Council price groups

		Weighting
A	High-cost laboratory and clinical subjects	1.6
B	Intermediate cost subjects	1.3
C	Others	1.0

research. This, as with other elements of the funding model, is based on far from robust assumptions about the nature of the PhD to which we have already referred, the diversity of the doctoral model and with the way in which the various doctoral models are developing.

The second element is the so-called supervision fee, paid to universities for second- and third-year students. Again based on quanta attributable to the individual academic subject categories, the supervision fee is approximately the same as that of the teaching fund in year 1 and is calculated with reference to cost weight ratio in Table 7.1. This element is only paid to departments rated 3a and above in England but to those rated 3b and above in Scotland and Wales.

Quality research

The final element of funding is included in the quality research (QR) part of the research block grant. Postgraduate Research (PGR) is one element of the so-called volume measures of QR which are assigned to RAE Units of Assessment (UoAs) based on the RAE score (3, 4, 5 and 5*) and the number of research active staff. A full-time PGR student is equivalent to 0.15 of a member of academic staff. Perversely, the level of funding is calculated assuming that each student takes 3.5 years to complete his/her work, but is paid over two years.

The amount of money received will relate to the 'cost weight' of the subject in which they are working and the figure will hence vary across the subjects within each of the three cost centre groups, as shown in Table 7.2. Cost weights are calculated to reflect the relative costs of research in each of the 68 Units of Assessment.

In addition to funds from the Funding Councils, universities also charge fees for the period of research. Fees vary between universities and across academic subject categories. In some cases fees reflect market conditions and can be substantially above levels advised by the Department for Education and Skills (DfES). A considerable level of university discretion appears to apply in the setting of fees with an increasing blurring of the line between full cost (usually overseas) and home/EU students. Similar variation applies to the charging of bench fees. There does not appear to be a clear rationale for fee levels in postgraduate research degrees, with many universities charging

Table 7.2 Per FTE rates payable in 2004/05

		Per FTE £
A	High-cost laboratory and clinical subjects	4,418
B	Intermediate cost subjects (part laboratory based)	3,589
C	Others (library based)	2,761

the same level as for postgraduate taught masters programmes. There appears to be 'no clear' relationship between the fee charged and access provided to supervisors in the ratio of supervisors to students and other forms of student support.

Issues related to funding linked to the RAE

We would argue that the current approach to funding universities for doctoral students is far from satisfactory as it appears to have little relationship to the realities of current doctoral practice and is inclined to encourage perverse behaviours. The linking of funding to RAE performance is of fundamental concern and associated problems are manifest in several ways. First, the inclusion of PGR in the QR volume measure encourages universities to recruit more doctoral students in order to inflate the multiplier for QR. It also creates significant differentials between universities in the level of funding available in similar academic subject categories as the calculation of QR is based on the variable RAE rating multiplied by research volume (of which, as we saw above, 1 FTE PGR = 0.15). As a consequence, a department (or more properly a Unit of Assessment) rated 5 will receive less to support each student than a department rated 5*. Currently a full-time doctoral student is worth about £12,000 per annum to a 5* laboratory-based department. Yet one can presume that there is no corresponding differential between the support needs of the student in the former as opposed to the latter department.

In the case of the English Funding Council, students who are studying in UoAs that are rated less than 4, and which as a consequence receive no QR, are potentially disadvantaged as the level of funding available to support them will be restricted to that relating to supervision. Indeed the notion that funding for PGR be related to the RAE and RAE scores has come under significant critical attention as it seems destined to produce inconsistencies across the sector. Those seven UoAs supported by the Higher Education Funding Council for England (HEFCE) Capability Fund receive funding when rated 3b and 3a; others similarly rated do not. Again, the rationale for this does not seem to relate to differentials of student need and the outcomes are therefore disadvantageous to some students for no apparent, justifiable reason.

The lack of funding directed towards the research environment may seriously affect the ability to provide a quality research environment for doctoral students in the many universities involved in regionally based knowledge transfer activity, such as that supported by the HEFCE Higher Education Innovation Fund (HEIF) in England, often undertaken by departments with RAE ratings below the current thresholds and frequently involving or requiring research student involvement. It is notable that in Scotland a more strategic approach has been adopted to develop structures that obviate the outcome.

The case for review

Funding through the block grant

At the heart of the funding debate are the level of overall funds and the balance between quality and numbers. There are increasing pressures to review the overall approach to the funding of doctoral programmes to remove some, if not all, of the inconsistencies observed in the current model. The case for funding through the overall teaching element of the block grant is persuasive. It would permit universities to manage PGR numbers in the same way as Undergraduate and Postgraduate Taught (PGT), and would ensure that the levels of funding available are consistent across the academic subject categories. Doctoral students would then be seen as part of the over-all student body rather than as a separate group, and this, in turn, would encourage universities to see provision in broad educational terms with PGR as one part of the totality of PG provision. This is especially the case as regards part-time and professional updating where research degrees are part of the spectrum of opportunity spanning PgCert; PgDip; MA/MSc; MRes; MBA; MPhil; Professional and Practice-Based Doctorates; and the PhD. It also resolves the problem we noted in connection with students supported from regional activity and those supported by HEIF funding and also by Research Council Doctoral Training Accounts, awarded to research groups, some of whom are not rated 4 and above.

Although inclusion in the funding stream related to teaching does offer an attractive alternative, it also raises potential problems that may affect university behaviours and standards. No matter what the level of the quanta used to calculate the PGR funds, it will not fund the required research environment for those departments that receive no QR funds. There will therefore be a need to demonstrate a suitable level of provision, as advocated by the QAA Code of Practice (QAA 2004).

Alternatively, satisfactory levels of funding may be achieved through the use of commercial income or by university collaborations. Such an approach, while logical in principle, creates major difficulties for universities and their sponsors, many of whom are reluctant to pay additional money. This will also be the case for those who do not receive the support for research training (the so-called 'Roberts money'), about which the Research Councils note 'Institutions should seek funding for additional skills training on non-Research Council funded PhD students and postdoctoral researchers from other sponsors of PhD training and research, to match that provided by the Government through the Research Councils' (Loeffler 2004: 2).

It may also encourage universities to transfer funds from undergraduate or postgraduate taught programmes to postgraduate research. However, as we move increasingly towards a more mission-driven approach to internal allocation of funds, such an approach seems entirely plausible.

Following the consultations on Research Funding (OST 2003; HM Treasury

2004) and *Improving Standards in Postgraduate Research Degree Programmes* (HEFCE 2003b) the HEFCE intends to modify and simplify its approach from 2005/06. Future funding of research students will be through a single funding stream. Funding will be for students registered in units rated 4 and above at the 2001 RAE level. Funding will also be made available for students in units rated 3a and 3b in receipt of Research Capability funding. The funding will be cost weighted according to the conclusions of the JM Consulting (2005) report. Funds will be profiled over three years, adjusted to account for the 3.5 years it actually takes on average to complete for full-time students (HEFCE 2004). The cost bands for 2005/06 will give allocations of £7,000 band A, £5,700 band B and £4,400 band C per student. In Scotland the Funding Council decided in 2002 to transfer the funding for postgraduate research provision from the teaching funding stream and establish a new Research Postgraduate Grant within the research funding stream.

The implications of the funding model

We have noted above some of the issues that have been driving a review of the current model. However, the discussion is perhaps more fundamental than the simple allocation of money. We are concerned that the model is driving us towards a two-tier system of research degree delivery in which one group of students, possibly those following the traditional route, are significantly better funded than others (with these others perhaps more likely to be part time and 'mature'). We argue this because many departments do not receive any QR funding for research, do not receive 'Roberts money' for research training, charge very low fees and, consequently, have very small budgets with which to deliver a quality research degree experience. Additionally, the raising of the stipend for Research Council students has placed many universities and their students at a disadvantage, as they are unable to apply the new levels of stipend.

Student tuition fees

The fourth element of the funding stream

The fourth element of the funding stream for research students comes from tuition fees and associated bench fees (such latter fees present, in some cases, a substantial additional cost to research in science and engineering to cover items such as materials and chemicals). The broad structure of full-time fees is set by the DfES and, as usual, is subdivided into three broad categories: Home and EU, Overseas and Channel Islands. With some variability between disciplines, there is broad parity of fees charged within the broad framework provided by DfES and little evidence that universities are exploiting the market by either significant variability between subjects within cost centres or between universities with different market positions for research. As we will note below, some universities even waive the fees for some students and hence, theoretically at least, we have a doctoral research degree process in some universities for which the university receives a negative fee!

Pattern of fees in relation to part-time students

For part-time provision the pattern of fees charged is of particular interest. A web survey of ten universities highlights the developing market in part-time provision as reflected in fees charged. For the session 2004/05, part-time fees for non-laboratory-based programmes varied from £580 to £1,900 (the latter being a post-1992 university). Three universities, all post-1992 universities, charged below £1,000. Such fee levels will reflect on the level of service that the student can expect and put considerable pressure on universities to deliver quality. Clearly, part-time students would be advised to shop around to get the best deal academically as well as financially.

Whether the fee charged reflects the real cost of delivery is again questionable and it is clear that many universities are responding to that question by raising the fee levels. The University of Wolverhampton, for example, has increased its fees substantially but noted that for students enrolling before September 2004, the old fee of £660 would apply. So even where fee increases are sanctioned, the impact on university finances may be lagged by anything from five to seven years until the part-time students work their way out of the system.

It is clear that in many cases there is a subsidy of the part-time student fee from the full-time and overseas fee. Unfortunately, the subsidy does not cover the full range of facilities that the full-time student receives. Many of the additional facilities, such as grants for attending conferences both in the UK and overseas, are not available to the part-time student (see, for example, University of Southampton 2001: 24). Cross-subsidy does not give equity.

The 'writing-up period'

For the many students who do not finish and submit their dissertation within the three to four years for which a stipend is paid, or for which some other sponsor is paying fees, many universities have a period referred to as the 'writing-up period'. In essence this is a period after research is completed and during which the student writes up the results and is examined. The concept of writing-up is not one to which all universities subscribe as it implies that writing-up is not part of the research process and is an afterthought – not an integral part of the doctoral programme.

Given that the writing-up period is one during which the student is no longer supported by a stipend, the fee is usually substantially less than the normal full-time or even part-time tuition fee. A survey in 2003 of 22 universities in the UK highlighted a considerable variation of both fees and practice (Leeds Metropolitan University, unpublished research, 2003). Only three universities had a full-time writing-up fee, confirming that writing-up is done when full-time research is finished. However, anecdotal evidence suggests that many students who are writing-up do in fact undertake the work on a full-time basis – often supported by part-time employment. The majority had a part-time writing-up fee that varied from £25 to £570. One university that charged a very low fee noted that this was to keep names on the register of the higher degrees candidates. If the student needed to use university facilities then additional charges were made. It is surprising to learn that these extra facilities included use of the library, inter-library loans, laboratory space and computing facilities. It is questionable as to how a student can write up a thesis without access to such facilities.

It does appear that for most of the universities the writing-up period is not a great drain on resources and that it is not a structured part-time activity. Two universities noted that they were abolishing the writing-up fee and would be charging students who had yet to complete their submission the normal part-time student fee, confirming the anomaly of the writing-up period in the overall structure of the doctoral process and legitimizing it by designating it as a formal part-time activity, with the associated access to facilities and supervision. One university adopted a novel approach to incentivizing completions by having a period of six months with no fee. Following that it charged the normal part-time rate.

Who pays the fees?

Tuition fees are paid by a wide range of sponsors, as can be seen in Tables 7.3 and 7.4.

Table 7.3 highlights several key facts about doctoral funding in the UK that tell us a lot about the way in which training is approached. The role of the Research Council funding has been declining over the period from 46.5% to 33.3% of doctoral student fees. On the other hand, the self-financing of fees, while only 15.4% in 2001/02 has increased by 85.8% during the period. Private industry, an insignificant funder at 4.6% of the total, has become increasingly *insignificant* with a reduction of 19.6% during the period.

Table 7.4 highlights the importance of self-financing for part-time doctoral students who form approximately 46% of students over the period. While not making such a significant contribution to the total number, both university and Government department funding have increased significantly, 37% and 66% respectively over the period. Notwithstanding the positive statements about the access agenda and the need to encourage more part-time research students, Research Councils make only a minimal contribution.

Table 7.3 Major source of tuition fees: UK-domiciled full-time first-year doctoral students in science, engineering and technology

Source	1995/96	1997/98	1999/2000	2001/02
Universities	813	896	800	950
Local Government	118	73	50	215
Government Departments	397	342	340	325
Research Councils	2,343	2,136	2,340	1,780
Other UK public	18	17		5
Self-financing	444	426	540	825
Charities	149	122	160	165
Private industry	311	342	290	250
EC	9	5		5
Other overseas	37	28	140	115
Others/unknown	390	306	630	700
Total	5,029	4,693	5,280	5,340

Source: OST *SET Statistics,* Table 5.7

Table 7.4 Major source of tuition fees: UK-domiciled part-time first-year doctoral students in science, engineering and technology

Source	1995/96	1997/98	1999/2000	2001/02
Universities	186	219	310	255
Local Government	10	1	20	20
Government Departments	99	58	150	165
Research Councils	13	13	20	5
Other UK public	2	1	0	0
Self-financing	782	730	820	915
Charities	14	6	10	10
Private industry	285	333	260	300
EC	1	0	0	0
Other overseas	0	1	20	20
Others/unknown	283	159	260	305
Total	1,675	1,521	1,850	1,995

Source: OST *SET Statistics,* Table 5.7

Student funding and stipends

The stipend and recruitment patterns

'Stipend' is the term used here for the maintenance grant paid to doctoral students for the period of their research. The word is used interchangeable with *bursary* and *scholarship*. It is expected that the stipend will cover all the domestic costs, including accommodation, subsistence and transport.

The level of the stipend has come under scrutiny in recent years, linked to difficulties in attracting good quality candidates to research programmes and the possible difficulties in completion as students are obliged to take part-time employment to complement the stipend. The Research Councils, for example, note an increase in unfilled studentships, both masters and doctoral, from 300 in 1996/97 to 618 in 1998/99, an increase from approximately 4.5% to 11% of the studentships available. EPSRC had particular problems in the period with 25% of masters and nearly 30% of MRes places unfilled in 1998/99 (*Research Fortnight* 1999a, 1999b; Hinde 1999).

The recruitment patterns of science, engineering and technology PhDs during the period 1994/95 to 1999/2000 suggests that there is some relationship between stipends and recruitment with a growth in 1998/99 following the 22% stipend increase in 1998. The growth is not uniform across all disciplines with mathematical sciences showing little change. A changing pattern of demand for postgraduate research awards has also been experienced by the AHRB and the ESRC. For the ESRC, the number of applications for the 2000 competition was 25% below that in 1993.

The implications of this apparent falling demand for studentships is fundamental to the future of research training and ultimately the science base, and is considered in some detail in the Roberts review (Roberts 2002). In the competitive academic environment where research student numbers are important at a disciplinary level, for RAE volume purposes and for departmental esteem, there is a temptation to maintain numbers by recruiting less-well-qualified candidates. Notwithstanding this observation, in their report on the 2003 competition for postgraduate awards, the AHRB noted a 14% increase in doctoral applications, an average success rate across all awards of only 28% and no shortage of highly qualified applicants.

Stipends and future career destinations

The postgraduate study intentions survey (OST 2002) is helpful in explaining the behaviours of (young) graduates in deciding on future careers and doctoral study and hence sheds light on the demand side of the equation. For many students the level of the stipend is one of the three key variables in their decisions, the other two being the long-term financial and career returns of undertaking doctoral study and the attractiveness of postgraduate study as opposed to other forms of employment.

Reviews of, and recommendations about, the stipend

The attractiveness of the stipend has been the subject of several reviews, particularly in the case of science and engineering and in some of the social science areas, notably economics (Hodges 1999). Roberts (2003) demonstrated that the level of the stipend fell by 4.5% in real terms between 1971/72 and 1991/92, while starting salaries for graduates with an upper second first degree rose by more than 42% during the same period. Despite the recent increases, from £6,800 in 2001 to £9,000 in 2003/04 (DTI 2000), stipends represent little advantage over the national *minimum* wage.

The Roberts recommendation that the stipend should be increased to £13,000 based on comparisons with mean net graduate salaries is a welcome recognition of the lamentable approach to PhD stipends and one which the 2003/04 and 2005/06 spending reviews agreed to fund. The analysis does not, however, include an international comparison – a major omission in the increasingly global market for high-quality graduate students. Such an analysis reveals that the UK continues to lag behind many of our competitors (including English-speaking competitors). Canada offers a useful example. In 2003 the Canadian Government announced a PhD scholarship scheme with 3,000 scholarships of 33,000 Canadian dollars. Whatever the relativities, it will be important to ensure that the stipend is both nationally and internationally competitive if the UK is serious in its demands to recruit the most able students onto its PhD programmes.

The Roberts conclusions, however, are based on average conditions and do not consider variability across discipline, even within science. It also neglects some of the more subtle aspects of funding such as national insurance contributions and maternity and paternity entitlement during and after the research period. While there is some evidence that starting salaries are higher both within and outside the academy for those with a Doctorate, the evidence is not overwhelming enough to compensate for low stipends – see, for example, the British Academy discussion (British Academy 2001: 35) and Conlon and Chevalier (2002).

Role of Research Council studentships and the sustaining of the community

The allocation of studentships to departments may be closely linked to the future of the department and in a wider sense of the discipline. Disciplines with large numbers of studentships, for example, will be involved in a virtuous circle. Those with few, such as art and design and nursing, will struggle to achieve the performance criteria and develop further. To exacerbate the problem there has been little consistency in approach across the Research Councils in their allocations of awards to universities and students. Approaches range from a simple demand-led model in which awards are given to the best applicants, regardless of any subject-based demand factors, to those in which the allocation is linked directly to peer-reviewed research grant success and hence research excellence. The demand-led approach, while ensuring that the best candidates are supported in their research, leaves little scope for strategic choice at the national, disciplinary or departmental level. Equally it introduces potential unpredictability and uncertainty into the system. It is noted that there is a shift in all cases towards a more planned approach in which allocations are made on the basis of quotas. The AHRB, for example, adopted a ring-fencing approach for a period of three years from the 2004 competition in which a small number of awards are ring-fenced for specific subject areas.

Approach to delivery of funds

The manner in which funds are allocated has changed significantly in the recent past, reflecting both the different approaches towards the PhD itself and attempts by the Research Councils in particular to reflect market conditions and university autonomy.

In 2001 the EPSRC began a shift away from quota of studentships towards awards to universities, which included both stipend and support funding with the introduction of their Doctoral Training Accounts (DTA). The DTA is a sum of money paid to research groups in receipt of EPSRC research grants to cover both the stipend and the associated costs of training a research student over a period of up to four years. The DTA allows much greater freedom of action to the individual research group as they respond to the training needs of the individual student and the market conditions for recruitment. The EPSRC (2002) aim was to:

- assist universities to attract the best people into postgraduate research and training in the UK;
- allow a maximum of local discretion in managing and organizing doctoral training within clear financial and accountability arrangements;
- provide resources in a succession of four year grants, to provide a flexible and transparent funding stream.

Although the EPSRC has specified minimum requirements that departments must achieve – for example a minimum stipend – there is concern that the approach may lead to increased variability in conditions for doctoral students in different universities (see, for example, NPC 2001).

Conclusion

There have been significant recent changes in the way in which doctoral education is funded. These changes have been driven by the need to simplify a model that has become increasingly complex and open to manipulation. It is intended that the new approach will relate more closely to costs as all universities move to full cost recovery in all their activities. Notwithstanding this apparent simplification, the addition of 'Roberts money' and the AHRB training money will continue to create complexity.

The rise in the stipend, which now brings the income of a research student into line with average new graduate salaries, will further support the recruitment of good graduates onto doctoral programmes – for recent graduates. It will, of course, do little to encourage more mature students into the doctoral research community which still remains very much a full-time young person's domain – in spite of the diversity of the overall student population. Although the funding models have become increasingly more market oriented, they still reflect this position.

With these positive changes we should not forget that they impact on only relatively small segments of the doctoral market. Many students and departments will remain under-funded for their Doctorate with a major impact on the quality of doctoral education.

Summary issues

- What will be the impact of funding changes on the number and quality of both university delivery and students?
- Will the funding models lead to a two-tier structure in which part-time, self-funded, mature students and under-funded universities are disadvantaged compared to well-funded research universities in which students receive Research Council sponsorship?
- Will funding models and funding sponsors and employers accept that the Doctorate is part of career development and life-long learning and provide appropriate funding?

8
Length of doctoral training programmes

Introduction

Attention was focused on the length of doctoral training programmes, submission rates and time to completion in the early 1980s with the events leading to the publication of the Winfield report (Winfield 1987). This was not a problem unique to the UK as is noted by Blume and Amsterdamska (1987) in their report to OECD. Noble (1994) notes similar concerns. Others have adopted submission and completion rates in funding decisions following Becher *et al.*'s (1994) observation that timely completion was 'strongly correlated with external coercion' (p. 157). Today UK completion rates, at least in the context of those students who are funded by the Research Council and other major sponsors, are envied by other countries. Maslen (1991a) noted how completion rates in Australia lagged behind those of the UK. In Canada, Smith *et al.* (1991) reported time to completion being over ten years for 43% of doctoral candidates. Although, as we will see, considerable critical attention has been given to the British completion record of doctoral programmes, the number for *fully funded* students, including the Research Councils and Wellcome Trust-funded students, is recognized internationally as very good. One of the major achievements in the delivery of doctoral programmes has been the dramatic improvement in submission rates, and this gives the UK a significant international competitive position. What is less clear, however, is the pattern of completion for other less fortunate students, either those self-funding or part time, for which until recently (HEFCE 2005) very little information exists.

There are significant sensitivities around this topic, not least because of the use to which such rates have been put in the managing of funding allocations and their more general use as performance indicators. The QAA Code (QAA 2004) shied away from an explicit expectation on completion rates and in the explanation under Precept 5 of the Research Environment it states:

Institutions will wish to put in place explicit expectations that are clear and readily accessible to students and supervisors concerning timely submission and successful completion periods. Such expectations are likely to be influenced by research council requirements where relevant, and by the mode of study of the student, i.e. full-time or part-time. They are also likely to vary according to the needs of subjects and individual students.

(QAA 2004: 8)

Of the many 'climb-downs' in the development of the 2004 Code this is perhaps the most significant. The original HEFCE document was much more explicit and addressed head on the need for a specific time period, the importance of which is discussed later in the chapter.

This chapter examines several elements that may be included in the overall discussion of the length of doctoral training programmes. In particular, it addresses time to submission, i.e. the time taken to produce a doctoral thesis, and attrition or wastage, i.e. the failure to submit a dissertation. In addition to their intrinsic value, submission, completion and attrition are increasingly being used as indicators of performance in research degree management and funding.

Submission and completion rates

Defining times of submission, completion and registration

There is some discussion over the value of adopting different end points when considering doctoral study. The literature tends to use the terms 'submission' and 'completion'. We will see, however, that when actually measuring such periods, a key date is the start date – and definitions vary for this date. There has, for some time, been a belief that the key time period in doctoral study is from initial registration to submission, as favoured in the Swinnerton–Dyer report (Working Party on Postgraduate Education 1982) and adopted by the Research Councils in their assessment of research degree performance. This period recognizes the time spent undertaking the research and writing the thesis as the most important element of the doctoral process. The date of submission is not, however, the date on which the award is made; this can be some considerable time later. Between submission and award there is the complexity of activities, including appointment of examiners, examination and *viva voce*, subsequent modifications and formal approval by the university. All this can add a further 24 months to the overall process, frequently because of either bureaucratic time lapse at the institutional level or the necessity to undertake additional work by the student for a variety of reasons, one of which may be premature submission. Many students will hence enter the labour market before they have been awarded the Doctorate.

Where completion is viewed as the key date, then the period involved in the production of the thesis is extended by the examination and subsequent administrative processes. It suggests that, from a student perspective, the key is having the award and hence matters of examination and institutional process should be focused on rapid examination and award.

Both approaches, however, have some important limitations created by institutional variability in the definition of the term 'registration'. For some universities, registration takes place when an individual enters the institution and enrols. For others, a student may enrol in an institution and become registered some time later when the programme of research has been formally accepted by the institution, which can be anything up to 12 months later. For recording purposes and the records complied by HESA, enrolment marks the start date. However, in relation to institutional regulation, including for example the maximum period a candidate can be registered for a Doctorate, the date of registration may be the key date. All this is very confusing and as a consequence we would argue that there is a need to develop a uniform and agreed metric and set of definitions.

Consequences of using submission and completion rates as indicators

Perhaps the most important reason for the particular importance of submission and completion relates to student advantage or disadvantage. It is self-evident that if we are to encourage students to devote several years to research and the production of a thesis, then there are significant opportunity costs involved. These will increase as time to submission increases. Second, significant amounts of public money are invested in the doctoral process and it is not unreasonable to expect an efficient use of this money in terms of timely outputs and outcomes.

The choice of indicator (submission or completion rates) may have an unintended consequential effect on performance. Submission dates may, if used as performance indicators, encourage students to submit their work earlier than would ideally be the case. Given that most universities allow students to make major or minor modifications to the thesis once examined, early submission is less risky in relation to successful outcome than might be expected. The use of the submission period in this context however would give a false indicator of the time period involved in completion of the thesis. It also creates a situation where the examination process may become a means to complete the work – it allows the candidate the opportunity, in one sense at least, to submit work that can be corrected later. As is noted in the chapters later in this book on examination of the Doctorate, this can skew the process by giving new levels of meaning and purpose beyond the judging of whether or not the candidate has provided evidence that is sufficient enough to claim the award.

Data related to submission rates

The only significant study of submission rates in the UK before the recent HEFCE work (HEFCE 2005) is that of Winfield (1987) in his report for the Economic and Social Science Research Council (ESRC). Winfield's report provides a useful, if partial, baseline on which to investigate submission rates. Winfield highlighted the problem of available data on the subject. As far as data is concerned, little has changed in the intervening period and the observation made by Berelson remains true today.

> *Considering that so many people held such strong views on the time taken over the PhD, one would think that the facts on how long it takes to get the Doctorate would be readily available and generally accepted. Yet that is not the case.*
>
> (Berelson 1960, quoted by Winfield 1987)

The Research Councils and AHRB keep time series data on submission rates for their students, as do other sponsors including the Wellcome Foundation. There is, however, no nationally comparable data set that allows the production of submission rates. Data is collected on completion by the Higher Education Statistical Agency (HESA), but until recently little if anything was done with it in terms of presentation and analysis. Consequently, analysis has to rely on submission data relating to an elite group of mostly full-time students, representing 40% at most of the doctoral student population.

Winfield provides early evidence of the low submission rates in the UK that in the case of Social Sciences led to a major policy change involving sanctions to departments that did not achieve target rates. Table 8.1 illustrates the patterns for the group of Research Councils in the late 1970s.

The table also highlights the variation between the different disciplinary groupings represented by the Research Councils. Although not high by today's standards, NERC and SERC (now EPSRC) have much larger numbers of students completing within four years. Although Winfield argues that there are disciplinary explanations for this variation, he recognizes that completion rates in the Social Sciences must be addressed, asserting that 'questions

Table 8.1 Submission rates: 1976–80 starters

Year	Less than four years				Less than five years			
	ESRC	DES/BA	NERC	SERC	ESRC	DES/BA	NERC	SERC
1976	11	15	50		23	29	69	
1977	12	16	53	48	25	27	71	
1978	15		47	48	26		62	
1979	17	11	53	48	29	24	76	
1980	18		49	50	24			

Source: Winfield (1987)

about effective performance in doctoral study are not attacks on academic freedom' (Winfield 1987: 35).

The sanctions policy implemented before Winfield, but subsequently endorsed by his report, has been paralleled by a significant improvement in submission rates. Whether this is a case of correlation or causality may be disputed. Those working in the sector in the early 1980s will certainly recall the increased attention given to submission by institutional and departmental managers.

The pattern of submission today shows a very different picture, as is highlighted in Table 8.2. Rates show considerable variability across institutions and disciplines. This is reflected in the AHRB figures, for example, where the institutional range is from 100% to 0% in terms of four-year submission. At the disciplinary level, Music, Art History and the Classics continue to have relatively low four-year submission rates, while much higher rates are observed for Law, Theology and Archaeology.

The HEFCE Project on Doctoral Submission and Completion Rates (2004)

Genesis of a system of quality monitoring

In 2002 HEFCE established the need to identify minimum standards for research degree programmes in co-operation with the Research Councils. It was decided that there should be a method by which institutions could be monitored in terms of compliance with a minimum set of standards. A significant part of this concept of standards was the notion that the quality of delivery of doctoral study programmes can and should be measured in terms of the time taken for students to complete their programmes of study. Funding would then be linked to compliance in this respect. HEFCE pursued a consultation process that included *Improving Standards in Postgraduate Research Degree Programmes: Informal Consultation* (HEFCE 2003a). One of the out-

Table 8.2 Submission rates: 1990–97: % submission within four years

Start date	BBSRC	EPSRC	ESRC	MRC	NERC	PPARC	AHRB
1990	70	67	73	64	73	82	45
1992	72	67	75	67	72	81	54
1994	85	72	76	72	73	81	57
1996	86	71	76	75	78	84	70
1997	90	75	81	75	88	85	71

Source: OST/AHRB

comes of this consultation was an acceptance by the sector that standards of research degree delivery should be open to quality review. However, there was little agreement about criteria for such reviewing and critical concern about the use of quantitative measures, particularly in relation to time taken to submit work for examination and/or successfully complete the award.

In 2004 HEFCE completed a study into doctoral submission and completion rates across the sector (HEFCE 2005). The study incorporated all degrees that are examined predominantly through research, thus including the Professional Doctorates and the so-called New Route PhD as well as the traditional MPhil/PhD. The HEFCE team that carried out the research used HESA data. This work presented a picture that was far from the more optimistic one coming from the Research Councils and AHRB. It emphasized the importance of funding, age, mode of study, discipline and institution in any explanation of time to completion. For all students, time to completion is more comparable with our international competitors.

Compliance with a standard of completion rate

Despite reservations from across the sector the HEFCE are effectively to monitor performance of institutions in terms of research degree provision in relation primarily, or solely (the likely uncertainty on the final nature of the monitoring remains uncertain), on the basis of completion rates. Institutions that are not 'compliant' will be asked to justify their position and, where the justification is deemed to be inadequate, the HEFCE will consider withdrawing funds. The likely scenario is that institutions will be measured against what is the median point for completion across the sector, taking historical data from HESA to create an initial baseline. Where an institution's completion rates are at a significant variance from this median point then that institution will first be asked if the statistics are accurate. If the statistics are correct, then there will be an assumption that the institution is not meeting a reasonable level of completions and QAA will be asked to conduct an inquiry. As a result of the inquiry, QAA will make recommendations to the HEFCE. Whether or not there will be allowance for discipline-specific variation (or indeed variation relating to any of the other factors in the HEFCE study) is not yet certain. When the detail of the system of monitoring is revealed, then undoubtedly its 'teeth' will become apparent.

Data used in the HEFCE study

The HEFCE study used HESA data from 1996 to 2002/03. Students who left before one year of registration were removed from the sample. The study then looked at those students, both full and part time, whose registration persisted past the one-year mark in terms of factors affecting length of time to completion. The sample comprised 13,700 full-time students (8,000 of whom were 'home') and 4,800 part-time students (4,000 of whom were 'home'). The data did not take into account anomalies such as students taking time out from their studies; in this way it focused upon overall time registered rather than time spent actually working on the research programme. So, for example, devices such as suspensions (where a student goes in a state of regulatory limbo – still registered but not active) were ignored in the study as this data is not recorded by HESA.

The study considered the following factors:

• Sources of funding
• Subject studied (in broad discipline areas)
• Institution type
• Age and sex
• Previous qualifications
• Home/overseas (non-EU) students.

Main findings of the HEFCE study

The study revealed that after seven years of study 71% of full-time students had completed (82% had completed *or* were still active). In terms of part-time numbers, 34% of students had completed (62% had completed *or* were still active); 38% were no longer active and within that group 4% (of the overall number) had left with an MPhil.

Of the Research Council-funded, full-time students, approximately 80% had completed after five years. Of the Research Council-funded, part-time students, 30% had completed by seven years, 30% were no longer active and 40% were still active.

The main conclusions of the study may be summarized as follows:

• Completion rates for full-time students were more consistent than for part-time students.
• Completion rates were improved if funding was received from the Funding Councils.
• Discipline areas were a factor in terms of completion rates for full-time students (less so for part-time students).
• Research Council students tended to complete more quickly than non-Research Council students.
• Overseas students tended to complete more quickly than home students.
• Sex was a minor effect (women's completion rates being lower than men's).
• Similarly, age was a minor effect (older students were less likely to complete or took longer to complete) – early 20s had a 80% completion rate; early 30s had a 60% completion rate.
• There was a slight advantage in terms of completion time if the student's previous qualification was a first-class degree.
• Institution type (pre- or post-1992) had no discernible effect.

- Discipline area had a significant impact with natural/medical sciences completing much more quickly than humanities and social sciences ('vocational subjects' fell between the two).
- Critical mass of research group was not a factor, i.e. there was no indication that students in small units were disadvantaged in comparison to students in larger units.
- The overall average times for completion of doctoral programmes were: 60% completed in four years and 70% in five years.

Attrition

The importance of attrition rates for students and institutions

Attrition (and rates of attrition) is another key element of doctoral performance. Berelson (1960), quoting Sir Hugh Taylor of Princeton noted, 'if the graduate schools of the country would solve this problem of attrition. We could raise substantially the output of graduate schools of the country without increasing enrolment or additional expenditures for faculty and facilities' (Berelson 1960). As with many aspects of Higher Education, certainly in the UK, attrition rates have been dominated by discussion and analysis at the undergraduate level (see, for example, Yorke 1999; Johnes 1990). At postgraduate level there is little or no current discussion or concern for attrition in the UK. The work of Wright and Cochrane (2000) is particularly interesting because it presents a detailed study of what drives success in a single institution, the University of Birmingham.

But first, what is meant by attrition? Straightforwardly, this may be defined as leaving without the award for which the student is registered. In most institutions this will be formally recorded as a withdrawal. Frequently, there is a significant gap between a student withdrawing from a programme and that fact being formally recorded. In some cases this may result from administrative delay. More often, however, it is because of the decision being implicit rather than explicit, or informal rather than formal. It is the case that many students simply do not work on their research, for whatever reason, rather than formally withdraw. Thus it can be in excess of 12 months between ceasing actively working on the research and formal withdrawal. The definition is further complicated by formal procedures such as 'suspension'; in the case of suspension, a student formally withdraws from a programme for a specific reason, usually ill health or similar non-academic reason, for a specific period of time with the intention and agreement to return subsequently.

An understanding of the nature of attrition is vital for the improvement of the doctoral delivery process. From the student perspective, dropping out of a programme represents a significant loss, both directly financial and personal as well as indirectly in terms of the opportunity costs of time spent with no material gain. From an institutional view, there is a significant cost in terms of administrative and academic time as well as financial costs as bursaries and other funding streams achieve no returns. There will be losses for other stakeholders, funding agencies, sponsors and families. Overall there is the loss to the national research base.

Lack of empirical data on attrition rates

Currently there is no direct, available data that would allow an analysis of attrition in doctoral study. The Research Council data gives indirect evidence that, assuming an asymptotic pattern of submission, almost 10% of candidates fail to submit and hence can be said to have withdrawn. Of this 10%, anecdotal evidence suggests that approximately 50% drop out in the first year of research. This supports the views of Becher *et al.* (1994) who identify the first year of study as the time at which students are most vulnerable and hence most likely to drop out. It is possible then that with the development of the MRes and the 1 + 3 models of the Doctorate, attrition will significantly reduce.

Conceptual issues in relation to attrition rates

Many of the conceptual and theoretical issues in relation to attrition rates derive from an understanding of attrition at undergraduate level that, as we have noted above, has been more thoroughly researched in recent years. The major elements that appear to be of importance are explanations that revolve around what we might refer to as:

- the individual and the structural – in this context one needs to consider explanations involving gender, age, ethnicity, social background, and levels of funding;
- academic – in which explanations relate to the nature of the research being undertaken, previous research experience and disciplinary understanding, and associated academic matters such as teaching commitments;
- environmental – in which explanations would look to elements of both the research environment and the processes within it, such as the rigour of recruitment, levels of supervision, mentoring and overall support and progress review; less tangible environmental attributes such as social fit, ambiance and culture are also involved.

Several other questions arise in the discussion and analysis of attrition. As in many other instances, there is a problem of measurement – what is a doctoral research student? Reference has been made earlier to some of the issues in terms of type of Doctorate. UK data does not differentiate. There are, however, more subtle problems associated with registration and enrolment, whether an individual is a member of staff or not: Graduate Teaching Assistants (GTAs), those writing up and no longer defined as full time, and those without funding.

Establishing benchmarks is a major challenge and one that brings in additional complications to those of the undergraduate sector. From the limited empirical evidence available it seems that attrition rates vary, for example, across disciplines, reflecting possibly the different research cultures.

Equally, what can be seen as an acceptable or good attrition rate is not a straightforward matter. The figures quoted in North America, which rise to between 40% and 50% are, in our view, not rates to which the UK sector should aspire. At present with very little UK data it is impossible to establish norms or benchmarks against which to work. The benchmarks for attrition in the undergraduate population vary significantly and range from as little as 3% to well above 40%. It would seem reasonable to expect variability in the Doctorate benchmarks, reflecting similar factors as in the undergraduate context. However, rates above 10% would seem unreasonably high for a group of students who, for the most part, will have successfully completed a first degree, are making an explicit choice to continue with their education and who have experience, if not complete understanding, of the education system and culture.

Wright and Cochrane's work suggests that the variability is not as clear-cut as convention might have us believe, particularly as far as gender, mode of study and nationality are concerned. Table 8.3 highlights some of their key observations for submission within four years or part-time equivalent. They also note that there is no significant difference between full-time and part-time students, those from overseas and home and EU students, male and female students and those who gained their first degree at Birmingham or elsewhere.

Finally, it is important to note any significance or emphasis that should be placed on the point at which the student withdraws. No matter how effective the recruitment and induction process a university adopts, a student who drops out at an early stage in his/her doctoral career is less a cause for

Table 8.3 Percentage submission within four years: University of Birmingham

Characteristic	%
Science	64
Arts and Humanities	51
Research Council funding	66
Other funding sources	58
Age 21–27	64
Age over 27	57
First or upper second (initial degree)	67
Other class or qualification	58

Source: Wright and Cochrane (2000)

concern than one who makes that decision well into the programme. The loss to the individual and the institution is far less problematic in the former than in the latter. Nerad and Miller (1996) confirm that there are two patterns to withdrawal from PhD programmes in the USA. In the former case, students realize early in the process that the doctoral programme is not for them; in the latter they lose interest or run out of motivation or money and take employment.

Reasons given for leaving doctoral programmes

The key question about attrition, of course, concerns the reasons why students leave. There is little recent survey evidence in the UK to help in our understanding of why doctoral students leave. Booth and Satchell (1995) and Bowen and Rudenstine (1992) both report higher completion rates in the sciences compared with the humanities and social sciences. Booth and Satchell also noted that men were more likely to complete faster than women, who had a tendency to withdraw earlier. Earlier work by Rudd and Hatch (1968; see also Rudd 1985) suggests that personal and individual problems are at the root of attrition. Most evidence, however, is anecdotal and intuitive and is of limited value in planning systematic strategies to improve rates.

Recent American work by Golde (2000) and Lovitts (2001) indicates that the key reasons for both attrition and longer times to completion are as follows:

1. Insufficient funding for graduate students.
2. Lack of transparency of supervision.
3. Inappropriate programme design.
4. Academic isolation.
5. Unreasonable scope of thesis.
6. Poor quality of admissions.

It is notable that each of these elements of explanation is discussed elsewhere in this text.

We have made little reference so far to the different types of Doctorate in considering attrition; and, of course, there is little or no data on which to make comparison. In considering the appropriateness and value of the newer Doctorate programmes – professional, new route and practice-based – it would be useful to have such data. Intuitively, however, we should expect all three to have lower attrition rates because they address explicitly or otherwise many of the issues involved and noted above. The Professional Doctorate, for example, usually has a work involvement and is delivered in smaller modular chunks making commitment more likely and ease of completion higher. The sense of belonging to a 'cohort' may reduce academic isolation considerably. In short, reasons for leaving may differ significantly across the range of kinds of doctoral programmes.

Length of doctoral programmes

The discussion of completion rates and attrition often takes place in isolation of the regulatory position with regard to the time permitted to undertake a doctoral award. This 'time permitted' is usually expressed in terms of a maximum and minimum time for which a student can be registered. Typically, this is independent of any time period relating to ideal completion times and duration of student bursaries or Funding Council fees. This rather confused position adds another dimension to the lack of clarity about doctoral study. There does appear to be little logic in the times allotted and it is difficult to establish why they were selected. Given the earlier observations about the differences in the nature of the Doctorate in different disciplines, it is perhaps surprising that there is not a greater degree of disciplinary variability that is observed. In many institutions the period is identical for the different types of Doctorate – PhD, Professional Doctorate and Practice-Based Doctorate – suggesting a lack of rationale behind the period.

Registration periods

Part-time and full-time periods of registration

The period for part-time provision is of particular interest as, typically, it requires twice that of the full time. This assumes that part-time doctoral study is half that of full time, which, while having a certain logic, fails to recognize the frequently very different approach and style of the part-time Doctorate often undertaken in spare time rather than in formally allocated 'half time'. Anecdotal evidence suggests that many students adopt the part-time registration to minimize the fees they pay, in some cases thus reducing payments from £3,500 for full-time registration to less than £1,000 for part-time. To compound the problem, HESA part-time data also includes students who are writing-up. Not only does this latter ambiguity create problems with the interpretation of the data, but it also further confuses analysis of length of maximum period of the doctoral programme. If a candidate undertakes three years' full-time study then one year part-time writing-up, the question arises as to whether this is completion within three-and-a-half years or four years. It quickly becomes obvious that four-year completion rates are academic as, unless a student is fully funded to undertake the work in the additional year, at least part of the study will inevitably be in part-time mode.

In differentiating full time from part time it is necessary in our view to be cognizant of the time spent on the project rather than the time spent within the university environment. It may be that within the science model, a full-time student is in the lab for 40 hours or more a week and the part-time student only 20 hours. However, there will be many cases where both full-time students and part-time students spend an equal or reversed amount of time on the project itself. In the case of a work-based study, it may be that a part-time registered student undertakes the research full time as part of their full-time job. The demarcation between full time and part time is not clear.

Funding in relation to registration periods

It seems to us that this discussion is significant because of the importance of the four-year cut-off in submission rates imposed by the Research Councils and the Funding Councils. Equivalence would suggest that the four-year threshold should only apply to those who are fully funded for four years; for the remainder, and we suspect the majority, the threshold should be five years or more.

The minimum period of registration for all Doctorates is also problematic and, as we have shown earlier, the nature of the work undertaken will vary enormously. This will be particularly pertinent where work-based research forms an integral element of the work, as in the Professional Doctorate. If it is possible to achieve the outcomes of doctoral study in a short period – perhaps because some elements of the work have already been completed in the work environment before registration – then logic suggests that a minimum period may even be inappropriate. In our view, as in so many aspects under consideration in this book, the outcomes must become the key elements under consideration.

Process and product of doctoral study related to timescale of funding

The discussion above is relevant to the current state of doctoral education in the UK for three key reasons. First, the various gatekeepers and funders appear to be developing thresholds which are based on a model of the Doctorate and its funding that no longer represents the reality of doctoral education. The diversity of provision needs to be reflected in the thresholds if they are to be adopted and employed with any level of seriousness. Second, the nature of academic delivery and supervision within the doctoral programme must better reflect the diversity of candidates if we are to achieve our objective of ensuring that all candidates are able to succeed and complete their studies in a timely manner. Finally, support programmes such as UK GRAD must respond to the reality of doctoral programmes across the sector and provide generic support for all those who will benefit in order to ensure equity across the student population.

Perhaps the most appropriate way forward is to adopt the approach used by the AHRB in its definition of Doctorate, in which it relates the process and the product more closely to the timescale of funding.

Doctoral awards provide support for up to three years of full-time study, or up to five years of part-time study, *to enable you to pursue and* complete *a programme of doctoral research and gain a doctoral degree.*

In awarding studentships for doctoral research, we assume that a doctoral thesis is a piece of work that:

- *exhibits substantial evidence of original scholarship and contains material that can be prepared for publication, and*
- *can be produced by a capable, well-qualified and diligent student, properly supervised and supported,* within the period of award.

(AHRB undated; authors' emphasis)

If the thesis is not completed within the period of the award, three or five years – then it will be deemed to have failed within these terms. This explicit link to timescale is a welcome approach, bringing clarity to the scope and management of PhDs. By extension, our own view is that the other Research Councils and the Funding Councils who give time-limited awards should similarly be linking the scope of the Doctorate to the time period of award far more explicitly.

While arguments are commonplace for longer periods to completion (taking account of mode of study, needs of student and disciplinary variation), it is unfortunate in our view that the regulators have not grasped the nettle more firmly. Equally, it is interesting that institutions appear to be so reluctant to accept such requirements. After all, the longer a student continues after the period of funding, the more likely it is that he/she will never complete. From an institutional point of view, once outside the Funding Councils' funding period, supervision and infrastructural support will no longer be funded.

Conclusion

Whatever the motivation for undertaking doctoral research, if that research is to contribute to the development of knowledge generally or to the specific knowledge and skills of the individual, then timely completion and dissemination is important. The growth in the number of doctoral candidates and the increasing complexity of research has tended to cloud issues of successful and timely completion. The discussion of such rates must not be seen as a stick with which to beat failing individual research programmes or university departments, but a powerful tool to force us to think about the Doctorate, the student experience and, in particular, the management of research degree processes. For those who cry foul, we would simply suggest consideration of those institutions and disciplines in which success rates and completion rates are high and reflect on well-managed, well-specified programmes of research.

Summary issues

- Is it possible to define how long a Doctorate should take to complete and, if so, how long should that period be?
- Is it desirable to design programmes in such a way that they can be completed in an agreed period and, if so, can this period be consistent across all disciplines?
- Is timely completion an indication of quality in well-managed departments and should it be used as a performance indicator of quality?
- What are the consequences of targets for completion or submission to institutional funding or student success?
- What are the factors that may best explain why some students drop out of their research programmes, others complete on time and others need to extend their registrations?

Part 4

Managing Doctoral Study

9

The nature of doctoral supervision

Introduction

Supervision in a changing context

Supervision and supervisory practice have received increasing attention in the literature and from regulatory and sponsor organizations. However, attention is variable in the research literature, dominated by the Australian literature and remarkably receiving little interest in the UK research literature. The report from the Wellcome Trust (2001) is one of the few analyses of the views of supervisors.

The nature of research supervision is challenged by the changes in the nature of doctoral study. The traditional model of a single supervisor supporting and encouraging the individual, young, full-time, highly motivated research student (in which this personal and individual contact supposedly ensures excellence) is no longer tenable. As Zhao (2003) notes, the changes in doctoral education and the increasingly complex research environment place new challenges for research degree supervision. The traditional model does not address the needs of a highly mobile, IT literate, frequently part-time and mature population of research student. Nor does it respond to the needs of new and emerging forms of Doctorate that demand different pedagogies such as the workshop model, course-work model, conference model and collaborative cohort model described by Conrad *et al.* (1992) and summarized in Table 9.1.

Worldwide concern with supervision

Interest in supervisory activity and its importance in academic discussion are not restricted to activity in the UK as already noted. In his study of international doctoral degrees, Noble (1994) notes that supervision is important to academics internationally, observing that faculty advising/directing/

Table 9.1 Changes in the contemporary landscape of research training

	Extending from	*Into*
Research degree programmes	Master's and doctorate by thesis	Increased diversity, e.g. prof. docs., doctorate by project
Form	Written thesis	Artefact
Location	Academy	Workplace
Knowledge production	Mode 1 (disciplinary)	Mode 2 (socially distributed)
Researcher	Individual	Collaborative
Research process	Open	Focused
Knowledge	Single discipline	Multi- and trans-disciplinary
Skill set	Research skills	Research skills + generic skills
Commitment	Disciplinary truth	Performativity
Graduate outcome	Independent researcher	Worker in the knowledge economy
Assessment	Of thesis (by academics)	Thesis or exegesis/artefact (skill mainly by academics)
Institutional intervention	Minimal	Managed
Research and academic life	Research is the central endeavour and focus of academic life	Commercialization of research is the central endeavour and focus of academic life

	Shift from	*To*
Time horizon	Open	Pre-set
Supervision	Unconstrained	Fast

supervising was the third most important issue identified by his group of international scholars. Equally, he notes a range of familiar issues such as 'supervisors and students fail to define sensible and manageable projects which can be completed', 'poor staff understanding', 'supervision is too permissive', and 'professors prolong the process because of overwhelming concern about total perfection' (Noble 1994: 32). We should, then, take research degree supervision seriously – more seriously than to date. This chapter considers various aspects of the discussion about improving both the approach taken to supervision and the practice and results of that supervision.

Supervision: research or teaching?

The challenge of defining the role of supervisors

Bound up in the discussion of the nature and purpose of the PhD is the nature of supervision. Is it a matter of researching, linked to the notion of the PhD being a piece of original research, or is it a matter of teaching, reflecting the view of the PhD as being the training of advanced researchers? Such a dichotomy is clearly too simplistic, but it challenges us to clarify the role and nature of doctoral supervision.

If supervisors are asked if research degree supervision is an act of research or of teaching then, in our experience, responses will vary considerably. At one end of a continuum are supervisors who see their role as engaging in research, enabling a novice to take part and verifying that the novice has achieved 'enough' (for the doctoral award) in terms of research findings. At the other end are those supervisors who see themselves as engaging in an act of pedagogy in which they impart a set of research skills and an amount of subject knowledge to a learner who then has to demonstrate that he/she has learned enough to be counted as a peer. We suggest that the focus of the efforts of supervisors will differ according to their place along this continuum. Indeed, the Wellcome Trust analysis notes that supervisors identify their role as 'teacher, trainer, mentor', or even as 'mother and father' (Wellcome Trust 2001: 15), with little reference to research, suggesting a role far nearer to that of teacher than to researcher.

The attributes of a successful supervisor have been discussed elsewhere, e.g. from the perspective of the supervisor by Delamont *et al.* (1997), from the perspective of the student by Cryer (1996) and from both perspectives by Phillips and Pugh (2000).

Supervising the learner about research

In the QAA Code there is recognition in Precept 5 that part of the research degree process is one of learning as well as of undertaking research.

Precept 5: Institutions will only accept research students into an environment that provides support for doing and learning about research and where high quality research is occurring.

(QAA 2004: 8)

The code also describes the characteristics of such a research environment, concluding that:

Such a learning environment will also enable research students to make judge-ments requiring creativity and critical independent thought, *accepting that uncertainty is a feature of the conduct of research programmes. This environment should enable students to grapple with challenges that* develop intellectual maturity *and encourage a high level of* reflection on the student's own learning about research *as well as on research outcomes.*

(QAA 2004: 8; authors' emphasis)

The attributes of supervisors

The attributes highlighted in Table 9.2 suggest a range of skills much broader than those of a successful researcher; they would be recognized equally as the attributes of a successful teacher. They are certainly skills that would not automatically be associated with the understanding of research.

In our own view, what is needed is a focus on the student as a learner about research (i.e. about the skills needed to do research effectively as well as knowledge about research findings and their implications) and the supervisor as a teacher about researching. Clearly, learners have to engage in research and will be judged on their learning in terms of the evidence provided within the thesis. In that thesis, they will need to demonstrate that they have made a contribution to knowledge *and* that they have understood that contribution in terms of its genesis and its implications. Therefore, we suggest that research degree study needs to be relocated (or accepted as being located) in the domain of 'teaching and learning'.

Supervisors and the need to produce critical thinkers

Further to the above, it seems to us that the kind of teaching involved at research degree level is one in which special attention needs to be paid to the independence of the learning and the creativity that the student needs to exhibit. The dangers of reducing teaching to the transmission of specific skills and knowledge are as acute at this level as they are throughout the rest of Higher Education. Indeed they are greater as the aim here is for critical thinkers of the highest order. Teaching for independence and creativity then become paramount. One of the issues here may be the relationship between the kinds of learning outcomes that are implicit in doctoral study and the

Table 9.2 Attributes of the supervisor

The supervisor role
• Facilitator (providing access to resources or expertise).
• Director (determining topic and method, providing ideas).
• Adviser (helping to resolve technical problems, suggesting alternatives).
• Teacher (of research techniques).
• Guide (suggesting timetable, providing feedback).
• Critic (of design or enquiry of drafts and interpretations).
• Freedom giver (authorizes and supports students decisions).
• Supporter (shows encouragement and interest and discussion).
• Friend (non-academic support).
• Manager (checks on progress, planning and feedback).
• Examiner (internal examiner, mock vivas, progress reports)

Source: Brown and Atkins (1988)

assessment for the award. There is no nationally agreed set of criteria about just what is being examined in the PhD examination process (though there may be suggestions within disciplines where professional organizations issue guidance) though of course there is guidance of a kind in the QAA's Framework Higher Education Qualifications. Certainly, in their assessment criteria many institutions will include originality, publishability and contribution to knowledge. But the way in which individual examiners assess the candidate's capabilities in this respect vary greatly (see Trafford 2003). Of course, assessing a candidate's potential to work creatively, perhaps across discipline boundaries, is necessarily difficult. But if creativity and independent critical thought are what are required then the teaching ought to be directed at those skills and abilities and the assessment ought to reflect their presence or absence. Both teaching and assessment need to recognize that the learning of these skills and abilities will necessarily require the taking of risks.

Supervision as workload

Attempts to specify workload in relation to research degree supervision

Given the complex and individual nature of research supervision, the question arises as to the number of students for whom an individual supervisor should be responsible. The HEFCE/Joint Funding Councils' consultation process highlighted this when it initially suggested specific limits to the number of students a supervisor could support at any one time. More recently the revised QAA Code of Practice has taken a more holistic view of supervision as part of an overall portfolio of activity.

> *In appointing supervisors, institutions need to be aware of and guided by the overall workload of the individual, including teaching, research, administration and other responsibilities, for example, external examining duties and other professional commitments, such as consultancy or clinical responsibilities.*
>
> (QAA 2004: 17)

Notwithstanding these observations, in our view it is unlikely that any supervisor can realistically deal effectively with more than approximately six students at different stages of the doctoral process and for whom the individual supervisor is the main supervisor or 'Director of Studies' (we are assuming here that no supervisor in an HEI within the UK is likely to be able to devote 100% of his/her time to supervising).

Evidence in relation to supervisory workload

Data from the Wellcome Trust study shows that the generality is for supervisors to have quite small numbers of students. Only 9% of the supervisors in the study were supervising six or more students, while the majority (72%) were supervising between one and three (Wellcome Trust 2001: 17). Other than the Welcome Trust data, there is little evidence to suggest that supervisors are allocated more students than they can reasonably manage. It appears that the current concern is based on anecdote alone.

Difficulty of a single metric in relation to supervisory workload

It is questionable whether or not there can be, or should be, a definable norm for the number of students for whom an individual supervisor may be responsible. The workload of supervisors needs to be seen in the context of their overall duties, research, teaching and administration. Consequently, some supervisors, for whom research and research supervision is a main activity, may reasonably have a larger number of students. Further factors that inevitably affect the way in which time is allocated are the nature of the programme of research and the abilities and potentials of the individual student. It is unlikely, therefore, that a single metric can be applied to a system which includes sciences, humanities and the arts, full-time, part-time and overseas students and MPhil, PhD and Professional Doctoral programmes. Each instance of supervision will have both specific needs and needs attributable to the discipline, award and mode of study.

Supervision as part of a tripartite process

The supervisor's responsibilities

The quality of doctoral experience is a tripartite responsibility involving the student, the supervisor and the institution (Elton *et al.* 1994). Emphasis has traditionally tended to be placed on the importance of the supervisor in this relationship, in part because of the way in which doctoral students have been recruited. Typically, supervisors have been expected to 'deliver' in terms of the following (based on the Royal Society of Chemistry 1995: 10 and 11):

- read papers in advance of meetings;
- be available at agreed times;
- be friendly, open and supportive and show a keen interest in the research;
- be constructively critical;
- enable the student to develop as an independent critical thinker capable of creative work;
- have good knowledge of the research area;
- be well organized and structure meetings usefully.

The student's responsibilities

We suggest, however, that any consideration of responsibilities should be widened to include the student. In this case it might identify responsibilities such as:

- production of a research proposal within an appropriate timescale;
- regular attendance at meetings with the supervisor;
- submission of written work to their supervisor regularly;
- taking cognizance of the supervisors comments and feedback;
- reflection on own thinking and learning as well as on project outcomes;
- discussion of any issues of access, provision of facilities or data with their supervisor in the first instance.

The institution's responsibilities

Similarly, the institutional responsibility is fundamental to the doctoral experience as ultimately it is the institution that is responsible for the quality and standards of all awards, although the majority now delegate the responsibility to Graduate Schools in one form or another (UKCGE 1998a; Woodward *et al.* 2004). The institution also sets the patterns and standards for the way in which it operates supervision (e.g. in terms of expectations and training requirements) and its various codes of practice (e.g. for students and for supervisors). Delegation of responsibility from a central body to Graduate School or Faculty or Department level should not in any way diminish the institution's basic responsibilities. Indeed, where delegation of supervisory practice (in its broadest terms) is delegated, then the institution creates a new need – that of monitoring the way in which the devolved responsibilities are carried out.

Expectations about responsibilities in relation to the process of supervision

When considering the overall quality of research degree provision it is particularly valuable to identify and focus on expectations within this tripartite structure. Without each of the three elements, the quality of the doctoral experience will be much diminished and the quality of the research award may therefore be impoverished. More importantly, there is a need for each party to be clear in its role and in the responsibilities entailed. Indeed, there may be a good case for linking the three partners explicitly within a contractual agreement that binds the parties more transparently than in the implied contract on the back of enrolment. For example, at the University of Oxford (THES 3 March 1995) the graduate committee has drawn up a charter (the Graduate Academic Charter) with 26 recommendations, including research supervision and a form of feedback, 'where graduates write reports on their supervisors, which can be acted on in such a way as not to damage the students academic future'. Such contracts or charters may be seen as useful tools in establishing relationships and responsibilities, but as Hockey (1995) notes, it is something that is little developed in the UK research literature.

In France this has been taken forward in the form of a charter, *la charte des thèses*. This document specifies the rights and responsibilities of each of the partners involved in doctoral study: the student, director of studies and the institution (http://cdt.jeunes-chercheurs.org/). Although applied in various forms within the French system, it addresses some if not all of our concerns about responsibilities and is something that we suggest institutions might be encouraged to develop. Whatever method an institution uses to clarify the roles and responsibilities, it is important that the institution ensures that all the different players in research degree study have their respective parts to play and should be held to account for their knowledge of their role and their effectiveness in carrying out their responsibilities.

Principles underpinning tripartite responsibilities

We suggest that the kinds of principles that an institution might wish to consider when looking at the supervisory element of the tripartite responsibility include:

- the need for supervisory teams rather than single supervisors;
- the need for supervisors to be actively researching in the area of the proposed research degree programme;
- supervisors to be trained specifically in the pedagogy of research degree training;
- the supervisory team to contain experience of successful supervision;
- a transparent system of allocation of time to supervise being in place;
- a recognition that supervision requires a regular pattern of meetings with the outcomes of those meetings being recorded in an open way;
- a recognition at institutional level of the roles and responsibilities of the various players in the supervisory context (to include here the student) at the various periods of the programme;
- an open, negotiated, agreement at the level of each specific degree programme of the responsibilities and commitments of individual supervisors and of the student;
- a transparent system in place which monitors supervisory success.

Supervision and overseas students

Recent literature has paid particular attention to the needs of international students, perhaps because of their importance (i) to the well-being of UK research, (ii) in terms of the income of most universities and (iii) because they bring particular issues for the supervisor (CVCP 1992). It is noteworthy however that almost nothing in this context is to be found in key reports such as Harris (1996), Dearing (1997) or the White Paper (DfES 2003), the last of which gave scant consideration to postgraduate provision in general.

In their review of unpublished research dealing with international students, Leonard *et al.* (2003) identify a substantial amount of unpublished material in both masters and PhD theses, which deals with international students and postgraduate study. The work of Okorocha (1997) is particularly notable as it relates specifically to supervision. As Okorocha notes, the principle issues for the international doctoral student derive from cultural differences and expectations. Usually, but not always, overseas students come from an education system, both secondary and higher, in which norms, relationships and expectations are significantly different. As a consequence, relationships with supervisors may be very formal, and some support colleagues may be condescending. Coming from didactic pedagogies, overseas students' understanding of how learning takes place may be very different to the understanding prevalent in the UK. Additionally, language and religious beliefs may introduce further barriers to the kind of interaction and debate that is typical within the UK system (Cryer 1998).

Research supervisor training

Training in the UK and overseas

The need to train supervisors has been recognized by policymakers and funders in the UK for over ten years. As early as Winfield (1987) it was noted that supervisors were attending seminars and workshops for training purposes. More recently other countries have recognized the need. For example, the Swedish Government (2000) passed a bill entitled *Research and Renewal (2000/01: 3)* part of which made it mandatory for Swedish universities and other institutions of higher education which offer postgraduate studies to arrange training courses for research supervisors. The Council for Renewal of Higher Education was allocated approximately 7 million SEK (approximately £535,000) to develop programmes of training over a period of three years. In the UK, the Government White Paper *Realising our Potential* focused attention on the issue stating, 'A period spent in PhD training represents a substantial investment in public funds and is important to ensure that it represents good value for money for the taxpayer, as well as the individual student' (DTI 1993: para. 7.15).

From the Science and Engineering Research Council to Harris

This theme is developed in the SERC (now the EPSRC) discussion paper on research supervision which 'observes that to become effective and productive managers, supervisors should *acquire* a range of skills including core research and management skills'. More recently the pressures to rethink the role of the supervisor, increased emphasis on the training of supervisors, and the importance of supervision, comes from a range of sources that may conveniently be referred to as those pushing institutional change and those pulling or encouraging institutions to change their practices. The push factors come from a series of initiatives and reports over the past ten years or so, each of which has, in one way or another, exerted pressure on institutions to pay more attention to supervisor behaviours. The Harris report (Harris 1996), itself a landmark in postgraduate education in the UK, initially identified the need for more careful supervision and indeed for the training of supervisors. Box 3, in which Harris identified the key attributes necessary for the successful delivery of research degree programmes, included supervisor training as a vital element.

The Research Councils

The Research Councils have begun to recognize the importance of the supervisory process to successful completion of award (in this they are led, arguably, by the ESRC). This has become formalized within the 2001 training guidelines from the ESRC in which it is stated:

> *The ESRC will expect to see a statement about the provision of professional development opportunities for supervisors in applications for recognition. It follows that the ESRC will expect outlets to have formal systems in place for monitoring the performance of supervisors, for identifying the training and development needs of supervisors and for ensuring that these are met.*
>
> (ESRC 2001: C3.2)

The UK Funding Councils

The Policy Paper, *Improving Standards in Research Degree Programmes* produced by the UK Funding Councils (HEFCE 2003b: Table 1, section 4a) states that in connection with threshold standards for research degree supervision, 'All new supervisors [are] to undertake mandatory institutionally specified training.'

QAA

The revised QAA Code of Practice is less specific than the HEFCE publication noted above but is also potentially more demanding on supervisor training. Precept 11 states that 'Institutions will appoint supervisors who have the appropriate skills and subject knowledge to support, encourage and monitor research students effectively' (QAA 2004). The use of the word 'training' is dropped from earlier HEFCE consultations, presumably for fear of alienating academics who feel that they are above being trained, although many spend much of their time training others.

While not using the word 'training' explicitly, under the revised Code *all* supervisors will be expected to engage in development of various kinds to equip them to supervise. The explanation beneath this Precept goes on to refer to development activities, 'to assure ... competence in the role', 'to demonstrate ... continuing professional development, ... in updating knowledge and skills' and '... sharing good practice' (QAA 2004). The Code then identifies the new supervisors who will 'participate in specified development activities arranged through their institution, to assure their competence in the role'.

As we have already identified, the role of the supervisor with all its associated responsibilities is very broad. If institutions are to be able to assure that their members of staff have the appropriate skills to address this breadth of responsibility, it will require a considerable level of development activity, underpinned by a monitoring or appraisal system capable of ensuring that the training is taking place and having the desired impact on supervisor competency. This approach is a long way from, and a significant advance on, running training courses which once completed can be ticked off and forgotten.

Beyond litigation

Perhaps the most significant driver of change, however, relates more fundamentally to quality assurance and the student experience. It also relates to the all too familiar consequences when things go wrong; that is, notably, complaints and appeals. It is important to note that there are significant benefits from supervisor development activity beyond those of compliance and litigation reduction. There is a danger that training course for supervisors are 'sold' to wary academics on the grounds that they need to know how to protect themselves against litigation of one sort or another. In our view there is a danger that such a selling point may undervalue the real purpose of such training, which is to improve the overall quality of the experience of research degree study for all concerned. For many staff in universities the opportunity to supervise a research student offers a valuable extension and diversification of their portfolio, and one that can stimulate new ideas and creativity. These things may, of course, then transfer onto taught postgraduate and undergraduate teaching. Consequently many staff, and particularly those who are new to academia, may well appreciate the support that such development activity gives them. Depending on how the development activities are arranged, they may also support intra-institutional or inter-disciplinary networking and collaboration. In our own experience, the sharing of practice from one discipline can make a significant contribution to the supervisory practice of another. For example, the teamworking approach of the typical Chemistry laboratory has much to commend it and its principles may be emulated, albeit in different contexts, by, for example, the social sciences, humanities or design.

Training for whom and in what?

The HEFCE guidelines noted earlier in this chapter emphasized the need for all new supervisors to have mandatory training, and this is reflected in the revised QAA Code of Practice, albeit using a different tone and language. Supervisor training is now regarded in the same way as training for more general university learning and teaching and is adopted as compulsory for new staff in many institutions in the UK. However, it is not only those new to supervision that are in need of support as the ESRC note, but also supervisors with considerable numbers of successful completions. The language used in the revised QAA Code of Practice explanation (set out under the Precept already mentioned) is more subtle and refers to 'specified development activities'. The key is the way in which the sector interprets and implements these 'activities' – what is understood by development activities, what do they contain and how should they be delivered?

Some elements of any such activities are relatively easy to identify. The Doctorate has changed significantly over the past ten years. Partially as a result of this change, institutional and national regulations have altered, as have institutional organizational structures and the management of doctoral students. Therefore, without updating on regulations and requirements alone, many so-called 'experienced' supervisors would be unaware of many of the current imperatives. Yet beyond this apparent, readily identifiable need, institutions are required in the current climate to assess the wider needs of supervisors. If training is about enhancing the quality of the supervisory experience then universities must identify the gaps in experience, skills and knowledge of that supervisor. Such identification moves the discussion towards a complex process that will involve time and ultimately expense and in which individual skills of supervisors are assessed – perhaps as part of annual appraisal and development review, with input from the student.

Of course, rather than an individual analysis of learning need it is more likely that those charged with organizing supervisor training within an institution will attempt to identify, across the supervisor population, areas of deficit in supervision and weakness in supervisory practice and concentrate on those. Again, there is little evidence of areas of weakness other than the anecdotal. Consequently, the activity of supervision needs to be discussed and understood in terms of improving professional practice – an activity that arguably should engage all academics. Perhaps what the longstanding supervisors should be encouraged to review is their own practice; they need to reflect on ways in which they undertake their supervisory duties. For example, existing supervisors need to be challenged on the relationship between supervision, teaching and learning and research.

Updating supervisors

As in all discussion of the research degree process, it is clear that for many supervisors, supervision is not as commonplace as other activities and hence needs frequent reinforcement. Research degree supervisors do not have the opportunity to gain the kind of experience that is possible when teaching cohorts of taught course students, where regular feedback is given and received. The importance of updating is emphasized by the Wellcome Trust survey (2001) which highlights that even for active supervisors in institutions that have significant numbers of research students, the frequency of supervision can be quite low and hence the level of experience may be highly variable. In the survey, 46% of the supervisors had supervised less than ten students in the previous ten years. In the context of the overall academic portfolio it might be suggested that in an absolute sense, very few of this group of supervisors could be said to be experienced. This is something of a conundrum and leads us to question when it can reasonably be asserted that a supervisor is 'experienced'. If we extrapolate from the Wellcome survey it seems probable that the majority of academics in the UK will supervise less than ten doctoral students in their academic careers.

Models of supervisor training

Differing expectations of the supervisory experience

Pearson and Brew (2002) introduced the various approaches to supervision development that relate to the different institutional and professional contexts in which students will develop. As Becher *et al.* (1994) observe, in general supervisors have a rosier picture of the process than students and tend to see problems as belonging to the student, not to themselves. It may be suggested that from a supervisor's perspective the student's role is to:

• produce a research proposal within an appropriate timescale;
• attend regular meetings with the supervisor;
• submit written work to the supervisor regularly;
• take notice of the supervisor's comments and feedback.

However, the student may have a different set of expectations that might include:

- supervisors to be available;
- supervisors to read the student's work in advance of meetings;
- supervisors to be friendly, open and supportive;
- supervisors to be constructively critical;
- supervisors to have good knowledge of the research area;
- supervisors to structure meetings usefully;
- supervisors to show a keen interest in the research;
- supervisors to display an interest in the career prospects of students.

It seems likely that the constructive reconciliation of these and other expectations is fundamental to successful supervision and successful research training.

Range of approaches to training supervisors

There are several models that have been adopted for supervisor training, ranging from formal accredited programmes to informal workshops (Clegg and Green 1995). The range of possible approaches is wide: the model adopted will reflect the type of institution, its size, the number of research supervisors, the current staff development structures, the level of commitment from senior managers and, ultimately, the level of funding available. Although there has been no national survey to establish the balance of approaches across the sector, there appears to be a wide variety, encompassing, for example: (i) in-house, (ii) externally provided, (iii) accredited or non-accredited, (iv) voluntary or compulsory, (v) new supervisors or all supervisors, and finally (vi) interdisciplinary or single discipline. Programmes are run by independent agencies from time to time.

Cryer[1] offers useful advice and frameworks to those setting up and running programmes for supervisors. The Gateway on Research-Supervision[2] provides additional information on all aspects of research supervision and thereby seeks to ensure that institutions and individuals need not reinvent ideas already employed elsewhere.

Interpretation of supervising as engaging in teaching

Frequently, training programmes have been developed in response to Research Council requirements in individual departments or because of perceived institutional development needs or through the personal interest

---

[1] www.cryer.freeserve.co.uk/supervisors
[2] www.research-supervision.man.ac.uk/

of research directors or heads of graduate schools. Arguably, the most developed programmes are found in some of the newer universities and university colleges (for example, the Universities of Bradford, Hertfordshire, Leeds Metropolitan, Staffordshire, Paisley and Edgehill College all have well-developed accredited courses for research degree supervision) where it may be that staff development programmes are more generally well established and regarded by academic staff. It is also in these institutions where, typically, the numbers of experienced supervisors are more limited than in some of the older pre-1992 universities. The more limited research culture also benefits from the interdisciplinary nature of most of these programmes. In some, the completion of a formal training programme – often a postgraduate certificate – permits a member of staff to supervise research students without undertaking a long apprenticeship. This approach lays claim, overtly or covertly, to the notion that it is possible to *learn* how to supervise through a process of learning and teaching that takes place outside the act of supervising itself (though clearly it may require reflection on that act). It is perhaps unsurprising that these courses often involve the use of mentors and reflective practice to support the potential supervisor in coming to terms with the many issues we have already discussed. In other words, the process of learning in such situations tends to interpret supervision as primarily a teaching activity rather than a research activity.

The pedagogy adopted similarly reflects the different traditions and circumstances of institutions. In many institutions, workshops in which more experienced staff share their experiences dominate the delivery. Typically, much use is made of role-play, for example, in the management of supervisory meetings or in the *viva voce* . The programme offered by the Institute of Animal Husbandry at Pirbright is an excellent example of how pedagogy is adapted to circumstance in the Training and Accreditation Programme for Postgraduate Supervisors (TAPPS).[3] The TAPPS model, which is accredited by the BBSRC, is based on the assembly of a portfolio that demonstrates the seven objectives and six personal values that underpin the competencies the programme expects of the supervisor – these are highlighted in Tables 9.3 and 9.4. The TAPPS programme places great importance on the supervisor as a reflective researcher.

The content of supervision development programmes

As we noted earlier, supervision requires a wide range of skills; indeed, some would argue that the requirement is too wide for a single person. Indeed, this is one fundamental reason for encouraging supervision to be undertaken in teams.

---

[3] www.iah.bbsrc.ac.uk/primaryindex/jobs_and_training/TAPPS.

Table 9.3 TAPPS objectives/competencies

---

1 Design a research project that is appropriate for a research degree.

2 Recruit and select an appropriate student for the project.

3 Plan, agree, implement and monitor an appropriate research supervisory process and team.

4 Make a personal contribution to situations that promote the development of students as scholars and researchers.

5 Provide appropriate support to individual students on academic and pastoral issues.

6 Use an appropriate range of methods to monitor, assess and examine student progress and attainment.

7 Reflect on their own practice, assess and plan their future needs and continuing profession development as a research supervisor/research worker.

Table 9.4 TAPPS underpinning values

---

1 An understanding of situations that support student development and achievement in their known research.

2 A concern for student progress towards independence.

3 A personal commitment to student scholarship, academic excellence and integrity.

4 A commitment to work with and learn from colleagues.

5 A commitment to, and practising of, equal opportunities.

6 Continuing reflection on their own professional practice.

Cryer[4] provides useful information on the content of programmes for both experienced and new supervisors. Of key significance is that all supervisors need to be aware of their roles and responsibilities and be capable of putting them into practice. The revised QAA Code of Practice gives a clear indication of these roles and responsibilities in the explanation of Precept 13. The Code (QAA 2004: 16) states that supervisory responsibilities may include:

- providing satisfactory guidance and advice;
- being responsible for monitoring the progress of the student's research programme;
- establishing and maintaining regular contact with the student (where appropriate, guided by institutional expectations), and ensuring his/her accessibility to the student when he/she needs advice, by whatever means is most suitable given the student's location and mode of study;

[4] www.cryer.freeserve.co.uk/supervisors.htm

- having input into the assessment of a student's development needs;
- providing timely, constructive and effective feedback on the student's work, including his/her overall progress within the programme;
- ensuring that the student is aware of the need to exercise probity and conduct his/her research according to ethical principles, and of the implications of research misconduct;
- ensuring that the student is aware of institutional-level sources of advice, including careers guidance, health and safety legislation and equal opportunities policy;
- providing effective pastoral support and/or referring the student to other sources of such support, including student advisers (or equivalent), graduate school staff and others within the student's academic community;
- helping the student to interact with others working in the field of research, for example, encouraging the student to attend relevant conferences, supporting him/her in seeking funding for such events; and where appropriate to submit conference papers and articles to refereed journals;
- maintaining the necessary supervisory expertise, including the appropriate skills, to perform all of the role satisfactorily, supported by relevant continuing professional development opportunities.

Accreditation and assessment

There is a considerable range of opinion about both accreditation and assessment of supervisor programmes.

Accreditation

Accreditation, the route followed by those institutions that currently run integrated programmes for supervisors offers both advantages and disadvantages, as follows.

Advantages
- an accredited award gives the supervisor recognition at a formal level;
- it is possible to devise ways in which credit can be built up;
- attendance at courses can count towards 'student numbers' and hence gains funding;
- can be 'sold' outside the home institution.

Disadvantages
- needs a formal development and approval process;
- needs a quality assurance infrastructure;
- needs to be located in a department or equivalent unit that has the appropriate quality assurance mechanisms (in most universities).

Several institutions have adopted the accredited route as noted earlier and now offer programmes that dovetail into the general structure of learning and teaching development programmes. The approach adopted will invariably reflect the nature of the university and flexibility of the university in terms of regulations and organizational structures.

Assessing the supervisor's learning

One question that arises in the context of development activities is whether or not to assess the supervisor at the end of the programme. Clearly if the programme is accredited in some way then assessment becomes an essential component of the programme; where this is not the case then the issue of assessment becomes a matter of judgement. The following notes summarize the advantages and disadvantages of assessment of learning in any supervisory training programme.

Advantages
• recognition of achievement;
• check on learning;
• gain credit towards award.

Disadvantages
• problems of peer assessment;
• problems of failure;
• time involved.

It is interesting to note that in some institutions, from our own experience, many members of staff favour assessment, particular where it takes the form of a reflective assignment, as it allows them to gain formal feedback on their own thoughts and learning.

Institutional collaboration

So far in the UK there is little evidence of institutional collaboration with regard to supervisor training. This is a field which is worthy of further development as costs and shared experience must be a powerful driver for those (the majority of) institutions who deliver only small numbers of doctorates each year. Collaboration was a key element in the development of the supervisory training systems in Sweden that we noted earlier.

Impact of supervisory training programmes

It may be too early to evaluate the impact of this growth of supervisor training on the doctoral process in general. Certainly, in institutions such as

Leeds Metropolitan University formal supervisor training in the form of an accredited course, has led to over 60 staff becoming approved supervisors; there is therefore evidence of substantial numbers of awards being made on the basis of assessed work in the realm of supervisory training. However, to our knowledge there is no evidence beyond the anecdotal that the overall quality of the doctoral experience has improved (e.g. as evidenced by improved completion rates), though there is some evidence that students respond positively to the notion that their supervisors have been trained.

The quality of supervision

The quality of doctoral supervision has been questioned and considerable emphasis has been placed on the need to improve poor supervision. Articles by Wakeford (e.g. Wakeford 2004) have, by producing anecdotal evidence, tended to overstate the lack of quality in the supervision (Green and Powell 2004). The Office of Science and Technology's (OST) study of postgraduates funded by the OST Research Councils in the late 1980s suggested that the vast majority of students were of the view that their postgraduate work had been supervised very or quite well (OST 2002). It is likely that given the attention to supervisory practice (i.e. the increase in training courses) in the intervening 15 years this figure should be even higher (though clearly we recognize that there is no necessary correlation between provision of training and enhanced performance).

It is perhaps too easy to identify supervisors as the principal cause of failure in research degree processes in which unsatisfactory supervision is frequently related to non- or late completion (Burgess *et al.* 1994; Moses 1984). In fact Moses identified three groups of factors which all contribute to such late completion: (i) personality factors, including interpersonal differences, personality clashes, and work style; (ii) professional factors, including supervisors who do not have the necessary level of subject expertise to 'manage' the project and (iii) organizational factors, which frequently relate to institutional problems and work overload. More recent work suggest that other factors such as funding are far more significant (HEFCE 2005).

Looking forward

The revised QAA Code of Practice (2004) devotes four precepts to the supervision process (Table 9.5) and these address many of the issues that we have noted in this chapter. The precepts are based on four key principles.

- Access to regular and appropriate supervision.
- The opportunity to interact with other researchers.
- Advice from one or more independent sources.
- Arrangements in the event of the loss of a supervisor.

Table 9.5 QAA precepts relating to supervision

- Institutions will appoint supervisors who have appropriate skills and subject knowledge to support, encourage and monitor postgraduate research students effectively.
- Each research student will have a minimum of one main supervisor. He or she will normally be part of a supervisory team. There must always be one point of contact for the student.
- Institutions will ensure the responsibilities of all research student supervisors are clearly communicated to supervisors and students through written guidance.
- Institutions will ensure that the quality of supervision is not put at risk as a result of an excessive volume and range of responsibilities assigned to individual supervisors.

The guidance that accompanies these precepts emphasizes the need for supervisors to have the appropriate skills and time to undertake the tasks, to be appropriately managed and to communicate clearly with their students. Implicit in much of what is outlined in the Code is recognition that supervision should be a managed process seen as part of a supervisor's overall workload and not an individual activity arranged and administered at an individual level. The opening up of the supervisory process with the advent of the use of supervisory teams may greatly improve the supervision process both organizationally and academically although it may challenge those institutions that have large volumes of research students. It also requires an understanding of the part to be played by all members of the team – otherwise, of course, team supervision will remain a paper exercise. Recognizing the need to be assured of levels of competence, the Code expects that all new supervisors will access *specified* development activities (authors' italics) and perhaps more importantly that all supervisors will be able to demonstrate their continuing professional development ... *to support their role as supervisors* (authors' italics). While shying away from the challenge of training more 'experienced' supervisors the Code implies a level of development associated with the teaching side of the process for which 'I have continued to be research active' is an inappropriate answer! It will be of interest to see how institutions respond to this challenge.

Finally it is worth reflecting on the potential of either supervisor or institution to develop a perfect supervisory system. It is perhaps worth looking at the picture from the consumer perspective. Table 9.6 presents albeit anecdotal information of why things go wrong from a student perspective and reflects the basic requirements or aspirations of research students. Most of the variables are covered by earlier discussion. The personal attributes should not, however, be underestimated. Power relationships, age

Table 9.6 Why things go wrong: view from the consumer

Personality factors	Research interest mismatch	Other responsibilities
• Age • Neglect • Language or cultural barriers • Gender • Approach to work	• Slow/poor feedback • Lack of interest • Elusiveness	• Ineffective management/ direction • Organization isolates students • Support/facilities inadequate

Source: Discussion with research students members

differentials and cultural misunderstandings are still important causes of friction and failure in the intimate student–supervisor relationship.

Monitoring and evaluating supervision

Although considerable attention has been given to standards of supervision, very little has been devoted to monitoring and evaluating supervision performance. Perhaps this is because of sensitivities in relation to evaluating individual performance or because students feel that they will be disadvantaged if they make negative comments (in what can be a very dependent, close, student–supervisor relationship). Different disciplines have different supervisory traditions, making a common system difficult to establish and different stakeholders may have different needs. Whatever the apparent difficulties or obstacles, we would argue that there is a need to develop an approach that will allow evaluation to take place as part of the developmental approach to supervision which is now common in the UK. Table 9.7 identifies five broad headings, all of which have been the subject of discussion in this book, on which evaluation might be based, with some key indicators for the assessment of achievement.

While such an approach might be developed for institutional purposes, it might well be useful for the individual supervisor to adopt such a framework as part of his/her personal development and reflection.

It may be useful to develop an evaluatory model similar to the Postgraduate Research Experience Questionnaire (PREQ) survey used in Australia to monitor the experiences of postgraduate students. It builds on the Course Experience Questionnaire (CEQ) that has been in use since 1992. Recognizing the need for a more appropriate tool for the increasing number of postgraduate research students in Australia, an instrument paralleling the CEQ was developed to gather specific data concerning the experiences of research higher degree graduates, and has been administered nationally since 2002. The PREQ does not attempt to be an all-inclusive measure of

Table 9.7 An approach to the monitoring and evaluation of supervision

Broad areas	Possible indicators
Supervisor/student relationship	Regularity of meetings Student comments at annual review Absence of complaints/grievances
Student performance	Student publications Examination success Referrals Attrition rate Employment success

Personal development	Attendance at professional development
	  activities
	Involvement in doctoral activity (committees,
	  training programmes, etc.)
	Invitations to examine

Supervisor performance	Numbers supervised successfully Completion times Numbers completing

Source: Adapted from Mullins (2004a)

graduates' experiences; instead it focuses on six dimensions that are common to all research degrees. The current form of the PREQ consists of 28 items and comprises the following six scales:

- Supervision
- Intellectual climate
- Skills development
- Infrastructure
- Thesis examination process
- Clarity of goals and expectations.

Conclusion

The role of the supervisor is changing as the nature of the Doctorate itself changes, reflecting a changing pattern of demands in both academia and society in general. As the prevailing pedagogy has shifted from one that emphasizes teaching to one where the focus is on learning, the demands on supervisors also change. We have noted that in these changing contexts the expectations of supervisors is greatly increased, both in terms of knowledge other than subject knowledge and skills other than those of the particular discipline-based research area.

Just as we no longer expect an apprenticeship model to satisfy the needs of the research student, then we should not have similar expectations for supervisors. Increasingly there are demands for supervisors to be better equipped to manage these new tasks. Training of supervisors is now an important element of the research award process. However, we suggest the need for care in the way such development work is introduced. It would be all too easy to discard practices that have worked in the past and in so doing alienate those responsible for the successful award of over 14,000 Doctorates in the UK each year.

Summary issues

- Is the nature of doctoral supervision changing as demands both pedagogically and from the marketplace are changing?
- Is it feasible to expect single supervisors to have the skills to deal successfully with the wide range of responsibilities placed on them?
- How far will a team approach to supervision help to resolve some of the apparent difficulties of supervision?
- Will the increasing expectation that supervisors are appropriately trained improve the position and quality of doctoral supervision overall?
- How far should development as a supervisor be regarded as just one element in the portfolio of an academic member of university staff rather than being singled out as a 'special case'?

10

Monitoring and assessment

Introduction

This chapter focuses, first, on the way in which doctoral programmes of study are monitored and, second, on the way in which research degree students are assessed on their progress. In this manner the chapter sets out what precedes the final examination stage, this latter being dealt with in the following two chapters. Issues of monitoring and assessing are addressed first in the context of the traditional MPhil/PhD route and then in separate sections in relation to the PhD by published work, the professional doctorates and finally the Practice-Based Doctorates.

The Framework of Higher Education Qualifications in the UK indicates that assessment of the PhD should be 'solely by a final dissertation or published work' (of course, this may not be true of all doctoral awards and indeed those other than the PhD are considered in later sections of this chapter). However, many universities adopt some kind of transfer or progression or upgrade point at which the work of the candidate is assessed and the potential for development judged. Indeed, the Revised QAA Code of Practice (2004) indicates that formative judgement-making should take place during the process of a research degree programme. There are then, in the UK, typically points of assessment prior to the final process of assessing for a doctoral award. These assessments are not usually award bearing – that is, passing a point of progression does not lead to the candidate gaining an intermediate award. This chapter examines the distinctiveness of ongoing, interim, formative assessments in doctoral programmes of study. It also considers the way in which individual programmes of study are monitored and the way in which institutions monitor their overall provision of research degree study. The chapter begins by distinguishing between assessing and monitoring.

Distinction: monitoring of programmes and interim assessments of candidate

A distinction is indicated above between, on the one hand, the assessing of a candidate's progress on his/her programme of research study and, on the other, the monitoring of that programme. The revised QAA Code of Practice – Postgraduate Research Programmes (QAA 2004) refers to 'review', where the current authors are using terms relating to 'assessing progress'. Although there may not seem to be much difference between these terms, we are clearly deliberately taking a slightly sharper definition. We interpret the phase of reviewing to involve acts of assessment – judgement-making about progress. Assessing the candidate's progress will be in terms of any outcomes from the research, mapped against the stated intentions of the programme, whereas the latter will involve monitoring all aspects of that programme and the way in which it is being supported within the institution. It may involve the submission of, for example, technical reports on investigations from the candidate and questioning of that candidate on progress and plans. The questioning here may go beyond the narrow remit of the project to encompass expectations of skills to be learned and experiences that should be engaged in. Monitoring the programme on the other hand may involve an appraisal of the ways in which the project is being supervised and resourced. It may also involve an appraisal of the kinds of generic and subject specific courses attended by the candidate. Where assessment necessarily involves the measurement of achievements over a given period of research degree study, monitoring is more properly conceptualized as an oversight of the way in which the programme is progressing in terms of the overall aims within the context of the working environment.

There is another dimension to monitoring and that concerns the way in which an institution monitors its overall provision in relation to research degree study. In a later section within this chapter the kinds of criteria that may be employed in this respect will be discussed.

Principles, purposes and practices of monitoring of individual programmes of study

Principles of monitoring of individual programmes

It has already been noted in this book that research degree study differs from other postgraduate work in being based upon individual programmes of study where specific learning outcomes are not predetermined. Following from this distinction it is reasonable to suggest that where taught courses are monitored in terms of the totality of students (i.e. in terms of provision of resources, quality of teaching, etc.), monitoring needs to be mirrored at an individual level in the case of research degree students. It may not be possible to aggregate the student experience in the way it is in cohort-based programmes but, nevertheless, the demands of a system that is required to monitor the quality of its learning programmes are not diminished because the cohort size is, effectively, one (remembering the distinctiveness here of the Professional Doctorates which are discussed later in this chapter).

Purpose of monitoring of individual programmes

The purpose of any monitoring process is to ensure that students are making appropriate progress towards the research degree(s) in question and that their programmes of study are being sustained appropriately. This process implies that all aspects of the programme should be reviewed, including supervisory arrangements and the material resourcing of the research project where appropriate, as well as the individual student's progress beyond the immediate requirements of the research project itself. This latter will include what the student is learning from programmes of related study that may contain generic and specific skills training.

Practice of monitoring of individual programmes

Ideally, annual monitoring should involve input from students and supervisors and perusal by academics, with specific responsibility for the process, who are outside of the immediate supervisory team. Indeed, the notion of external review prior to final examination is increasingly seen a key feature of quality provision (again, it figures prominently in the revised QAA Code of Practice 2004). The way in which institutions provide for research degree study has been criticized in the past for the lack of such review – that is, for the way in which some doctoral students have pursued their research projects in isolation of any feedback from outside the immediate supervisory team.

Principles, purposes and practices of monitoring of institutional provision of research degree study

Feedback mechanisms

The revised Code of Practice for Postgraduate Research Programmes (QAA 2004) requires that UK HEIs put in place mechanisms to 'collect, review and, where appropriate, respond to feedback from all concerned with postgraduate research programmes' (QAA 2004: Precept 21, p. 22). The reviewing and responding clearly needs to be both open and constructive – collecting feedback with no intention of using it to improve quality of provision, or with no mechanism to enable effective responses, would be counter-productive. Further, when an institution does respond it will need to have in place an effective way of disseminating its response to all concerned parties. The Code is then concerned with mechanisms and ways of communicating – it is taken as accepted that a good use of feedback is central to an institution's quality agenda. However, the matter is not as straightforward as it may seem. Because of its individual nature, research degree work is notoriously difficult to manage in terms of getting representative views from all of those who are involved in the process of study and assessment. However, while views of, for example, individual examiners on institutional processes and standards will necessarily be constrained by the 'snapshot' view they have (typically one instance only), where a theme appears from the collected views of examiners, then the institution may feel the need to recognize and respond. The same applies to the views of students, supervisors, members of review panels, administrators as well as external sponsors, collaborating establishments and employers.

As well as the difficulty of getting representative views, the individual nature of research degree study creates a problem in terms of the confidentiality of feedback. Because of the vulnerability of students in particular (but also in relation to the ease of identification of individual examiners and other players), it is arguable that the feedback gained is more likely to reflect accurately the perceptions of the subject when its source cannot be identified. Institutions therefore need to find a way of ensuring confidentiality in at least some aspects of their mechanisms for gathering feedback. In the UK, getting and making use of feedback is seen as part of the general quality assurance processes of institutions. There is an expectation (see, again, the revised Code of Practice, QAA 2004, Precept 21) that feedback about research degree provision will be a part of a regular reviewing of academic standards and will take place at least annually.

Indicators in relation to institutional monitoring

The kinds of indicators of quality in delivery of research degree programmes in general that institutions might employ are both internal and external and will need to take account of both the range of disciplines and the diversity of student population. It is likely that a combination of indicators will reveal an accurate picture of the quality of an institution's research degree delivery. Any single indicator taken in isolation is as likely to mislead as to reveal anything useful for the reasons given below.

Key indicators of quality of delivery are described here, not in any order of preference because we suggest that no such order exists. Again, indicators need to be taken as a whole because giving undue weight to any specific indicator might be misleading.

- The submission and completion rates are clearly important indicators of success. Indeed, in the UK, the Research Councils use submission rates as measures of success. Submission rates are determined as the time it takes a student from enrolment to submission for examination. Of course this may prove to be an unreliable measure of real quality if no account is taken of the success of those submissions and, indeed, the time taken from examination to final gaining of the award (in the UK it is common to be awarded the degree 'subject to' either minor or substantial amendments and the making of such amendments and their subsequent verification by examiners can be a lengthy process). Conversely, making judgements about the time taken for students to be successful that rely on completion rates alone, would fail to take account of variable delays in examination, or amending of dissertations following examination, due to factors such as the availability of examiners.

- Pass, referral and fail rates all play their part in giving an overall picture of the quality of the work and of its assessment. However, considering failure rates in isolation of the number of students who withdraw prior to examination would be potentially misleading. This leads to mention of another measure commonly used: withdrawal rates. Here it is clear that in an extended programme of study stretching over some years, there will be an element of natural attrition and therefore there is a need to factor into any overall view the number of students who withdraw before the final submission and for what reasons.

- Further indicators are the number of appeals and complaints and the reasons given for them. Again, outcomes of any analysis are not straightforward. Complaints and appeals procedures that are well communicated are more likely to be pursued than those that are cloaked in secrecy or hard to access for one reason or another.

- Many institutions analyse comments from examiners. Here there is a difficulty in relation to the range of expectations that an institution may have of an external examiner and the opportunity he/she has to fulfil them. If, for example, there is an institutional expectation that an examiner will comment on provision of resources (material and/or human) within the department then clearly that examiner has to have access to information on that provision and some way of 'inspecting' it to see if his/her experience matches up to information given. Given the time frame of most examinations and the fact that most involved would see the examination of the candidate on the evidence presented in the dissertation as the prime responsibility of the examiner, then it becomes hard to see how a wider brief can legitimately and effectively be met without a fairly substantial reconceptualization of the role of the examiner.

- In terms of the world outside the institution, feedback from alumni, employers, sponsors and other external funders as well as recruitment profiles and information on employment destinations and career paths of former students all play their part in giving an overall picture of the quality of provision.

In all of the above, institutions need to build into their procedures some formal opportunities for consideration of feedback gained – be it qualitative and/or quantitative. There are questions here about how fully the research degree community within an institution can be expected to effectively reflect on the outcomes of its monitoring processes without the support of critical input from those outside its immediate circle.

Kinds of interim/formative assessments (e.g. upgrades/transfers, annual assessments, assessment of course work)

Transfer from MPhil to PhD registration

One of the features of the traditional route to a PhD in the UK has been a paucity of formal points of assessment. Typically, a candidate would only be assessed on his/her progress at one point in the programme of doctoral study. This point was often defined as a transfer or upgrade from MPhil to PhD registration. Candidates would enrol on an MPhil programme with the possibility of transfer to PhD registration after, typically, one and a half to two years of full-time study. This process involved some mechanism for applying for and being granted (or not) the transfer or upgrade – usually a transfer report would need to be written, which would then be assessed by a team consisting of supervisors as well as those external to the supervisory team. The assessment would be made on the grounds of achievement to date and the potential of both candidate and project to succeed at doctoral level; it may also have taken into account the candidate's ability – judged essentially on how much had been learned since enrolment.

Objectives of a progress assessment

The progress of an individual student will, in the natural course of an appropriate student–supervisor working relationship, be assessed informally as the work progresses. Regular tutorial meetings will invariably involve reviewing progress and giving feedback – at best such reviewing and feeding back will be a transactional process between student and supervisor(s). It is worth stressing here that effective ways of keeping appropriate records, which at the very least outline the outcomes of informal meetings and any agreements reached, are important if the informality is not to become an excuse for lack of action. Also, there is a responsibility on all parties to ensure that meetings take place and that a shared record is kept. The revised QAA Code of Practice (QAA 2004) raises the possibility of electronic logging of records of meetings and recommends that such record keeping should be seen as a part of personal development planning. Whatever may be claimed about informal meetings and their potential in terms of monitoring progress, many (e.g. Delamont *et al.* 1997; Leonard 2001; Phillips 1994; Phillips and Pugh 2000) would argue that as well as this informality there should be formal situations in which reviewing and assessing should take place. Certainly this is a key aspect of the revised QAA Code of Practice (QAA 2004). The Code gives examples of the context for 'reviewing' programmes – for instance, that it might take the form of an annual review by a panel specified by the individual institution (see, in particular, Precept 16 and the explanation beneath it).

Individual institutions will vary in the way in which they interpret the main objectives of any such formal progress assessment system. However, the list below perhaps summarizes satisfactorily the common features that might be expected within any such system. The objectives would include:

- to assess the candidate's progress to date on the approved programme of training in research methodology;
- to agree the next phase for a candidate's approved programme of supervised research training and to attach a timetable for the completion of the next phase of the programme;
- to agree that the programme, if competently and diligently carried out, has the potential to satisfy the requirements for the final (doctoral) award;
- to assess the candidate's general knowledge of the relevant subject area and awareness of the specific context of the research carried out to date specifically in relation to extant knowledge of the subject;
- to give the candidate experience of defending his/her report and general knowledge within the setting of an oral assessment;
- to give the candidate the opportunity to have work completed and in progress scrutinized formally by academics outside of the immediate supervisory team;
- to enable revision of the original targets within the defined programme of study;
- where a student's progress is not deemed satisfactory then an institution's system should be able to ensure that there is adequate support for the student concerned to reach the required standard or to work towards an alternative award;
- where the intention of the candidate is to submit, ultimately, for a doctoral award, assess the potential of the candidate to make a successful doctoral submission.

What the revised QAA Code (QAA 2004) requires is that the above should be transparent to all parties concerned and reasons, obligations and responsibilities understood by all. The evidence (e.g. Phillips and Pugh 2000) suggests that research degree education is characterized by conflicting perceptions of roles and responsibilities. These issues are considered more fully elsewhere in this book but here it suffices to note that where individuals perceive their role in the assessment processes in a light that is not consistent with perceptions held by others, then the conditions are present for confusion at best and conflict at worst. It is important, therefore, that all concerned know what the progression assessment involves, what the criteria are against which progress is being measured, who is making the judgement and why, what the possible outcomes are and their implications, and what the student is expected to produce by way of evidence to support his/her case.

In our view it is essential that the student should be present at any formal review/progression assessment meeting – though this is not a universally accepted viewpoint. Certainly, the student must have the right to present a case for progression in such a way as to give an accurate account of personal achievements and the outcomes of the project and to receive a fair hearing. Institutional procedures will need to be constructed on these bases. In short, we would argue that student involvement and engagement are vital if the process is to be effective.

Our use of the term 'assessment' in the context of this reviewing process leads to the notion that there need to be criteria against which the student's progress can be measured. If decisions are to be made about approving the continuation, extension, suspension or termination of the student's registration, then they need to be made against criteria that are both understandable and realizable in terms of the individual project. There also needs to be clear time frames within which progressions may happen and final submissions made.

Objectives of a written progression report

Typically, the process of assessing the progression of a student would include the submission of a progression report (indeed this is part of the examples of good practice as stated in the QAA Code (QAA 2004)). Again, the perceived objectives of any written report as part of the assessment process will vary but are typically a subset of the above objectives and may be summarized as follows:

- to record in outline the design, methodology and outcomes of the research programme to date;
- to set both rationale and outcomes in a critical context in relation to the existing literature;
- to indicate the rationale for amendments to the original programme of work (typically, this original programme would have been approved by a research degrees committee at one level or another);
- to indicate the research work to be undertaken in the next phase of study;
- to give the candidate experience of writing in the style of, and to the standard required for, a doctoral submission.

Oral presentation at the progression stage

The progression stage would typically involve some kind of an oral presentation and an assessment of both that presentation and the written report at a meeting conducted by at least one member of the supervision team and at least one suitably qualified independent person (that is independent of the project itself). Again, this is taken to be an example of good practice in the QAA Code (QAA 2004). Many institutions would use the term 'oral examination' – clearly this is not synonymous with final examination though it may share many of the features of the final *viva*. Clearly, in mirroring the final examination *viva*, the progression *viva* would give the student some experience of what to expect in an oral examination setting.

The use of an independent assessor at the progression stage

The progression stage provides an opportunity for the candidate and his/her progress to date to be subject to independent review. Accordingly most universities require the appointment of one or more independent assessors (independent that is, of the candidate's research programme). The role of this person or persons is similar to that of an examiner in the doctoral *viva* inasmuch as he/she should attempt to assess objectively both the report and the candidate using the same kind of criteria as, for example, the external [doctoral] examiner is likely to adopt. Clearly, assessors at any interim stage are not seeking to make final judgements of the work at doctoral level – rather they are required to assess whether or not the work is on track to achieve that level and whether or not the candidate has learned enough to enable him/her to pursue the project to its conclusions and, again, is on track to achieve the required level of doctoral knowledge, understanding and skill.

In consideration of the above it may be seen as vitally important that the person invited to take on the role has appropriate expertise and experience. That person needs to know enough about the extant literature to judge how the project sits in terms of contributing to knowledge and, more significantly perhaps, to judge its potential to do so (given the work that is to follow in the intervening period before final examination). Also, that person needs to know enough about how research students learn independent mastery of research skills. Again, in this respect the person is required to make judgements about potential as well as the existing state of the work (and the candidate's abilities). Ideally, then, the interim assessor should have experience of examining at doctoral level at least, and also of supervising. It is also important to stress that, in the case of interdisciplinary research programmes, the assessment panel should have collective expertise across the breadth of the programme.

It is important for the candidate, supervisors and assessors to appreciate that the whole process is an assessment of potential at one point in time. It gives no guarantee that a Doctorate or any other award will eventually be made and is not necessarily confirmation that the process equates with the award of an MPhil because it may not be a matter of judging work completed against MPhil criteria but rather about making judgement about progress towards doctoral level. We suggest that if the purpose of the assessment stage *is* possibly to award the MPhil, then the assessment process should be different to the way in which we describe it here and specifically it ought to relate more directly to assessing against the criteria for the award.

The relationship between interim and final assessments

It is perhaps necessary to reinforce the point made above. To return full circle to the beginning of this chapter, it is commonly accepted that the PhD (if not other doctoral awards) is assessed 'solely by a final dissertation or published work'. It is the case therefore that assessments prior to the final assessment are not (typically) used in any way to indicate how that final stage will proceed. Progression assessments may be interpreted in this way as indicators of progress but they do not necessarily predict the outcome of final examination. At this final stage the criteria will be different; essentially 'the bar' will have been raised and the examiners need to measure the work against the standard for the Doctorate. In this sense it is possible to conceive of a candidate passing points of progression comfortably yet failing to achieve the doctoral standard ultimately – however unfortunate that may be. While there is then a necessary relationship between passing a progression point and being able to submit for, and subsequently pass, a final examination, the former is not sufficient in itself to guarantee the latter. Here we are assuming a hierarchical notion of progression assessments – wherein standards increase and lower standards are subsumed within higher ones.

Interim assessment and the PhD by Published Work

Prima facie stage

The PhD by Published Work often involves a *prima facie* stage where the candidate may be required to make a case for progressing to a full submission. Typically, the candidate will be asked to write a summary of the contribution to knowledge that his/her publications have made and to give an indicative list of the range of publications likely to be entered into a full subsequent submission. Implicit in this stage is the notion that some element of gate keeping is required before the candidate can gain access to the process of full assessment. This stage of making a case at face value, that the collected work is worthy of consideration, is similar to the registration stage common in traditional PhD training where a candidate has to propose a programme of work and make the case for it being able to deliver work that will (i) indicate his/her prowess as a researcher and (ii) have the potential to make a contribution to knowledge. But in the case of the PhD by Published Work, of course, the 'work' will have already been completed. The assessment at this *prima facie* stage then is more a case of judging if there is a case to be made – with the final judgement being left to others.

In the UK, different institutions take differing views as to what the purpose of this stage is (Powell 2004). For some it would seem to be a simple matter of checking through the application and making sure that the candidate is appropriately qualified (e.g. in terms of connection to the institution) where for others it is a matter of making a preliminary judgement as to the quality of the publications and subsequently the likelihood of a submission being made that will meet the criteria for the award.

Change in the number of institutions requiring a prima facie stage

In its report on the PhD by Published Work, UKCGE (1996b) recorded that 62% of responding institutions offering the degree of PhD by Published Work required a two-stage submission: the first designed to establish a *prima facie* case for the application (generally consisting of the submission of a list of the publications to be submitted and a short analysis of the contribution to knowledge made by them), and the second consisting of the compiled, cited publications themselves with or without an accompanying analysis. In Powell (2004), where the same question was asked ('is a *prima facie* case required?'), albeit of a different sample size, it was noted that this percentage had increased to 86% of those responding. There was then an increase in the prevalence of the notion of a *prima facie* case over the period from 1996 to 2004.

It seems that the need for some kind of *prima facie* stage has increased over the time of the two surveys (UKCGE 1996b; Powell 2004). However, this overall trend should not obscure the range of how institutions interpret such a stage. Powell (2004) noted that the information entered by institutions by way of comment on the *prima facie* stage indicated considerable variation in the way in which institutions were gatekeeping the process of applying for a PhD by Published Work. For example, some institutions describe the stage as 'initial registration', whereas others describe it as a stage of 'pre-admission' where a senior academic reads the publications and in one sense or another 'vets' them for appropriateness of level.

Named post-holder judging the prima facie case

Powell (2004) noted that in 13 of the institutions in his sample making the requirement for a *prima facie* case, the case was judged by one or two named individuals (typically a Head of Department, Graduate Dean or senior academic) while in a further 25 the decision was made by a committee of one sort or another (typically a Research Degrees Committee or a defined sub-panel); 13 institutions did not specify how the decision was made. Again, it seems reasonable to suggest that where an institution allocates the task of judging a *prima facie* case to a named post-holder at senior committee level then that person is making the decision without necessarily any subject-specific knowledge. The decision is therefore perhaps appropriate to the meaning of *prima facie*. It is of a general kind – at face value rather than as a preliminary academic judgement. The questions that arise are rooted again in reasons for the stage – on the one hand, it may be to prevent waste of administrative and academic time (for both candidate and institution); on the other it may be more akin to the transfer/upgrade/progression stage in the traditional PhD route where a case is made for the work continuing to PhD submission with a reasonable chance of success.

Interim assessment and the Professional Doctorate

Progression assessment as a key feature of professional doctoral awards

One of the roots of the current professional doctoral awards in the UK was the kind of doctoral award in the USA that included a series of progression points through a pre-ordained programme of learning about research (pre-determined, that is, in contrast to the kind of PhD wherein student and supervisor in the first instance negotiate an individual programme of study that is unique to the student). Indeed, the idea of assessing progress through a set programme of learning skills and knowledge lends itself, at least super-ficially, to the basic concept of the Professional Doctorate. Professional knowledge and the skill to apply it can be seen to set the parameters for the kind of client group that is to be attracted to the doctoral programme and the progressive assessing of those skills and that knowledge in turn become part of the way in which candidates are inducted into higher (i.e. doctoral) levels of the profession. This may be a particularly sharp distinction where the Professional Doctorate is also a licence to practise; here some specific skills might be deemed essential for progression to the final stages of the course and, similarly, knowing a set menu of things may be a necessary prerequisite for later learning of doctoral level skills and knowledge.

A key feature of professional doctoral programmes in the UK is that most contain elements that are taught and assessed as coherent entities and sub-sequently contribute to the final judgement-making about the professional doctoral award. (Of course, as is noted elsewhere in this book, many PhD programmes in the UK now contain taught elements – though the distinc-tion remains at the level of the way in which any outcomes may contribute, as in the Professional Doctorates, to the final doctoral outcome.) In the report by Scott *et al.* (2004: 81) all 12 of the institutions surveyed included in their professional doctoral programmes assessed components, other than the final dissertation, that contributed to the final assessment for the award. This report goes on to note, drawing here from evidence of developments in this respect from Australia (as discussed by Maxwell 2003), that there is some movement towards submission by portfolio rather than the simple course-work plus dissertation model. Certainly, the complexity of the situation as revealed by the Scott *et al.* report indicates a range of ways of treating assessments other than the final dissertation of the 'contributing to knowledge' kind. For example, one of the instances cited was based on an initial profiling of the candidate's professional knowledge and abilities and a subsequent planning of a programme designed to address, professionally relevant, personal developmental needs. Progress towards a final doctoral submission then becomes a matter of meeting the targets that have been negotiated and of providing evidence that they have been met. In turn, the dissertation then becomes the focus of the later stages of the programme – there is an expectation that within it the skills of researching in the particular profession will be realized.

It is possible in the above example to identify two fairly distinct phases to the programme – at least in terms of assessment. First, there is the meeting of personal development targets as a foundation for later learning and, second, there is the presentation of a research-based dissertation founded upon that earlier learning. There is a similarity here with the 'traditional' PhD programme where the plan is individual to the student (accepting the existence of collaborative projects) – the difference lies in the nature of the target setting. In professional doctoral education the targets relate to the professional development of the candidate, whereas in the PhD they would, normally, relate to development in the state of knowledge.

We should stress here that the example we cite above (from Scott *et al.* 2004) is just one exemplar from a range of differences. The common thread, again, is the likelihood that in a professional doctoral programme a more flexible approach will be taken to the balance between, on the one hand, progress assessments and, on the other, examination of the candidate on the basis of the evidence presented in a dissertation. According to the evidence from interviews conducted by Scott *et al.* (2004) the move in recent times has been away from prescribed, required research skills – at least in Doctor of Business Administration (DBA) programmes. This move is not sustained, however, in all professional doctoral fields. In the Education Doctorate (EdD), for example, the structure tends to be characterized by a sequential structure in which mandatory taught courses with required assignments lead to the later research dissertation stage – sometimes divided in itself into preparation for the dissertation (including, for example, reviewing the literature) and the final researching and its presentation within a dissertation.

In all of the professional doctoral programmes surveyed by Scott *et al.* the assessment involved a 'substantial, conventionally defined thesis, varying in length between 30,000 and 50,000 words. This was in addition to, and in a sense regardless of, any interim assessments.

Progressing through a set number of learning outcomes

The areas in which professional doctoral study is offered tend to be areas that encompass a range of disciplines. For example, in the EdD, psychology may be studied though not with the purpose of producing psychologists but rather of producing practitioners in education who can understand and apply psychological knowledge in the context of learning and teaching. Where it is deemed necessary for a candidate for a Professional Doctorate to understand and be able to apply particular aspects of contextualized discipline-specific knowledge, there is a clear case for assessment of that particular knowledge and attendant skills. In such Doctorates it becomes possible to begin to deal in quite specific 'competencies' and in the candidate's ability in applying them in a range of situations. Clearly, at least some of these assessments can be interpreted as ways of accessing the next level of study; that is, this kind of learning outcome may be seen as hierarchical and the candidate must therefore demonstrate competency at one level before moving up to the next level. It is also the case that interim assessments of this kind will need to address the issue of contextualization – in short, the candidate will need to demonstrate his/her abilities in the particular professional context, or the university has somehow to recreate the conditions of that context in any assessment process that takes place within the university itself.

Some of the programmes surveyed by Scott *et al.* (2004) made use of highly targeted tests in the earlier stages of the candidate's programme, which were prerequisites for progression to later stages that involved in turn broader and more flexible assessments. Programmes differed in the way in which the assessments were collected together. In some, each interim assessment was discreet and self-standing and was assessed on its own as a necessary requirement for progression, whereas in other programmes assessed work was collected together and presented as a portfolio. In some, work to be assessed was presented for assessment in portfolio format. Issues raised by the use of portfolio are discussed in the section below.

The use of portfolio as a product to be assessed

A portfolio can be distinguished from a dissertation in as much as the latter requires the presentation of a thesis (an intellectual argument) in a coherent and unifying sense – there is consistency of argument and a single audience is intended. A portfolio allows the inclusion of disparate pieces of work, written for different purposes, illustrating different kinds of skill application and is intended for a range of audiences. This is not to say, of course, that a portfolio might not include a unifying theme and a singular sense of purpose, but rather that these things are not necessary for that portfolio to achieve its aims of conveying to the assessor the range of knowledge and skills that the practitioner has acquired. Nor is this to say that a portfolio might not include an integrating commentary; indeed such a device is fairly common in current UK Professional Doctorates (Scott *et al.* 2004). The commentary might be interpreted as a *post hoc* rationalization of work achieved or as a summarizing of the contents of the portfolio – whatever the interpretation, it is an artefact of the disparate pieces of work rather than an integral driver for them.

Some of the above features of the portfolio lend themselves to the realm of the Professional Doctorate and many (e.g. Usher 2002) would argue for its usefulness in this context, in particular perhaps because the use of a portfolio enables the inclusion of both academic and professionally oriented work. Where boundaries are perceived between these two elements, the portfolio allows for them to be broken down in as much as it enables the candidate to target different audiences and purposes within a unifying submission. For our purposes in this chapter it also accommodates an approach to learning that is typified by distinct phases of specific learned outcomes that can be collected together to give an overall pattern of achievement. That pattern may of course include an element of progression – the candidate is not expected to be operating at doctoral level throughout his/her programme of study but rather may be seen as a learner needing to exhibit what he/she has learned over a period of years. Here the portfolio allows the candidate to indicate progress made from 'novice' (assuming this to mean a level of noviciate in relation to specific tasks) to expert and, in turn, gives the assessor the opportunity to plot a curve of development rather than merely assess a final, doctoral standard. A portfolio might then include work that has been assessed at an early stage in the candidate's learning and therefore at a lower level than subsequent work.

In this scenario the user of the portfolio is recognizing a need for relative standards to be applied as a candidate progresses through a programme. Of course, a portfolio does not have to be constructed on this progressive basis – it is quite possible for the candidate to assemble a portfolio that indicates only doctoral level work, albeit in different areas within the remit of the Professional Doctorate. However, it may be argued that the notion of a portfolio as containing work indicating how a candidate has progressed from novice to expert (or more properly from experienced practitioner to advanced, doctoral level practitioner) fits with an underlying ethos of professional doctoral education which suggests that a strict demarcation of academic and practitioner knowledge, with the former somehow superior to the latter, is unhelpful and ultimately non-productive of moving forward knowledge and skill in the context of specific professional work.

Interim assessment and the Practice-Based Doctorate

In direct contrast to the Professional Doctorates considered above, the Practice-Based Doctorates may not lend themselves so readily to progression points where interim assessments may be made. It is harder to conceive of discrete stages of learning being amenable to assessment in this latter kind of Doctorate. There might well be an accumulation of skills that are required for a practice-based outcome to be realized but even here it is unlikely that they would be predeterminable in the way that is implied in many professional doctoral programmes. Of course it is still possible for a candidate for a Practice-Based Doctorate to report on progress and be assessed on that progress. That assessment might be at an interim stage or indeed it might be that the final assessment could include appraisal of the earlier stages of the finished work. In this sense much of what is written about interim assessing within PhD programmes in general applies in the case of practice-based awards. The difficulty in this area comes when the candidate is concerned to enable new understandings in his/her audience – assessing an interim stage in this 'enabling' is problematic because the effect can only be realized when the final artefact is available. Such assessment could not be a matter of illustrating stages in the development of new knowledge – it does not seem possible to show how something that has not yet happened (i.e. the audience's response to the artefact) is developing. The only way forward would be to offer recorded stages in the preparation of the work for appraisal at the completion of the work – such reflective appraisal of processes is not the same as the kind of interim assessing that has been discussed in this chapter.

Conclusion

This chapter has explored the use of interim assessing within different kinds of Doctorate. In so doing it has perhaps revealed something about both the usefulness and the limitations of such assessing in doctoral study. We may also suggest that it has, to an extent, indicated some of the key differences between the processes of learning that go on within these different kinds of Doctorate. In all of this there can be little doubt that the feedback gained from effective interim assessing is vital for the progress of both the student and the research project. Again, as noted elsewhere in this book, it is important to step back from the usual practices of progression assessments (upgrades, etc.) and consider the relative and distinct purposes of monitoring and assessing progress at both individual and institutional levels. If doctoral study is essentially an educational process (and we would argue that it is) and assessing progress is typically accepted as an integral part of such a process, then we would conclude that parallels need to be drawn between this general interpretation of good practice in education and the way in which progress may usefully be assessed within the realm of research degrees.

Summary issues

- To what extent could and should monitoring processes used for taught programmes be adopted at both individual and institutional level for doctoral research?
- To what extent should the transfer from MPhil to PhD be regarded as part of the overall assessment process for the award?
- Should individual annual monitoring of doctoral processes be equally rigorous both in implementation and outcome?
- To what extent should intuitional monitoring of the Doctorate be regarded as part of overall institutional quality monitoring or as a separate process specifically for the Doctorate?

11

Principles and purposes of doctoral examination

Introduction

This chapter and the one that follows address issues surrounding examining for doctoral awards. This should be a simple matter of the candidate being given the opportunity to provide sufficient evidence that he/she has met the criteria for the award in question. However, the ways in which that opportunity is realized, the kinds of evidence that are deemed worthy of consideration, what counts as 'sufficient' and how the criteria are expressed and interpreted are not constants across the sector. There are differences in custom and practice between disciplines, between institutions and across the kinds of doctoral award. In short, providing evidence to merit the award is not a simple matter.

The issue of the final examination brings us full circle to the difficulties encountered earlier and throughout this book. The question that needs resolution in any assessment process such as this is first to understand just what is being examined and here there is lack of definition in some if not all aspects of doctoral study. Certainly in the case of the PhD there is evidence to suggest that there is little consensus between disciplines, institutions and individuals about the nature of what is being examined (see Underwood 1999 for a fuller exposition). Tinkler and Jackson (2004) suggest a distinction between process-oriented and product-oriented definitions of the PhD. For some, the PhD is a training programme; for others, it is a piece of work that represents the outcome of the candidate's research work. Similarly, Powell (2004) notes in relation to the PhD by Published Work that examiners may differ in their understanding of where the 'contribution to knowledge' lies – in the publications themselves or in the critical appraisal that is submitted with them. The specific case of examination for the award of PhD by Published Work is considered later in this chapter and more fully in Chapter 12.

Research degree examination as assessment

Doctoral examination is frequently viewed as distinct from other aspects of examining in higher education. It has developed its own custom, practice and mystique – specific to the UK – with the *viva voce* or oral examination seeming to take on significance beyond assessment of the achievement of research outcomes. Yet the examination phase of any programme of doctoral study is one of assessment. The candidate's progress as a learner about the business of research needs to be assessed if an institution can claim with confidence that he/she is capable of operating as an independent researcher (and, ultimately, of supervising others in the act of researching). Similarly, an assessment has to be made about whether or not a candidate has met the assessment criteria laid down for the award – typically this will be expressed in terms of 'contribution to knowledge'. The tensions between these two aspects of the assessment agenda are explored later in this chapter. What we suggest here is that, however high level the work and however distinctive research degree study may appear – its assessment retains core similarities with all other aspects of postgraduate study. Students engage in study that is set against explicit criteria, present their work and are assessed on how closely it matches those criteria. What sets research degree study apart in the UK (in addition from the tensions noted above) is typically the individual nature of the work, the focus on one project or set of linked projects, the length of time spent on it and the dependence in the assessment phase on one, relatively short, oral examination.

As with many aspects of research awards the approach adopted is significantly different from that of taught awards. This is the case with assessment in which for example the QAA Code on assessment does not apply. This is indeed unfortunate, as it would bring into focus some of the issues that we should consider and what we are attempting to achieve when we discuss assessment in the Doctorate. The QAA definition of assessment that is noted below is a useful starting point for discussion

> *Assessment is a generic term for a set of processes that measure the outcomes of students' learning, in terms of knowledge acquired, understanding developed, and skills gained. It serves many purposes. Assessment provides the means by which students are graded, passed or fail. It provides the basis for decisions on whether a student is ready to proceed, to qualify for an award or to demonstrate competence to practise. It enables students to obtain feedback on their learning and helps them improve their performance. It enables staff to evaluate the effectiveness of their teaching.*

(QAA 2000: 4)

Assessments are frequently referred to as *diagnostic, formative* or *summative* which the QAA describes as:

- *diagnostic assessment* provides an indicator of a learner's aptitude and

preparedness for a programme of study and identifies possible learning problems;
- *formative assessment* is designed to provide learners with feedback on progress and inform development, but does not contribute to the overall assessment;
- *summative assessment* provides a measure of achievement or failure made in respect of a learner's performance in relation to the intended learning outcomes of the programme of study.

The extent to which the assessment procedures of doctoral work reflect this categorization will be considered during the chapter. In principle, however, it is worth emphasizing that, other than in the context of the professional doctoral, assessment has successfully avoided addressing them head on.

The role of oral examination: the *viva voce*

The necessity of an oral examination

Institutions vary in their stance with regard to the obligatory nature of the *viva*, with some insisting on it being held regardless of the quality of the doctoral thesis and others offering various kinds of dispensation, for example 'where no useful purpose would be served'. Institutional stance with regard to the necessity for an oral defence relates to the underlying perception of the examination as being (a) of the intellectual argument expounded by the candidate in his/her written thesis or (b) of the process of research training that led to the development of the argument and the production of the thesis. In essence, a product might conceivably be examined in the absence of its author whereas judging the outcomes of a process of training would seem to require some questioning of the individual who has been trained.

Despite the lack of clear criteria that relates specifically to the *viva* (as discussed in a later section in this chapter) the oral examination is usually seen as an essential part of the overall assessment process. Indeed, many institutions have a regulation that requires that no student can be judged to have failed the doctoral award without the chance to demonstrate his/her knowledge and accomplishment as a researcher in a *viva* situation. Similarly, many institutions operate the notion of a posthumous award only where there is evidence that the candidate would have passed the *viva* 'had he/she survived to be in a position to undertake it'.

By way of contrast it may be noted that, in Australia, oral examinations are, typically, not held. However, judgements are made on the basis of lengthy and detailed written reports. It is perhaps worth adding that, in Australia, examination processes may take one year to complete. It may be, then, that holding a *viva*, at the very least, focuses collective minds on completing the process.

The presence of the supervisor(s) at the oral examination

Powell and McCauley (2002) note wide variation in terms of institutional practice regarding whether or not a supervisor should/could be present at the oral examination and his/her role if allowed or encouraged to be present. In some UK institutions where supervisors may be present, they are invited only at the discretion of the examiners, in others only at the discretion of the candidate, and in others they may be required to be available on request ('on campus') but normally not be expected to attend. In some institutions attendance requirements or restrictions relate only to the principal, or first, supervisor. Possibility of verbal contribution from supervisors during the examination varies from being expected to speak, being allowed to speak at the request/discretion of the examiners, to not being allowed to speak. Commonly the supervisor's unspoken role is that of acting as 'candidate's friend'. The pros and cons for all players of attendance by supervisors at their student's *viva* are discussed in detail in Tinkler and Jackson (2004: 90–4). All of this is, of course, in stark contrast to the situation in many other European countries where the oral examination is very much a public affair and supervisors will invariably be present and often be expected to comment after the oral examination itself to the assembled examiners who meet to discuss the performance and the result.

The viva as a public event

As far as the authors are aware, only two UK institutions (Universities of Manchester and Oxford) make the *viva* a public event, though some departments claim openness within certain categories of staff. Indeed, the openness within the two named universities above is restricted, in the former to all supervisors, academic staff at the university and all its PhD candidates and, in the latter, to, 'any member of the university in academic dress'. There is no evidence that the merits and demerits of public defence are discussed within UK institutions. Clearly, differences in current UK practice relate largely to differences in the relationship between prior consideration of the work (in public fora and specifically in publication) and final outcome. In short, the bases for assessment differ between UK and many other European countries. There are also differences in the nature of the doctoral examination in the UK that relate to the kind of Doctorate undertaken – some which are considered later in this chapter.

Lack of clarity of purpose of the viva

There is evidence in the literature about a lack of clarity with regard to the purpose of the *viva* (a) from an institutional perspective (Powell and McCauley 2002) and (b) in terms of the perceptions of the various participants (Tinkler and Jackson 2004). For example, the *viva* may be interpreted as an examination in the broadest sense of the term (and here questioning may extend beyond the work presented in the thesis to encompass issues of the candidate's knowledge of related subject matter) or as merely a matter of verification of authenticity. Indeed, many oral examinations seem (to examiners and students) to become effectively opportunities to fine-tune the written work of the candidate in order that it reaches a notional standard that is acceptable for scrutiny by peers in the relevant intellectual community. Tinkler and Jackson (2004: 16) list nine main distinct 'roles' that were cited by respondents in relation to the purpose of the *viva*; no one role was mentioned by more than 40% of respondents. Therefore there was no real consensus about the purpose of the *viva*.

The viva as non-examination

Given the lack of consensus with regard to the purpose of the *viva* it is perhaps not surprising that, for some, the *viva* is interpreted as an event – important as a rite of passage – but not as an examination in the true sense of the word. When an examining panel tells the candidate the outcome of the *viva* at its outset, the event ceases to have any relation to examination, inasmuch as 'to examine', in any real sense, requires that the work and/or the candidate is tested against some criteria and subsequently is deemed to have met those criteria or not, as the case may be. Yet in the survey reported by Tinkler and Jackson (2004: 29), 32% of UK candidates reported that they were informed of the examiners' decision at the start of the *viva*. This kind of scenario is similar to that which pertains in other European countries – for example, in Sweden, where the 'result' is not in any real doubt. However, in this latter situation the whole purpose is more clearly defined. The event is not called an examination – it is referred to as a 'defence' or a 'disputation' (see Powell 1999b for a fuller description).

Certainly, the candidate is required to defend his/her thesis but there is less of a pretence that an examination is taking place. The defence here is part of the doctoral standing and the experience of gaining a Doctorate, but the assessment has already taken place (typically, by publication). Again, it seems that the issue in the UK concerns the relationship between the *viva* as a putative oral examination and the process of assessment itself, be that of the candidate and/or of the written submission.

The viva as a context for testing a candidate's broader knowledge and skill

Part of the agenda that many examiners bring to the oral examination situation is a desire to test out the candidate's knowledge of the subject (i.e. beyond the immediate concerns of the thesis) within which the thesis sits. For many, carrying a doctoral title should necessarily indicate that the title-holder is adequately conversant with his/her subject and the *viva* is an opportunity to assess whether or not this is the case. Many institutional regulations specifically allow the examiners to question the candidate on subject matter related to the thesis, but not directly addressed within it. Indeed, some regulations allow examiners the possibility of setting the candidate tests to judge subject knowledge. All of this takes on a particular significance in the context of professionally based doctoral work and this is dealt with in more detail elsewhere, but in all doctoral work it can be argued that there is a requirement that the candidate be worthy of the doctoral title and able to work as a practitioner (however loosely interpreted) in a knowledgeable and skilful way. It is not unknown for a doctoral candidate to be asked to read and summarize a research paper in the *viva*. Similarly, a *viva* may involve practical demonstration of one kind or another.

The use of the *viva* to test out the candidate's knowledge is, in part at least, a discipline-specific matter – see Wood and Vella (2000) for information on doctoral standards in molecular bioscience, where knowledge and skill (in such as 'laboratory manipulation') are prominent.

Assessment criteria

Commonly used doctoral criteria

The UK national qualifications framework (QAA 2001) describe doctoral level work as that which makes a significant contribution to knowledge and is original. Institutions interpret this description in the way in which they set out criteria (a description of a level clearly differs from the assessment criteria that need to be attained to meet that level). Some use 'contribution to knowledge and to the application of that knowledge'; others include the notion of 'publishability'. This last indicator is usually expressed in a somewhat imprecise way; however, in some disciplines the pressure to publish is more explicit, for example, BPS/UCoSDA (1995) suggest that a doctoral submission should be equivalent to at least two articles in refereed journals. Notions of doctoral level in relation to Professional Doctorates will invariably include some reference to contribution to professional practice and/or knowledge. The liberal interpretation of all of this would include contributions to research procedures and processes (for example, the refinement of particular domain-specific research tools) as well as revised theories or interpretations and syntheses of different aspects of existing knowledge – perhaps from related but distinct research disciplines – into new understandings. Knowledge, its application in different spheres, ways of learning about the world and new interpretive stances or paradigms are often available to the examiner in a heady mix that is undifferentiated in institutional regulations. Again, there are significant disciplinary differences in criteria used and the way in which they are employed. In molecular bioscience, for example – according to Wood and Vella (2000) – being judged to be an independent, self-directing scientist takes on more significance than any 'original' findings.

None of the above is, however, a satisfactory approach to the development of criteria for assessment that would give confidence of a reasonable level of commonality in understanding and equity in application across doctoral awards. This is not to argue that all doctoral awards are equal in terms of achieving a level against criteria. It is, however, to argue that if there is a standard for the Doctorate, then there must be criteria that allow us to determine whether that standard has been achieved. Most importantly, candidates must be aware of the criteria that their work is being judged against.

In all of the above there is little evidence that attempts have been made in a systematic way to describe the benchmarking of doctorateness, though Shaw and Green (2001) use the QAA Framework (2001) to explore the possibilities of doing just that. In their work they identify the elements of the doctoral outcomes from the QAA's doctoral learning outcomes and develop a series of performance standards against which these can be assessed. In this way they demonstrate how each of these elements may form the basis for criteria in the assessment process. While not concluding with a definitive framework of criteria, they do demonstrate some of the strengths and weaknesses of such an approach, as illustrated in Table 11.1 in consideration of research skills.

This approach provides clarity to both the expected outcomes but highlights the difficulties of determining relative and absolute expectation of candidates. Is the criterion to be present in all cases or only in some? How many of the standards need to be achieved before the candidate has reached the required standard? Although requiring additional work the approach does offer an interesting approach that brings clarity for both the student and examiner in terms of what we mean by doctoral standards and a metric to reconcile the criteria question across all doctorates.

Learning outcomes are, however, used widely in the approach to assessment of Professional Doctorates, as noted later in this chapter.

Pass/fail examination outcomes

In the UK doctoral system, it is generally the case that a doctoral award is seen as the pinnacle of academic achievement and is awarded on a pass/fail basis. Very few institutions offer any differentiation within the doctoral award, though note of particular merit or distinction is possible in some. Similarly, there are in some instances (notably professional societies) 'prizes' for particularly significant theses. Certainly, some of the Professional Doctorates may include the notion of a doctoral award 'plus' professional qualification, but the PhD is generally seen as a mark of excellence – with the implication that there are no gradations within that; in short, one cannot have a 'really

Table 11.1 Learning outcomes and performance standards: research skills

Learning outcomes	Performance standards	Alternative criteria
R1	provides evidence of:	
general ability to conceptualize, design and implement a project [for the generation of new knowledge, applications or understanding at the forefront of the discipline] and to adjust the project design in the light of unforeseen problems	• a valid, coherent and planned approach to *all* aspects of the specification, design and implementation of the project/ study	*most, main, majority*
	• *all* instances where the specification, design, implementation, organization, management required adjustments	*most, main, major*
	• *detailed* argument and critical evaluation to support the validity of *all* adjustments made	*full, complete* *main, major*
R2	provides evidence of:	
make informed judgements on complex issues in specialist fields, often in the absence of complete data	• valid and appropriate judgements made in *all* contexts such as data sampling, data analysis, data interpretation in the subject area of the study	*some, most, majority, main*
	• valid and appropriate judgements made in *all* aspects of derivation of results, interpretation of results, extrapolation, generalization	*some, most, majority, main*

Table 11.1 continued

Learning outcomes	Performance standards	Alternative criteria
R3	provides evidence of:	
able to communicate their ideas and conclusions clearly and effectively to specialist and non-specialist audiences	• *fully* developed research-oriented communication (written, oral, listening) skills	*highly, well*
	• *absolute* clarity of message to *all* audiences	*good, acceptable* *most, a range of*
	• ability to design and apply *all* communication methods and techniques as appropriate to *any* audiences	*many, most, a range of* *many, most, main, typical*

good excellent' [*sic*] award. This view was contested by the Committee of Vice Chancellors and Principals (CVCP) in 1988, where a suggestion was made that a 'PhD with Distinction' should be introduced and further that an estimated 10% of PhD candidates should receive this level of award. This suggestion has not, to date, been taken up by the sector in any significant way although Phillips (1994) suggests, from a survey of external examiners, that some favour for the notion of mapping the divisions used in undergraduate degrees (3rd, 2.2, 2, 1) onto doctoral awards – thus allowing acknowledgement of work that is not truly excellent but which reaches some 'pass' criteria.

Of course, the status quo of pass/fail with no gradation is not universally agreed, indeed it is in direct contrast to the system in France where PhDs are stratified into a series of classes or 'mentions'. To gain access to an academic career it is generally seen to be necessary to gain a top-level award ('la mention très honorable avec les felicitation du jury à l'unanimité') or at least a second level ('la mention honorable') (Brown 2003).

Inconsistency of criteria

There is little consistency between institutions in terms of the level or kind of guidance that is given to examiners on criteria for assessing submissions (Powell and McCauley 2002). Many institutions cite the need for criteria such as originality and 'publishability', but detailed checklists of criteria for assessing theses are not commonly in evidence. This area is explored in some detail in Shaw and Green (1996). This kind of variation reflects the underlying lack of clarity about threshold performances that might define differences between degrees at Masters (e.g. MRes), MPhil and PhD levels. Also, there is lack of clarity concerning any weighting that might be given to different components within a thesis and to different aspects of the examination. For example, it is an open question upon which examiners would most probably fail to agree as to whether critical self-appraisal be allowed to compensate for poor research design or not.

There is variation in terms of how institutions apply criteria to the written submission on the one hand and the oral examination on the other. Tinkler and Jackson (2004: 14) in their survey found that while the majority of respondents 'offered specific criteria for assessment in the *viva* and/or provided more general aims for the thesis and *viva* in combination' a number gave an indication of criteria in relation to the written submission but not to the oral examination.

Assessment of process or product?

There is a tension in the PhD examination, as noted above, in respect of the extent to which it is the process of research training or the finished product that should be examined. Different approaches to this tension will lead to differences in views of the way in which the *viva* ought to proceed and indeed the breadth of the remit that should be given to examiners. For example, should examiners be:

- able to 'explore records of research supervision' (CVCP 1993) or other documents such as progression or transfer reports;
- asked to comment on quality of supervision, training opportunities and facilities provided by departments – seen in the BPS document, UCoSDA/ BPS (1995), as 'an important subsidiary role of the examination board';
- given access to a candidate's critical self-appraisal of their own learning as well of the research findings and interpretations?

The answer an individual examiner gives to these questions, regardless of the institutional strictures, will clearly colour the way in which that person goes about his/her task.

There might well be a consensus suggesting that what is being examined is more than the written words in the submission. The key research skills, identifiable within the work and the way it has been presented for examination are being judged and the candidate's learned skills and abilities are central points of scrutiny. Examiners pose questions that enable them to make judgements about the candidate's integration of key skills and understandings. The oral examination is the context in which this questioning can take place, yet this dimension is in danger of being lost if the marking of the thesis and the subsequent oral examination become contexts for checking text and improving the literary qualities of the work.

Assessing skills at doctoral level

The issue of assessment of skills learning is raised here in that it is often dislocated from the main focus of doctoral assessment. It is necessary at this point to distinguish the PhD and the PhD by Published Work from the Professional Doctorates inasmuch as the latter may well involve some assessment of professional skills that is integrated within the student's programme of work. But the award of PhD is typically made on the basis of an assessment of the candidate's ability as evidenced by his/her presentation of an intellectual position (expounded and defended within the thesis) and defence of it in an oral examination. Learning about, for example, how to communicate ideas in an oral context may obliquely come into play but it is not typically, specifically assessed. Such a skill is deemed secondary to, or supportive of, the research project itself. In short, generic skills are often required in the process of learning but are not assessed as outcomes of learning. Of course, a generic quality within the learning of a skill would mean that it could only be assessed within a context unrelated to that original learning. This becomes problematic in the context of conventional PhD examination and in any case returns us full circle to some of the difficulties noted above about demarcating the generic from the specific and the skill itself from the learning of that skill. The current climate in the UK where generic skills training courses are propagated with lack of clarity about the issues raised above can only lead to confusion about purpose and the monitoring of delivery – it is difficult to judge how effective an HEI's delivery of such courses is when the only thing that seems certain is that they should exist.

In these respects the PhD by Published Work sits somewhat anomalously. It is difficult to see how a PhD awarded on the basis of published work could be seen to directly indicate that the successful candidate had demonstrated a range of generic research skills. Clearly, an assumption might be made that the acts of publication in themselves indicate that skills of communication and negotiation had been demonstrated. However, it is unlikely that the whole range of the skills indicated in the Joint Research Councils' skills requirements could be assumed from those acts. There is a tension here then between the move towards European harmonization (e.g. the Bologna process) where publication is the typical route to a PhD award and the skills agenda that pervades current thinking in the UK.

Issues arise (discussed further in Chapter 5) concerning the extent to which a sense of parity between doctoral awards can be maintained when some (e.g. Professional Doctorates) focus on the learning of skills (defined as both generic and specific even though this is not a distinction that we find useful) and others (e.g. PhD) focus almost entirely on 'contribution to knowledge'. Skills can be defined, the learning of them can be predetermined and delivered in a didactic context and the measurement of them is readily manageable. On the other hand, contribution to knowledge cannot be easily defined or predetermined; a student may be guided towards it but cannot necessarily 'teach' it in a didactic context and it is not readily measurable. If amount and kind of focus on skills learning differs across different doctoral awards then questions of the parity of doctoral awards arise.

Transparency of criteria

Criteria for successful doctoral achievement are necessarily difficult to standardize across disciplines and across HEIs, and it is not certain that such standardization would be desirable. Nevertheless, there is a need for more transparency. At present the situation across the sector is opaque as well as varied and this makes auditing of quality and standards a difficult exercise. As indicated by the findings of Tinkler and Jackson (2004), this opacity disadvantages the student who may enter the context of assessment unaware of the differing, and often hidden, agenda in operation.

The criteria of 'publishability' and 'original and significant contribution to knowledge' that are used commonly by institutions, often depend on a number of complex interdependent factors and are linked to discipline. Experience has shown that it is common for there to be little or no agreement between examiners with regard to criteria – by default decisions are therefore based on implicit criteria, which may remain idiosyncratic to individual examiners.

Status of viva performance versus the thesis as submitted

The structure of the examination process in the UK results in the written submission itself becoming the prime medium for assessment. Because of its length and the pressures towards specific outcomes (pass with amendments, etc.), it is difficult for the oral examination to function as a means of reflecting the student's expertise accurately enough for judgement to be made. The individual student's learning during the research programme must be seen to be secondary. It is then primarily or wholly the thesis that is assessed, though one might claim that examiners are making judgements about the candidate on the basis of what was presented in the thesis.

As noted earlier in this section, institutions do not always have criteria that are specifically applied to the *viva* phase of the overall examination process. Where no specific criteria are available then it becomes hard to see the basis on which a candidate could be said to have failed in the oral examination phase of the overall process.

There is a sense in which the nature of the oral examination depends on the perceived quality of the submitted work. If the document is seen as strong, then the oral part of the examination may become a summative process whereby the examiners sum up the strengths of the thesis and discuss postdoctoral extensions of the work. If, on the other hand, the document is felt to be weak then the *viva* might become more of a formative process whereby the examiners inform the candidate of the weaknesses, and/or demonstrate those weaknesses through questioning, and then lead the candidate to an understanding of what is required in a resubmission or re-examination. Tinkler and Jackson (2004: 12) discuss in some detail the ramifications of 'referral' and a 'second viva'.

The process of learning reflected in the final examination

If the view is taken that a doctoral examination should include some assessment of the process of a candidate's learning throughout his/her course of study, then it is arguable that the final examination of a Doctorate could be informed by previous stages in the process, such as a first year or transfer/upgrading report. If this is to be the case then clearly there would be some sense in examiners having access to these earlier reports. Further, some might argue that the same examining panel should examine throughout the process of a programme of study and at the final thesis stage. This would be analogous with assessments of taught postgraduate courses where examiners might have access to records indicating the whole of the progress of an individual student through a programme of study. In this context it might also be suggested that a report should be included at the final examination stage that describes any specific difficulties encountered and perhaps overcome successfully during the research process.

Conclusion

The purpose of doctoral examination is clear; it is to assess whether or not the candidate has attained the appropriate doctoral level. But beneath this singular purpose are layers of interpretation that differ according to perceptions of what counts as doctoral (e.g. in terms of originality, significance and necessary breadth) and how best the examiners can gain access to the candidate's abilities in order to make judgements about them (e.g. in terms of the extent to which the evidence is evident in the contribution to knowledge made). In the following chapter the processes reflecting these layers of interpretation are explored.

Summary issues

• How far does the current examination process reflect the progression of learning and research, including generic skills development, encountered in the doctoral research process?

- Should greater emphasis be placed on the development and assessment of specific criteria at doctoral level?
- Is there a common understanding of the relationship between the submitted thesis and the oral examination in the assessment of doctoral work?

12

Processes of examining the Doctorate

Introduction

This chapter examines the processes that underpin the final examination for a doctoral award. As noted at the start of the previous chapter, the process of examining a Doctorate should be about judging the evidence that the candidate presents in justification for the award. If the candidate is to be successful then the evidence must meet the criteria for that award. However, the differences observed in the previous chapter across disciplines, institutions and types of Doctorate may serve to obscure the essential nature of the task in hand. Issues in the processes of examination become complex where the relationship between evidence, criteria and judgement-making is not clear. In exploring these issues, the way in which examining panels are constituted and the roles that individual examiners play are discussed. There is then a discussion focusing on the oral examination as one distinct aspect of the process as well as possible outcomes and subsequent actions. The chapter considers the final examination within the context of different doctoral awards.

Examiners and examining panels

The composition of examining panels

Different notions of what is being examined and how examinations should be carried out lead to different notions of the composition of panels. Some institutions have an 'Independent Chair' of doctoral examination panels – many do not; some have regulations that allow the appointment of such a Chair in particular circumstances (e.g. where two external examiners have been appointed but where there is no internal examiner). Institutions differ in the extent to which they allow assessors at any progression stage to become examiners at the final assessment stage. Some institutions routinely appoint two examiners; one internal and one external; other institutions and many outside the UK routinely appoint three examiners. Institutions vary in whether or not they require that an examiner should hold a PhD. The extent and nature of any student input into the appointment of the examining team differs.

The relative status of individual examiners

The differing status of examiners within the panel is also far from being well defined. In the CVCP (1993: 73) document *Handbook for External Examiners in Higher Education* it is stated that 'an external examiner of a PhD is the examiner. He or she decides whether the thesis passes or fails'. This is a view held in some universities but not in others. In some the external examiner overtly holds the key vote whereas in others all examiners are equal – though implicitly some may be more equal than others. Clearly, the role of the internal examiner is defined in relation to that given to the external.

The nomination of examiners

The procedures for nominating examiners, and the mechanisms that enable institutions to monitor them, are generally seen to be important if independent and fair assessment is to be achieved – see, for example, QAA (1999) Precept 10a, which stresses 'the mechanisms used for communicating procedures relating to the nomination of examiners'. In the revised Code, Precept 23 states: 'Research Degree Assessment procedures must be clear; they must be operated rigorously, fairly and consistently; include input from an external examiner; and carried out to a reasonable timescale.' The explanation gives more detail of what is seen as good practice. These are summarized below.

- Each examining panel to have a minimum of two appropriately qualified examiners at least one of whom is external to the institution.
- The supervisors of a student are [normally] excluded from being his/her examiners.
- Examiners are not to have had substantial direct involvement in the research programme.
- Examiners are to submit separate, independent written reports prior to the *viva* and a joint report after it.

For the most part these strictures may not be contentious, though the definition of 'appropriately qualified' of course may prove problematic. It is also difficult to define independence in terms of an individual. The revised Code of Practice (QAA 2004) suggests that a potential examiner might be excluded 'whose own work is the focus of the research project' (QAA 2004: 24, under Precept 23). There is a sense in which the work of the candidate may be best examined by someone who has worked on similar research problems – and indeed one could argue that this is a prerequisite for an examiner to be considered as 'appropriately qualified'. The problem comes perhaps when the focus of the potential examiner's work is the same as the candidate's rather than similar to it. In short, to examine a doctoral submission fairly and rigorously requires that the examiner knows about the subject and understands what learning has necessarily gone on in the project and what questions need to be asked of the research design and the relationship between the methods of exploration of the topic and the presentation and interpretation of the findings. All of this requires that the examiner be competent within the same field as the candidate – to be part of it but still separate from the actual project concerned. This is a fine line and judgements about appropriateness need to be made on a case-by-case basis. There are other issues related to the independence of the external examiners, concerning formal links between individuals and institutions as well as frequency of contact between supervisors and examiners. These are explored in Jackson and Tinkler (2001) and Tinkler and Jackson (2000).

Qualification to examine at doctoral level

In terms of qualifications to examine at doctoral level, UCoSDA/BPS (1995: 8) suggested that 'an external examiner should possess a PhD or other evidence of a similar level of scholarship and should normally have been principal supervisor of at least one successful PhD student'. Yet it is not common in the UK for either of these conditions to be set by awarding institutions; neither are these criteria mentioned in the QAA Revised Code of Practice: Postgraduate Research Programmes (QAA 2004). The criteria that are usually applied relate to expertise within the field (usually ill-defined but sometimes judged by *curriculum vitae*) and experience of examining itself. So, it is quite possible in theory for someone to examine at doctoral level – without the doctoral qualification and without ever having engaged in research degree supervision. The relationship between examining, scholarship and supervising remain unexplored by most institutional regulations. Many institutions require an examining team to have experience of examining but are less concerned to consider supervisory experience, presumably on the grounds that these two activities are discrete.

Beyond the regulatory requirements there is a fairly substantial hidden agenda with regard to the choice of external examiner(s). In many disciplines the status of this examiner is seen to reflect on the quality of the examination and hence, obliquely, on the quality of the work itself. Delamont *et al.* (1997) take this further, suggesting that the examiner can have a strong and continuing influence on the professional, academic career of the candidate. Similarly, Leonard (2001) points to the need to see the examination as a chance to gain respect via the professional status of the examiner. The same kinds of points can be made about the institution where the doctoral award was made. Here, again, status is all.

The examiner as gatekeeper

Powell and McCauley (2002) suggest that the role of examiner is conceptualized by examiners and institutions as being on a continuum from 'teacherly' to 'confrontational'. In the first instance the notion of being part of an educational process is highlighted and examiners of this type tend to act as positive gatekeepers allowing access into the research community. In this conception, examiners may explore with candidates not only what they have learned while doing their research but also where the research may lead in terms of future investigations. They act in a pedagogical way, encouraging the learner and setting out for that learner the next stages in their personal – and sometimes professional – development. At the other end of the continuum the role assumes more the function of a gatekeeper in the negative sense – that is, of assessing who should and who should not be admitted to the community of scholars. The danger of this later conception is that examiners may end up seeing their role as to keep others out of the research community, disallowing those students who do not share the same ideology or methodology and passions. Along with this negative gatekeeping, the notion is suggested (Powell and McCauley 2002) that some examiners may even use the examination process, consciously or otherwise, as a chance for 'settling old scores' with other academics.

The findings of Powell and McCauley (2002) suggested that views about whether or not an examiner should be used at the progression stage and then again at the final examination stage varied along with the view taken of the gatekeeping role. If one sees the role as teacherly then there would be a tendency to see the role of formative assessor as positive and as compatible with that of final assessor. Conversely, those with a more confrontational view would tend to see a need for the examination at the final stage to be 'blind' to processes that had gone before. Judgements here would be made on the final product only. Roles would tend to correspond with 'assessment of process' (teacherly) or 'examination on the day as single event' (confrontational).

The individual examiner in relation to institutional regulations

Anecdotal evidence suggests that many doctoral examiners do not address institution-specific criteria or procedures either when making judgements about the candidate's work or when deciding how to proceed with the examination. Such anecdote is supported by Mullins and Kiley (2002) who found that only one-third of experienced examiners in their sample took note of institution-specific doctoral criteria when assessing doctoral level work. In short, examiners tend to bring their own conceptions to the assessment process, many assuming that all regulations are similar and that all concerned share a common understanding about the level of doctorateness required for a doctoral award to be made. In reality, there are significant variations in regulations and few common understandings of doctoral level.

Examiner fee

A final issue with regard to examiners is the level of fee involved as payment for examination. In the UK it is common, though not universal, practice *not* to pay internal examiners for their work in the examination process – presumably on the grounds that as members of staff the work falls within their paid employment. However, external examiners are, typically, paid for their efforts. There is no universally accepted fee – the level differs significantly across the sector. To our knowledge the only formal survey undertaken into fee levels for doctoral examination was that undertaken by the Modern Universities Research Group (MURG) (Brown 2002). Here most institutions surveyed (post-1992 universities) fell within the range £100–£150, with just a few exceptions paying between £200 and £220. The report notes that this is hardly commensurate with the amount of effort expended and expertise applied.

The 'mock' *viva*

In many institutions the candidate for a doctoral award is given a practice *viva* prior to oral examination itself. This practice is often termed a 'mock' *viva*. Perceptions of its purposes and its usefulness differ across the sector and from one individual academic to another. Tinkler and Jackson (2004) give six different kinds of approach to this practice event:

- where students take part in a 'practice run' organized by the candidate's supervisor(s);
- where students take part in giving each other mock *vivas* as part of a training course;
- where students undergo a *viva* as part of the procedure for upgrading from a Masters to a Doctorate – perhaps at the end of the first year of three years of full-time study;
- where students observe a video of a real or simulated *viva* as part of a training course;
- where students observe staff members simulating a real *viva* as part of a training course;
- where students observe an actual doctoral *viva* taking place.

Hartley and Fox (2004) add a seventh approach to this list:

- where the students read a 'mock thesis' and suggest questions for a subsequent *viva* role-play.

In these various approaches the student takes the perspective of candidate, examiner or observer. All of the approaches involve a degree of role-play and this distinguishes them from the kind of meeting organized by supervisors where possible questions are discussed and the procedures of the *viva* explained. There is little hard evidence about the extent to which mock *vivas* are used in preference to such meetings or indeed to no overt preparation at all. However, only about 25% of students in the studies of Hartley and Jory (2000) and Tinkler and Jackson (2002) had experienced one of the kinds of mock *viva* listed above. Of those listed above, the most common is probably the first (Hartley and Fox 2004) – that is, a dry run in which the student is questioned on his/her own thesis by people who are familiar with it.

One of the main criticisms of the use of mock *vivas*, of whatever kind, is that they do not necessarily replicate the questions that are asked in the actual *viva* itself. In this context, some attendees at workshops led by the current authors have criticized the use of mock *vivas* as, at best, leading the student into making unnecessary preparations and, at worst, misleading the student on crucial aspects of what he/she might realistically expect of the *viva* (that is, of particular questions arising and of particular approaches and themes being taken). There is some evidence to support this notion that questions arising at the mock stage will not be repeated at the actual *viva* stage. Hartley and Fox (2004) reported that 52% of the students in their sample who had been given a mock *viva* stated that there were important questions in the mock that did not come up at the actual *viva*. Similarly, 90% of respondents said 'yes' when questioned as to whether or not they had been asked important questions in the real *viva* that they were not asked in the mock. However, the noted difference in questions posed did not diminish the enthusiasm of the students in the Hartley and Fox study for the notion of a mock *viva*; indeed 90% of the respondents found the mock *viva* to be helpful to 'some degree' and 90% again recommended it for other students. The main advantages seen by the students were: rehearsal, getting a feeling for the type of questions they would be faced with (rather than the questions themselves), having the opportunity to see their thesis as a whole rather than as separate chapters, revisiting the original purpose of the studies reported in the thesis, and having a chance to experience the fear prior to the actual event.

Following the *viva*

Student perceptions subsequent to the viva

Research has indicated the kinds of disappointment felt by some, though not all, students following the experience of the *viva* and further that this disappointment does not relate exactly to whether or not a student passed, passed with amendments or failed (e.g. Hartley and Jory 2000; Hartley and Fox 2002; Jackson and Tinkler 2001; Leonard 2001; Tinkler and Jackson 2004; Wallace and Marsh 2001). Students in these studies reported variously on feelings that the questioning was not sufficiently searching, that examiners behaved in a negative way and that there was quite simply a sense of anti-climax when after years of study and much effort the whole event passed off in an unremarkable and, in some senses, unmarked way.

In terms of reactions to the event rather than perceptions of it, students reported various feelings ranging from relief, excitement, delight and frustration to 'sick, weepy and tired' (Tinkler and Jackson 2004: 205). Some who expressed satisfaction did so in the context of having been supervised by someone who, they claimed, gave little or no feedback of any kind during the period of PhD study. To them, the successful outcome to the *viva* was their first experience of having their work 'validated'. What is perhaps interesting in students' reports of the experience from their perspective is that, in general, few seemed to be simply happy. Indeed, many women respondents seem to continue to be reticent about their abilities and their achievement, even subsequent to a successful *viva* (see Leonard 2001 and Tinkler and Jackson 2004 for fuller explorations). For some candidates the whole business of post-*viva* corrections needing to be made marred any sense of satisfaction at the outcome.

Effects upon candidates following the viva

Clearly, any doctoral examination process will have effects on the candidate in terms of his/her future career and/or feelings of personal worth. Tinkler and Jackson (2004) cite some fairly depressing findings suggesting, in broad terms, that for many candidates (one in six of their respondents) the overall effect of the examination process was negative. Of the respondents 17% reported decreases in their perception of their own academic competence and similarly, 16% noted a decrease in their desire to work in academia (Tinkler and Jackson 2004: 208). Clearly, there are differences in effects according to the kind of examination result achieved but nevertheless all the studies seem to point to a less than satisfactory relationship between examination process and subsequent effects on perceptions and desire to continue researching. What is also noteworthy is the complex relationship between gender and levels of confidence. This complexity is explored in terms of the examination process by Tinkler and Jackson (2004), more generally in the context of access to research cultures by Deem and Brehony (2000) and in terms of subject in Thomas (1990).

Further work after the viva

In the UK it is common practice for examiners to award the doctoral degree subject to amendments and/or corrections that may be deemed 'minor' or 'substantial'. This has become part of the institutionalized culture of the doctoral examination. The purpose of this phase is not always clear. In some circumstances it is an opportunity for the candidate to rectify deficiencies in the work – at the extreme end there may be a need to gather further data and analyse it to meet the perceived deficiency in the work. It is perhaps worth noting that this practice distinguishes the UK PhD from those in many other parts of Europe where a thesis is (in some cases literally) 'nailed to a mast' and remains unchanged following examination.

It is usual in the UK for the same examiners to continue to sit in judgement on the candidate and his/her work when the first examination has not progressed satisfactorily. This would normally be the case whatever the level of re-examination or further work required. The exception would be where there is some dispute about the fairness of the process in the first examination – here an awarding committee at university level might decide that, in fairness to the candidate, there should be a new examination panel.

Some examiners in the UK see the post-*viva* stage as an opportunity to fine-tune the literary presentation of the work. Such examiners may arrive for the examination with a list of 'minor corrections' which may comprise anything from typographical errors to mis-labelling of tables and graphs to grammatical inexactitudes. Others see the phase as one in which fundamental flaws can be corrected and here it is likely that examiners will require the candidate to be given time to undertake 'substantial amendments'. Of course there are many variations and combinations of these kinds of approach to the task but in the UK both institutions (through their regulations) and the examiners they employ (through their practices) make heavy use of the post-*viva*, 'amendment' phase. This heavy use has implications for all concerned, but perhaps most specifically for the candidates and their supervisors.

Candidates often report being unclear about the amendments that are required of their work (Tinkler and Jackson 2004) and many express dismay at the prospect of revisiting their work – feeling that the sense of completeness and closure is [albeit temporarily] denied to them. Supervisors typically encourage their students to 'just get on' with the amendments. Again, typically institutional regulations allow a situation to develop wherein students can be given further work to do in a non-negotiated context where clarification can often be sought only via a third party (i.e. the supervisor). Given that amendments are often 'explained' during or at the end of what can be a very stressful situation for all concerned, but particularly for the candidate – there is clearly room for misunderstanding and lack of clarity about what is required. Subsequent written instructions as to what is required may go some way to resolving problems but again are the result of a non-negotiated process. Conversely, allowing a negotiation between candidate and examiners and giving the candidate open access to the examiner in terms requests for clarification on what is needed by way of amendment can lead to a kind of tutoring that is not wholly compatible with an examination phase of a learning process. It leaves the process open to appeal where a candidate can argue that the 'tutoring' failed to lead to a successful outcome (for example, where ultimately the amendments are not accepted by the panel despite substantial guidance by one or more of the examiners).

In our own view, the 'amendments' phase of the examination process would be well served by a closer focus on the purpose of the examination (and the *viva*'s place within it) which we believe should be judgement-making about the evidence provided by the candidate in relation to the criteria for the award. Making amendments may of course be about providing evidence, or the continuation of that provision; on the other hand, it may be serving some other, ill-defined purpose.

A second viva

Most institutional regulations allow the possibility of a second *viva* as part of the referral or re-examination phase. Typically, examiners have the possibility of a second *viva* at their disposal if they think that it is important for their judgement-making to question the candidate again on his/her work. In some cases, a second *viva* is mandatory. Clearly, a second *viva* offers the candidate the opportunity to retrieve any mistakes or misrepresentations that he/she made in the first event. If the former event can be interpreted as a learning episode, then the second *viva* also offers the chance to put that learning into practice. Conversely, a second *viva* may seem to the candidate to be no more than a re-run of an unpleasant experience – with the same examiners who have already found fault sitting in judgement for a second time in a situation that has some necessary similarities with the first. Tinkler and Jackson (2004: 212) cite different reasons why examiners from their sample might require a second oral examination (accepting that in some institutions some situations may require such a second *viva* regardless of the examiners' wishes); these may be summarized as follows:

- authentication of any substantial rewriting and testing of any new ideas findings;
- retesting of the candidate's knowledge;
- discussion of new developments in terms of possible publication and further work;
- the offering of a ritualistic 'closure' on the episode.

Clearly, reasons will vary according to the level and kind of work that has been required in the referral phase. In some cases – where it was the *viva* itself that the candidate was deemed to have been unsuccessful in – then clearly the only way to make a revised judgement is to rerun the event. In short, decisions about any second *viva* relate (a) to whatever was judged to be inadequate in the original examination and (b) to what one perceives to be the purpose of oral examinations generally. Presumably, an examiner who perceives the event to be a matter of rite of passage would subscribe to the final bullet point in the list cited by Tinkler and Jackson (2004) and summarized above.

Access to examiners' reports

Access to examiners' reports as a contentious issue

Access to examiners' reports has long been something of a contentious issue in the UK. The contention has been brought to a head by the Data Protection Act 1998. The argument may be polarized as follows:

- On the one hand, there are some who argue that a doctoral thesis represents at least three years of learning and is undertaken in an educational establishment and that an important part of learning is gaining from feedback given and further that an important aspect of any feedback system is the process of assessment. In the light of this argument, for a student to complete years of intensive study at the highest level and then get virtually no written feedback on their work from the assessors of it seems unfortunate at best and invidious at worst. A student in our experience noted that it (i.e. the doctoral thesis) was the greatest amount of work he had ever completed throughout his university education and yet he received the least amount of feedback on it.
- On the other hand, there are some who would argue that examiners are required to make a summative assessment of a high level piece of work and that it is not their place to give feedback – that should be given by the supervisors as part of the process of supervision and support through the examination process. According to this argument, examiners are likely to give their most honest and fair judgements when they make their comments to the relevant committee in confidence.

The current situation

Whatever the merits of the two positions (and clearly they are presented here as polarized views in reality many academics would fall on a continuum somewhere between the two viewpoints) the introduction of the Data Protection legislation noted above has shifted the balance so that, increasingly, institutions are interpreting the situation as one in which they will have to make examiners' reports available to candidates, at the very least, if those candidates make a formal request under the Act. The situation is then in a state of flux, with practices changing for various reasons and views being affected in turn (what seems an intrusion into an examiner's privacy at the one moment may come to seem less threatening when that 'privacy' is actually breached). Certainly, Tinkler and Jackson (2004: 213) note that despite the law 'many universities are not keen for candidates to see them (examiners' reports), and will not allow access to them without a formal request'.

The tension around giving access to examiners' reports is in part at least a by-product of the fact that the oral examination takes place in most UK institutions behind closed doors. As noted earlier, this is in direct contrast to the situation overseas – and in particular in many parts of Scandinavia and other parts of northern Europe – where the event is a much more open affair and where questions are asked and answered in a public forum.

The availability of preliminary reports and 'final recommendations'

Most of what is written above relates to reports written by examiners prior to the oral examination, usually known as preliminary reports. It is also the case that many institutions require that examiners make a final report after the oral examination. Wherever possible this is in the form of a joint recommendation; however, where agreement between examiners is not possible then most institutions will allow some kind of separate reporting. The matter will then be reviewed by a university committee that will have various options open to it (typically, to accept a majority view or to require a new examiner or new panel to make a judgement, often in isolation of the previous recommendations).

Making the reports available before the viva

Where examiners' reports are made available, this is usually but not universally restricted to the candidate and/or the supervisor(s) and to a period after the examination process is completed and the result approved by the relevant university committee. There is an argument – rarely heard in the UK but existing nonetheless – that the reports should be made available to the candidate before the oral examination itself. This argument suggests that, given the substantial and complex nature of the work, it is only fair that the candidate has the opportunity to reflect upon the issues that the examiners wish to raise. It is suggested that such openness before the event is likely to lead to a more rigorous and thorough examination rather than the reverse. This process of making reports available prior to the *viva* occurs in many universities in France, where examiners' reports are given to the candidate and the director of studies with the intention that they can prepare for the oral with a better insight as to what questions to expect.

Examination for the award of PhD by Published Work

There may be differences in the process of examination for the traditional PhD as compared with the PhD by Published Work. This sections explores some of these differences.

Parity between kinds of doctoral award

It seems reasonable to suggest that a PhD awarded on the basis of Published Work should reflect the same academic standards as those for a traditional PhD based upon a programme of supervised research. As noted by UKCGE (1996b), this requirement for comparability of standard presents different challenges to the examiners for the award of a PhD by the two routes (p. 15). While many would argue that parity should be attained if the award is to retain any credibility, it is not clear in the published literature just how institutions view this matter of comparability and what actions they take to ensure it. Clearly a key issue is how institutions seek to establish and maintain a system for ensuring that judgements from examiners take cognizance of the need for parity. It may be that implicit in the system is the notion that examiners who are experienced in examining the traditional PhD will be able to make judgements about a PhD by Published Work submission by reference to that experience. However, if the aims of the latter degree are unclear – for example, if the kinds of learning that they might expect the candidate to exhibit are not specified – then it is difficult to see how they can be confident in the judgements they make.

The task facing examiners of the PhD by Published Work

Currently there is no published guidance at national level for examiners of the PhD by Published Work. However, in UKCGE (1996b) suggestions were made about the main tasks facing examiners within the PhD by Published Work route. They are repeated here in a modified form because they seem, at the very least and in the absence of any specific national guidance, to be a useful starting point for debate about any differences between the tasks facing examiners within the two routes.

In the case of the published work route, the examiners' main tasks may be interpreted as to:

- evaluate the intellectual merit of the candidate's cited published work;
- establish if a satisfactory case is made for coherence between the publications;

- assess the contribution to knowledge represented by the publications and made apparent in any critical appraisal;
- evaluate the rigour with which the candidate has contextualized and analysed his/her publications in any critical appraisal;
- evaluate the appropriateness of the methods employed in the research and the correctness of their application;
- assess the candidate's contribution to the various phases of the research embodied in multi-authored works;
- establish the candidate's 'ownership' of the published work and appreciation of the state of [historical and current] knowledge within the candidate's research area;
- assess the candidate's research skills in terms of his/her potential as a continuing, independent researcher.

In undertaking these tasks the examiners would need to make their judgements while taking into account the position of the publications within their historical time frame and with recognition of the range of facilities available to the researcher across that time frame. One of the difficulties that may face examiners in undertaking these tasks is that publications themselves may not contain sufficient detail to allow some of these judgements to be made (UKCGE 1996b). For example, many academic journals prescribe succinctness, and this may result in general lack of experimental detail or background material. There may be instances where little or no evidence is available to the examiner about the quality of the work and the raw data on which important conclusions are based. This contrasts with the traditional PhD thesis where contextualizing is seen as part of the requirements of the text and where details of data can be accommodated in the main body of the text or within an appendix.

Locating the evidence within the assessment process

In the PhD by Published Work lack of crucial evidence in the publications might be at least partially addressed within any accompanying document within the submission (e.g. a critical appraisal). Whether or not any accompanying documentation can be effective in this way, however, depends on the remit given to it within institutional regulations and its possible length. In addition to the above, lack of evidence can be addressed to an extent in an oral examination. Powell (2004) noted that such examination was compulsory in the majority of institutions while discretionary in a few.

Examiners of the PhD by Published Work

UKCGE (1996b) noted that all institutions required the appointment of at least two examiners, and this situation is repeated in the survey reported by

Powell (2004). UKCGE (1996b) reported that, in ten institutions from their sample, both examiners were required to be external to the university and that in all the others a combination of internal and at least one external were required. It was further noted that the appointment of two external supervisors for members of staff was common practice. This basic pattern was repeated in the study reported by Powell (2004). Here, all institutions that responded to the question about examiners noted that at least one external examiner was required and further, ten of those who offered the degree to staff and others, responded that members of staff were required to have at least two externals. A number of institutions (24% of those responding) reported that only external examiners are used. Again, without data relating to practice with regard to the traditional PhD examination it is impossible to make comparative comments about whether or not the PhD by Published Work is being treated differently in this respect.

Oral examination of the PhD by Published Work

Almost exclusively, the PhD by Published Work is examined by *viva voce* (UKCGE 1996b; Powell 2004). There is similarity with the PhD. However, the nature of that oral examination will differ according to the importance given to the critical appraisal. Examiners will focus on the published works and/or the critical appraisal according to their view of the relative importance of these elements. There is likely to be a difference in kind between the oral examination for the two awards. In the PhD the examination is in part a judgement of whether or not the work is of a quality that merits peer-reviewed publication, whereas in the PhD by Published Work that judgement has, by definition, already been made (at least to some extent). Certainly, both awards require an examination in which the candidate must defend the contribution to knowledge that he/she has made, but there is a level of prior 'validation' in the latter that does not [necessarily] exist in the former.

Summary view of examination of the PhD by Published Work

The kind of rigour that is required if the degree of PhD by Published Work is to become more openly available can be argued to be a matter of establishing some sense of clarity about what is being examined in a doctoral submission of either kind and about the expectations of examiners regarding criteria for success. Clearly, examiners need to have understanding about the assessment process in which they are involved as well as knowledge of the candidate's research area.

Examination for a Practice-Based Doctorate

The differences in the examination of a Practice-Based Doctorate as opposed to the examination of a traditional UK PhD relate to the differences in the way in which the various parts of what is submitted for assessment (which may include a performance or an exhibition) are weighted either formally in institutional regulations or informally in the understandings of the various examiners. These matters have been discussed in Chapter 6, but for our purposes here it is enough to say that the focus of the examination process should be on how well the research question(s) is defined, explored and 'answered' (given that answers may take the form of further ways of, and understandings of, exploration); it should also be on the coherence of the way in which performance, critical appraisal and oral defence are integrated.

Examination for a Professional Doctorate

Examiners' focus in professional doctoral examination

In Chapter 5 it was noted that the assessment of such degrees is typically by a mixture of course work and *viva voce* and may involve the testing out of professional skills and knowledge to a level of acceptable professional [doctoral] competence. As an outcome of this it is clear that the assessment of the Professional Doctorate is likely to involve various elements rather than judgement-making on a single presented piece of work (i.e. on a PhD thesis). However, it is also the case that the research component of a Professional Doctorate is likely to be assessed in a traditional situation where the candidate is required to defend an original piece of research (originality is discussed further below) in an oral examination. This research is likely to involve a number of contributing projects – the degree to which these are linked by overt themes as opposed to being diverse and distinct will vary between professional contexts and between institutions. This variation will affect the way in which the assessment is conducted inasmuch as it will affect the examiners' focus on overall contribution to knowledge as opposed to learning of particular research skills, as evidenced by individual reported projects. It also affects the way in which individual institutions organize the assessment process. Where assessment is focused on the final, research-based thesis, it is likely that the process will mirror the kind of PhD examination prevalent in the UK, i.e. examination by at least two examiners, one of whom will be an external with the outcome recommended to a research degrees committee who act as an Examination Board. On the other hand, where assessment is focused on the outcomes of taught components it is more likely that the process will mirror the kind of assessment of postgraduate taught courses where a board of examiners sits and considers all the results of assessments that have made up the programme of study.

In all of the above there is the matter of the weighting of the various components of study. UKCGE (2002) indicates that institutions in the UK tend to give emphasis to the research component of programmes of professional doctoral study. Certainly, it would be extremely unlikely that a final examination board would award a professional doctoral degree to a candidate whose performance in the 'thesis and its defence' component was judged unsatisfactory. Compensation by excellent earlier work would not typically be enough to redeem the doctoral candidate. Conversely, it is more likely that compensation for earlier inadequacies in taught components might be awarded following an excellent thesis and *viva voce*. There remains a tension therefore in reconciling the importance for professional development of the professional doctoral award and the importance of being able to demonstrate independent abilities as a researcher is a key signifier for that award.

The use of portfolio as a product to be assessed

A portfolio can be distinguished from a thesis inasmuch as the latter requires the presentation of an intellectual argument in a coherent and unifying sense – there is consistency of argument and a single audience is intended – and the former allows the inclusion of disparate pieces of work, written for different purposes, illustrating different kinds of skill application and intended for a range of audiences. This is not to say, of course, that a portfolio might not include a unifying theme and a singular sense of purpose, but rather that these things are not necessary for that portfolio to achieve its aims of conveying to the assessor the range of knowledge and skills that the practitioner has acquired. Again, this is not to say that a portfolio might not include an integrating commentary; indeed such a device is fairly common in current UK Professional Doctorates (Scott *et al.* 2004). The commentary in this sense might be interpreted as a *post hoc* rationalization of work achieved or as a summarizing of the contents of the portfolio – whatever the interpretation, it is an artefact of the disparate pieces of work rather than an integral driver for them. There is a similarity between the portfolio and many science theses that are really collections of chapters reporting on a series of experiments – rather than a thesis in the sense of the development of an argument.

Some of the above features of the portfolio lend themselves to the realm of the Professional Doctorate and many (e.g. Usher 2002) would argue for its usefulness in this context in particular, perhaps because the use of a portfolio enables the inclusion of both academic and professionally oriented work. Where boundaries are perceived between these two elements, the portfolio allows for them to be broken down in as much as it enables the candidate to target different audiences and purposes within a unifying submission. For our purposes in this chapter it also accommodates an approach to learning that is typified by distinct phases of specific learned outcomes that can be collected together to give an overall pattern of achievement. That pattern may, of course, include an element of progression – the candidate is not expected to be operating at doctoral level throughout his/her programme of study but rather may be seen as a learner needing to exhibit what he/she has learned over a period of years. Here the portfolio allows the candidate to indicate progress made from 'novice' (assuming this to mean a level of noviciate in relation to specific tasks) to expert and, in turn, gives the assessor the opportunity to plot a curve of development rather than merely assess a final, doctoral standard. A portfolio might then include work that has been assessed at an early stage in the candidate's learning and therefore at a lower level than subsequent work.

In this scenario the user of the portfolio is recognizing a need for relative standards to be applied as a candidate progresses through a programme. Of course, a portfolio does not have to be constructed on this progressive basis – it is quite possible for a portfolio to be assembled by the candidate, which indicates only doctoral level work, albeit in different areas within the remit of the Professional Doctorate. However, it may be argued that the notion of a portfolio as containing work indicating how a candidate has progressed from novice to expert (or more properly from experienced practitioner to advanced, doctoral level practitioner) fits with an underlying ethos of professional doctoral education, which suggests that a strict demarcation of academic and practitioner knowledge, with the former somehow superior to the latter, is unhelpful and ultimately non-productive in the sense of moving forward knowledge and skill in the context of specific professional work.

The examination of research projects and taught course elements

There is a difference in the perceptions that examiners hold of what they are examining at PhD level (Powell and Green 2003). One crude distinction is between those who see themselves as examining the learning process that the student has undergone during his/her PhD studies as opposed to those who see themselves as examining the end product as encapsulated in the thesis. This distinction takes on a new light in the Professional Doctorate where an examiner may well assess a candidate's work throughout his/her doctoral studies, including taught components as well as the final research-based thesis. Here the clear focus is on the development of the candidate as a learner about professional practice and about the role and impact of research on that practice. Again, the way in which Professional Doctorates are examined differs across the sector but typically the systems used tend to borrow from both the PhD and taught course models of examination.

Appeals against examination outcomes and complaints about examinations

Grounds for appeal

It is important to stress at the outset of this section that there is much variation in the UK in the way in which universities deal with appeals and complaints regarding examination outcomes. Those concerned with the specifics of making a complaint or an appeal should refer to their institutions' individual regulations in these respects. To give just one example of variation: in some universities there is a regulatory mechanism that automatically generates an appeals procedure when a doctoral candidate fails outright to achieve the award or is awarded a lower degree than the one for which he/she was registered, whereas in others the onus is on the candidate to appeal if he/she thinks there is evidence to support an appeal on the grounds set out in the institution.

The issue of appeals against examination outcomes is a current issue in the UK and has been referred to earlier in this book. Here, however, we deal with appeals without reference to their incidence. All UK universities have appeals procedures and such are referred to in the QAA Code of Practice for Research Degree Programmes (QAA 2004). To our knowledge none of these allows appeals against the academic judgement of the examiners and indeed the Courts in the UK have ruled in the past that universities are correct in maintaining that candidates cannot challenge academic judgement. Typically, appeals that are made against examination outcomes are therefore targeted at one of three possible grounds: (i) procedural irregularities, (ii) circumstances that might have affected the candidate's performance at the *viva* and (iii) bias, unfair or inadequate assessment.

Of these three possibilities the first is perhaps the most commonly pursued. From the institution's perspective any irregularity on the part of administrators or any others involved can undermine an examination process and this is one of the reasons often cited for the introduction of an independent chair of examining panels. The second possibility is usually restricted in regulations to circumstances of which examiners were unaware at the time of the examination. Here there would be a question as to whether or not the examiners would have reached a different decision if they had known the particular circumstances in question. The final grounds would require evidence that one or more of the examiners acted in an unfair way in the examination of the thesis and the candidate. Clearly, there may be a thin line between 'unfairness' in this sense and academic judgement (which, as noted, is usually beyond the scope of any appeal). The candidate who believes that his/her work has been misjudged academically may see that as unfair. Appeals panels have the task of unpicking the rights and wrongs of any appeal on a case-by-case basis.

Outcomes of appeals

Institutional policies vary in respect of the grounds for appeal and in respect of possible outcomes. However, it is clearly the case that appeals can be accepted or rejected – differences come in what may happen following acceptance of an appeal. What may happen following acceptance is to some extent driven by the grounds upon which the appeal was based and then accepted. Where circumstances are revealed that were not known to the examiners at the examination stage, the panel may have the option of requiring the examiners to review their decision in the light of the 'new' information. Where a procedural irregularity is identified, the panel may have the power to set the examination aside – effectively declaring it null and void – and rewind the examination process to a point untainted by the irregularity. Typically this would mean requiring a fresh examination with new examiners. Similarly, where evidence is found that there was unfair or inadequate assessment, then a new examination may be required. In addition to the above, panels may occasionally have the option of allowing the candidate to revise and resubmit his/her thesis.

Complaints related to doctoral examination

It is necessary here to draw a distinction between appeals against examination outcomes, as discussed above, and complaints against individuals or procedures involved in the examination process. Most UK universities have an appeals process that is separate from its provision for dealing with complaints. In the case of a doctoral examination, candidates might wish to complain against some aspect of their examination even though the outcome was in their favour. Where appeals must be made on one or more of a number of carefully defined grounds, a complaint might be made on any grounds. Where an appeal is made with the aim of overturning or redressing an examination outcome, a complaint seeks to redress a perceived wrong, irrespective of outcome.

Doctoral candidates who have a grievance against some aspect of the examination process but feel that the grounds for appeal, as set down by the institution, do not cover the grievance in question, may decide to complain in the hope that a successful complaint might lead to a change in the outcome. This 'back door' approach will only be successful where a particular institution's regulations permit such change. A successful complaint may, however, be seen as an opportunity to appeal.

Office of the Independent Adjudicator

In 1996 the Committee on Standards in Public Life, chaired by Lord Nolan, questioned the traditional role of 'university visitor' and recommended that students in UK universities should be able to appeal to an independent body. Subsequently, the National Committee of Inquiry into Higher Education, chaired by Dearing in 1997, suggested that universities should review the way in which they handle student complaints. Following a consultation period in 2002 regarding the future of higher education, and the resulting White Paper of January 2003, the Government of the day stated its intention to establish an independent adjudicator for higher education.

The Office of the Independent Adjudicator (OIA) was established in 2003 and commenced a voluntary student complaints scheme on 29 March 2004. Over 100 higher education institutions joined the voluntary scheme. The OIA was designated the operator within England of the student complaints scheme with effect from 1 January 2005. All higher education institutions in England and Wales are required to comply with the scheme. It should be noted here that the OIA is not a regulator. It handles individual complaints against universities. However, it may also make recommendations about how universities should deal with complaints and what constitutes good practice.

Conclusion

Traditionally, the process of doctoral examination in the UK has been something of a private affair, taking place typically behind closed doors with few participants and few or no witnesses. Reports from examiners have often been withheld from candidates and indeed from their supervisors unless they make specific efforts (often in the form of legal challenge) to gain access to them. This kind of scenario is in direct contrast with the situation in many other parts of Europe. Increased openness is, however, a likely feature of future examination processes because of (i) a legal climate where access to information pertaining to the individual is seen as a right, (ii) an increasing isolation in contrast with other European countries, (iii) a QAA Code of Practice (QAA 2004) which leans towards giving students full and fair feedback and makes reference to 'independent chairs' of panels and (iv) the range of new kinds of Doctorate that bring to the overall scene new understanding of what and how doctoral level work may be best assessed. In response to all of this, universities may well need to challenge their own practices in respect of the processes of doctoral examination that they have developed over time – what has 'always been done' may no longer suffice.

Summary issues

- Given the significant variation in process, should there be a greater drive for standardization of the examination process?

- How can institutions ensure that external examiners approach the task with both rigour and independence?
- Does the establishment of an independent chair model offer a practical solution to many of the perceived problems of examination?
- How should both the candidate and the examiner be best prepared for the examination of the Doctorate?

Part 5

The Future of the Doctorate

Part 5

The future of the doctorate

13
Future directions

Introduction

The previous chapters have described and analysed the changing nature of the Doctorate in the UK, identifying some of the key changes and unanswered questions. In so doing we have attempted to raise questions that we feel are vital to the future success of the Doctorate as an academic award. We have not attempted to answer all the individual questions in detail (though this chapter does address the general substance of them), in part because their purpose was to encourage debate and challenge current practice and in part because we do not claim to have all the answers. We are, however, clear that failing to recognize and respond to the questions will ultimately devalue the Doctorate and disadvantage both individual students and UK research in general. Indeed the very fact that we can pose so many reasonable questions points to a worryingly fragile position.

In this final chapter we return to some of the broad questions we have raised and, in addressing them, take a forward look to how the award may be developed and delivered in the future. We do this with some trepidation, as anticipating change is a science in itself. We suggest, however, that change does not take place very rapidly in doctoral education. If one looks back and compares the changes that have taken place in the pedagogy of undergraduate education with those of the Doctorate, it seems reasonable to anticipate a significant amount of inertia in the doctoral system. As Noble rightly says, 'any changes to the (doctoral) process must not be radical if they are to be adopted and accepted within traditional universities' (Noble 1994). Perhaps, however, he will be proved wrong in the next decade.

The challenge in Europe

The European Higher Education Area

The UK Doctorate is still a world leader as far as the international market is concerned. There are, however, changes that are taking place both in Europe and at a global level that will influence the future, particularly in view of the Bologna declaration, which set out a framework for a European Higher Education Area by 2010 (Reichert and Tauch 2003; Ahola and Kivinen 2001). The original declaration covers six areas of activity, to which four more were added recently in the communiqué *Realising the European Higher Education Area* following the Berlin Conference in 2003. These are noted below.

1. Adoption of a system of easily readable and comparable degrees.
2. Adoption of a system essentially based on two main cycles: under-graduate/postgraduate (masters).
3. A common system of credits (ECTS).
4. Increased mobility of students, teachers, researchers, etc.
5. European co-operation in quality assurance.
6. Promotion of the European dimension in higher education.
7. Lifelong learning.
8. Higher education universities and students.
9. Promoting the attractiveness of the European Higher Education Area.
10. Doctoral studies as a third cycle.

Each of these elements is seen to be interdependent, so a common system of credits will enhance the mobility of students within a common two (now three) cycle system. The recent addition of the Doctorate is of particular interest here because it is arguably the area of European education that displays the greatest diversity. The Doctorate programme is an essential link between the Higher Education Area and the emerging research area. If Europe is to increase the number of researchers by 700,000 as the Commission outlined in its action plan 'More research for Europe – towards the 3% objective' (European Commission 2003) then research training will be vital. It is interesting to note that as part of this process the Directorate General (DG) Education and Culture supported by the Directorate General (DG) Research is currently co-ordinating a project proposed by the European University Association (EUA) to establish exactly what is happening in doctoral education in Europe (EUA 2004). In true European style, the project is being undertaken by six networks, involving 49 universities and covering four broad themes: structure and organization, financing, quality, and innovative practice.

The competitive advantage of the UK Doctorate

Currently the UK Doctorate has a competitive advantage in the European market, first because, particularly in the sciences, English is the dominant international academic language, second because of the rigorous quality assurance processes that are in place and third because of the timely completion rates as far as Research Council students are concerned at least. However, these competitive advantages may diminish as the EU model introduces common standards for quality, delivery and completions in the move towards 2010, and increasingly individual universities across Europe teach and research in English. The recent HEFCE analysis of completion rates will not be helpful in this context.

The European Doctorate

Despite the diminishing of some of the advantages inherent in the UK system, the Higher Education Area does offer opportunities for the UK provided that its universities respond and take advantage of developments such as the European Doctorate in which universities or groups of universities across Europe set up partnerships to deliver a common award. The European Doctorate is an award of an individual European university, made in accordance with the criteria set out by the Confederation of European Union Rectors' Conferences. It is a variation of the existing PhD, under which the following conditions have been met.

1. The thesis must be prepared as a result of a period of registration at a UK university that includes a period of research in another European country normally of not less than ten weeks.
2. Part of the *viva voce* examination must be conducted in a European language other than English, normally an official language of a European country. The examiners conducting the *viva voce* must include at least one from a university in a European country other than the UK.
3. The thesis examiners must include at least two from universities in two separate European countries other than the UK.

Several UK universities already offer the European Doctorate, usually in defined areas of study between groups of partner universities such as the European Doctorate in Sound and Vibration Studies at the University of Southampton. Others, such as the University of Sussex, offer the award in all subjects. It is worth noting that in this case the individual student is responsible for establishing the placement in mainland Europe. The university does offer help though through 'the international office'.[1] Yet other UK universities team up with mainland European universities and are

---

[1] http://www.sussex.ac.uk/International/europe/europhil.

involved in programmes that differ significantly from the UK doctoral model – of any description. The University of Warwick, for example, is a partner in a programme led by the University of Barcelona's Department of Business Economics and Management, entitled 'European Doctoral Programme in Entrepreneurship and Small Business Management'. To ignore such opportunities and developments will simply emphasize the UK's insularity in general and in research terms in particular. These types of Doctorate offer the opportunity to enhance the UK position in a collaborative rather than a competitive manner.

It is notable that eight of the 49 universities taking part in the EUA project are UK universities: Kingston University, University College London, and the Universities of Bournemouth, Leeds, Newcastle-upon-Tyne, Salford, Strathclyde and Wolverhampton. It is probable that one of the outcomes of this work will confirm the great variety of Doctorates and doctoral practice in Europe. This places even more pressure on the UK system to clarify its practices within a commonly understood framework so that the UK can continue to demonstrate its leadership in doctoral education.

The UK Doctorate and the international setting

The globalization of higher education and research has created a major market for UK universities; indeed it has been suggested that UK research increasingly relies on the attraction of overseas students. This international market does, however, introduce many of the considerations normally associated with international trade. For example, exchange rate fluctuations can have a significant effect on the attractiveness of particular countries for study. At the time of writing the decline of the US dollar against the euro and other currencies makes study in the USA more attractive for European students. More fundamentally, the General Agreement on Trade in Services (GATS) has alerted us to the fact that Higher Education is considered as a service within the terms of GATS. While there have been deliberations about the exception of Higher Education from the GATS discussions on the grounds of it being supplied in the exercise of governmental authority, it is difficult to see how this might be the case with the increasing commercialization of postgraduate research and increasing levels of international competition for students.[2] At present it is difficult to speculate on the impact of the GATS process on postgraduate research not least because of its complexity and at times ambiguous language. Perhaps the key point that can be made here is the recognition that research students are part of the global trade environment and as such all the associated paraphernalia will come into play.

---

[2] http://www.eua.be/eua/en/policy_global_GATS.

Producing doctoral candidates – supply or demand led?

The purpose of the Doctorate was a key concern of earlier chapters in this book where we noted the difficulty of matching the PhD to the job market. We suggested that the future number of Doctorates in the UK was largely unplanned and left instead to the vagaries of market forces. The question of the supply of doctoral candidates has recently come to the fore with the closure of some science departments and hence the potential long-term reduction in research capacity in some subjects. While not wanting to enter detailed discussion of funding, recruitment and national needs it is useful to note how some of our international competitors are realizing their needs.

Currently there is little relationship between the supply of PhD places at universities and the demand for the services of doctoral candidates once their studies have been successfully completed. If unemployment rates of PhDs in the UK are an indicator then demand does appear to be particularly buoyant. Patterns in countries like Finland, however, appear to be even more favourable with unemployment rates as low as 0.6% in engineering and 1.8% in the natural sciences. It is worth noting that it is countries such as Sweden and Finland that have taken the analysis of the demand for research capacity seriously. Not surprisingly they too are the only countries to have already exceeded the EU Research and Development investment target of 3% of GDP [targeted for 2010]. The work by the Academy of Finland on this subject demonstrates how a small but advanced economy such as Finland takes the development of a trained research base seriously (Academy of Finland 2003).

In contrast, and as we have already noted, there has been little attempt to control the supply of Doctorates coming on to the labour market in the UK. While the Research Councils have some influence on their own parts of the market, universities are free to recruit – or not – as many research students as they think fit (Triggle and Miller 2002). More often than not, their decisions are based on financial returns rather than any policy linked to national or regional labour market needs. It is notable that in a period when the knowledge economy and science in particular is emphasized by Governments, there is little encouragement to reflect market needs. There seems little appetite on the behalf of UK Governments to attempt to control or influence numbers at present. Perhaps this is something that we can look forward to in the future. Certainly, if the UK is to meet its EU investment target of 3% of GDP by 2010 then we suggest that this will necessarily be something to consider.

Innovations in doctoral study?

Diversity in doctoral awards and the need for coherence

Our discussion of the various types of doctorate has highlighted a confusion that is similar to that identified by Harris in 1996 when he spoke of the problem of nomenclature in postgraduate taught provision, 'Idiosyncrasies of nomenclature . . ., have been less of a problem in the past when the postgraduate sector was smaller and focused on fewer centres . . . however, change could bring national coherence and hence clarity in an international marketplace' (Harris 1996: para. 4.29).

His proposals in 1996 in the field of the Doctorate were limited to the PhD/DPhil:

> *This title should be reserved for a qualification awarded on the basis of an individually produced piece of research which is free-standing and makes an original contribution to the subject area. The target for completion of the degree should be 3 years for a full-time student.*

The 'Taught Doctorate', 'should be distinguished by referencing the relevant subject area, such as the EdD' (Harris 1996: Box 2).

The current profusion of research Doctorates in addition to the traditional MPhil/PhD, e.g. Practice-Based, New Route, European, and by Published Works, challenges Harris's vision of a level of standardization. Add to this list the tens of different Professional Doctorates, all with their own idiosyncratic structures and greater or lesser involvement with kinds of taught delivery, and the doctoral scene may seem to have taken on a complexity over the last ten years similar to the Masters in the mid-1990s. We suggest that there is an urgent need to pull this diversity into a more coherent structure if students and employers are to fully comprehend what they are dealing with.

Real innovation in patterns of doctoral study?

The confusion that we note above raises the question as to whether or not there has been a fundamental shift in differentiation in the Doctorate in which divergent processes and outcomes have been developed to address changing needs. We suggest that the answer to this question must be 'No'. What has been evident is a tinkering at the margins to satisfy particular needs without a fundamental review of purpose and intent.

The New Route PhD has added an additional year to the programme in order to accommodate extra elements directed towards a specific market. But it is not entirely clear if these elements are part of, or in addition to, the Doctorate. As we noted in earlier chapters when discussing assessment, it matters if these 'additional' periods of study are part of the Doctorate itself and are assessed as such. If they are such a part, then one might ask legitimately where they are assessed within the typical submitted thesis and oral examination. If, on the other hand, they are elements in addition to the Doctorate itself then, however laudable and important they may be, they should be interpreted not as part of learning to operate at doctoral level but as a precursor to that level of learning. In this latter case the elements should carry the possibility of failure on their own criteria alone and also the possibility of stepping off with a lower [non-doctoral] level award. In all of this it is hard to see what 'New Route' really means. Certainly there is nothing new in front-loading elements of taught courses in research methodology to doctoral programmes. For the route to be accurately describable as 'new' it would need to involve pathways that do not exist in the 'traditional' doctoral programmes. Given that there is diversity across the sector in what counts as a doctoral programme and given that doctoral education in the UK is typified by the range of approaches taken to teaching students to a doctoral standard of submission, then it seems unlikely that the descriptor of 'new' is indeed being accurately applied in the case of the 'New Route PhD'. In fact, what *is* new is not the route so much as the way of marketing and branding the award and collaborating in these respects.

In the case of the Practice-Based Doctorates, the question arises as to whether these are simply awards within different research paradigms with outcomes expressed in different ways – or fundamentally different products. What we described in earlier chapters are the former: that is, awards where research is defined in specific ways that do not conform to the traditional, science-originated, ways of operating. Any differences in teaching methods or ways of assessing arise from the paradigmatic differences in the relationship between knowledge, contributions to that knowledge and ways of judgement making about such contribution. In essence, the doctoral product itself remains the same as in other doctorates across the sector – the awards are just recast to address the particular demands of the disciplines concerned. However, the Practice-Based Doctorate, and particularly the potential for creative approaches to the submission itself, may challenge the conventional submission particularly in terms of appropriateness in demonstrating research capability and outcomes. We suggest that this challenge is no bad thing and indeed that the 'practice community' puts its own creativity at risk if it attempts to emulate a science model of doctoral research where that is not appropriate. This community needs to address the inherent intellectual structures within its domain rather than seek to emulate [inappropriate] structures from others.

We would argue that the additive behaviour described above to satisfy the needs of the different disciplines is simply avoiding the key issues which relate to what the nature of the Doctorate is, how it relates to the particular methodologies or paradigms of specific subjects and how the outcomes of this research learning might be evidenced.

And finally, when considering the Professional Doctorate, we suggest that what is required is the asking of fundamental questions about the research demands of the professions and how competences in these areas should be evidenced, rather than inventing new routes or rather new named awards. The notion of 'contribution' may need to be revisited to accommodate a new interpretation of the boundaries of an intellectual field (in particular where differing traditional academic disciplines may be brought to bear on specific, professional, decision-making contexts) and the ways in which those fields can be progressed. In our view what research seeks to do in many professional areas is, for example, to refine understandings of how professional workers may operate more effectively. In this sense 'contribution to knowledge' is redefined. The concept of professionally oriented research, as opposed to academic research, gives rise to a false dichotomy. The sole issue is the ways in which a contribution can be claimed and the kinds of evidence that may be presented to support that claim.

The innovative possibilities of electronic submission

The development of electronic submission and storage has major potential for the development of the Doctorate and the bringing together of the various doctoral forms as it allows us to focus on a single form of submission for the diversity of disciplines and their traditions.

The interactive potential of electronic submission will, for example, permit both musician and chemist to demonstrate their competences in performance and experiment respectively and will potentially offer an entirely new approach to the presentation and testing of evidence. Electronic submission will also, of course, enable wider and quicker access to research findings that form part of doctoral submissions. This increased accessibility will bring benefits both in terms of spreading the knowledge base and in increasing the transparency of standards of doctoral work across international borders.

The innovative possibilities of the Personal Development Plan

The Personal Development Plan (PDP) required of UK universities for all award bearing provision, including Doctorates, follows the Dearing report recommendation (Dearing 1997) that HEIs should develop:

- a transcript recording student achievement which should follow a common format devised by universities collectively through their representative bodies;
- a means by which students can monitor, build and reflect upon their personal development.

The QAA has subsequently developed policy and practice which requires universities to put in place PDP initiatives to ensure that students:

- become more effective independent and self-confident self-directed learners;
- understand how they are learning and relate their learning to a wider context;
- improve their general skills for study and career management;
- articulate their personal goals and evaluate progress towards achievement;
- encourage a positive attitude to learning throughout life.

They define the PDP as 'A *structured* and *supported* process undertaken by an individual to *reflect* upon their own learning, performance and/or achievement and to plan for their personal, educational and career development'.[3]

The approach builds on a clutch of earlier initiatives concerning ways of recording doctoral student achievements such as *The Royal Society of Chemistry Postgraduate Skills Record* (MacDonald 2000) and *Making Your PhD Work for You* (University of Leeds 2000). These projects developed an approach to the recording of, and reflection on, learning by doctoral students. Most were self-administered by students on a voluntary basis.

This development, now embodied in the revised QAA Code of Practice, reinforces the development of the employability agenda that we discussed earlier in this book. As the UK GRAD Programme survey (2004a) demonstrates, PDPs have so far received a mixed reception from students and supervisors alike – the benefits being perceived as countered by the time involved for the completion of PDPs and their current status outside the formal requirements of the Doctorate itself. As observed in our earlier discussion of examination and assessment there is a growing concern about what the subject of the final assessment of the Doctorate should be. As students are now expected to include the PDP process within their doctoral programme, it is reasonable to expect at least that there will be some discussion of this process in the final assessment of the programme. The fact that this expectation is rarely met indicates a further need for clarification of the purposes and content of the examination itself. It is notable that in its report *The Chemistry PhD – the Enhancement of its Quality* (Royal Society of Chemistry 1995) the Society observed, with reference to the expectations of the examiners, 'to assure themselves that the candidate possesses the necessary professional competencies, both those specific to a chemist (such as safety consciousness) and those of a more general professional kind (such as communication skills)' (p. 11).

Funding

The current structure of funding for universities and students is complex at best and confusing at worst; the complexity and confusion lead to degrees of games playing. The HEFCE costing review and the move towards the

---

[3] QAA, http://www.qaa.ac.uk/crntwork/progfilehe/guidelines/uidline.pdfd.

recovery of full economic costs will have significant impacts on universities and the availability of doctoral programmes. One outcome will surely be a more critical review of the Doctorate and its place in the higher education system. The system proposed for future funding of doctoral work (HEFCE 2004) reinforces the current concentration of doctoral programmes in the more research intensive universities.

It does appear to miss an opportunity to examine more fundamentally those areas in which national and regional agendas require doctoral research of particular kinds to be undertaken.

The discussion of the stipend and fees highlighted the great diversity of funding – and as a consequence the status and employment relationships of doctoral students and universities. This raises the question of whether or not the relationship is appropriate to the work undertaken, the status of the individual and the demands that are made of them. Within any group of doctoral students at present it is possible to have students who are funded by Research Councils, by employers or by other sponsor organizations; students may also be members of academic staff, research assistants, or may be employed by sponsor organizations, or may be retired or unemployed. Such diversity generates different perceptions of status, but more fundamentally of the relationship between students and the universities in which they undertake their research and the associated rights and obligations on all parties. If a comparison is made between a student receiving a stipend from a Research Council and a research assistant receiving a salary, one will be treated as a student within the conditions of the sponsor whereas the other will be an employee – even though ultimately both are funded by the same Research Council. The one receiving a stipend will have a set of conditions that will be far less favourable to that of the employed person. Although far from straightforward to resolve, there are strong arguments, not only to treat all doctoral students as employees, but also to develop their contracts explicitly in that way to ensure absolute clarity on rights, conditions and expectations.

Two-tier system

It seems to us that within the UK there is the possibility of a two-tier system of delivery developing with regard to doctoral education. This matters if it means that the experience of doctoral study for those in the lower tier is less than for those in the higher, and if the final doctoral outcomes (both 'contribution to knowledge' and candidate) are in any way diminished. This question is particularly relevant to the way in which students and institutions fund the Doctorate and the resources and opportunities that are made available. Institutions are increasingly aware of the costs of delivery, as are students of the costs to maintain themselves, part or full time. We are not confident, however, that these matters are fully examined when doctoral students are offered places and, consequently, many will be under-funded.

It is notable that the explanation of Precept 8 of the QAA Code states:

The student's ability to complete the programme may be affected by financial support, and for this reason institutions may wish to assure themselves that students have sufficient funding in place for the duration of the programme. It is equally important to ensure that students are made aware at the earliest opportunity of the financial implications of registering for the programme.

(QAA 2004: 10)

It is difficult to be fully satisfied that all students are adequately resourced, particularly if they are self-funded and, of course, circumstances change during a period of registration. It may be that universities should consider moving away from self-funding or require bonds or similar vehicles to ensure adequacy of funding.

Equally, and yet not included in the discussion of student recruitment in the Code, is the adequacy of institutional funding to secure an appropriate level of support for all students. While some of this is covered in the discussion of an appropriate research environment, there are nevertheless specific direct costs that institutions need to sustain if they are to deliver a single-class service.

Our concerns about the developing two-tier structure are, however, more fundamental than simply the adequacy of funding to ensure national research needs. They go to the very heart of the equality of opportunity for all capable and willing to undertake research. Heartened by the explicit statement in the QAA Code that suitability to undertake a Doctorate may evidenced by 'professional practice or learning that meets the institution's criteria and good practice guidelines for the accreditation of prior experiential and/or certificated learning (AP[E/C]L)' (QAA 2004: 10), we would not wish to see those students in receipt of anything other than a first-rate training.

Completions: product or time

Length of study

The length of period of study is not an absolute marker for the Doctorate – that is, it is not true to say that a Doctorate must take three or four years to complete. If a candidate can meet the criteria in less time then a registration period might be shorter. On the other hand, if more time is required then it is arguable that this might be equally appropriate. In the former situation a candidate might have prior publications that can be used as part or all of the evidence to support the intellectual position taken; in the latter situation, the candidate may need to engage in some longitudinal studies to provide appropriate evidence and such studies may necessarily require a longer timescale. Thus to place an entirely rigid time frame on researching may be inappropriate across all research degrees. Having said this it is quite reasonable to set out an expected time from registration to completion. It is also reasonable for those funding research degree studies to have a clear expectation of the duration of the stipend in order to ensure that the student has a reasonable chance of completing successfully. There is a danger, however, that what funding councils may, legitimately, require becomes a marker for quality of delivery of an institution in terms of its general research degree provision. Here the marker becomes illegitimate if completion times are used to judge quality in isolation of success rates. To use our example above, it would be unreasonable for the student undertaking a longitudinal study and producing a wholly satisfactory doctoral level thesis, though over a longer period of time than the 'norm', to be penalized (or for his/her institution to be penalized); what matters is that the evidence is provided to support the intellectual position in terms that meet the criteria for the award.

We suggest that, while it may not be possible to define how long a Doctorate should take to complete in absolute terms, it is nevertheless possible to identify an expected period and it is reasonable to assume that three years of full-time funding should be adequate for the task. It follows that it is indefensible to encourage students to enter into programmes that are clearly unachievable within the time period for which funding is available. This may deny the diversity of researching we have alluded to above and be inconsistent across disciplines, but we should accept that disciplinary idiosyncrasy is no excuse for poor research management. A mark of a well-rounded researcher is, after all, the ability to conduct and complete projects in a timely fashion.

Completion rates

The HEFCE report (HEFCE 2005) highlights an additional tension in the relationship between registration periods and completions – that of actual completion times. Although the report takes as the end point the time at which the award is made and, consequently, potentially adds perhaps a year onto the actual time taken to successful examination, it does highlight that many students, 29% full time and 66% part time, are not completing within seven years, which for many institutions is the maximum period of registration for part-time students. So we have a position in which students are working outside the period of both personal or stipend funding, outside the normal registration period for the award, and institutions are supervising students for whom they receive only tuition fees at best. The compounded loss to the individual and the institution appears on the face of it to be a major concern.

Managing the process

Inter-institutional collaborations

Our discussion about the management of the doctoral process highlighted the development of graduate schools during the 1990s and the way in which they had greatly improved the 'cottage industry' nature of PGR. Indeed, one may argue that the diffusion of the graduate school in its various guises across UK universities is one of their great achievements of the last ten years. The future does, however, present us with new organizational challenges not least because of the pressures to focus activity, to collaborate, to further develop interdisciplinary research and to respond to the regional agendas and the growing influence of the Regional Development Agencies.

We have already seen the development of a regional agenda in the hub structure of UK GRAD with regard to the development and delivery of research training. This follows other regional developments – for example, the White Rose Consortium between the Universities of Leeds, York and Sheffield and the joint research studentships offered by Sheffield University and Sheffield Hallam University.

It seems that as the QAA puts pressure on universities to provide a well-developed research environment (see the revised Code of Practice for Postgraduate Research Programmes; QAA 2004), so our graduate schools may begin to think more creatively, working at discipline level across universities in discipline-based graduate schools. If the reluctance of universities to work together in a formal sense is a result of a belief that RAE funding mechanisms do not encourage it, then this will be a major challenge for the future. Disciplinary collaboration across universities is not unknown, however, and there have been isolated schemes in the past, such as the Scottish Graduate Programme in Economics supported by the ESRC involving the Universities of Aberdeen, Dundee, Edinburgh, Glasgow, St Andrews, Stirling and Strathclyde and Heriot-Watt University. The European Doctorate discussed earlier also offers possibilities in this field.

Models of collaboration from overseas

Organizationally it would not take a great deal to develop discipline-based graduate schools following the Finnish model where there are now two, the National Graduate School in Materials Physics (NGSMP) and the East Finland Graduate School in Computer Science and Engineering (ECSE).

The NGSMP is part of the new graduate school (doctoral) system launched in Finland in January 1995. The aim of the system is to co-ordinate and organize research training at the Finnish universities. At present, the NGSMP has about 120 postgraduate students enrolled. The School organizes postgraduate courses and workshops, invites international lecturers and supports conference participation of its students.

The ECSE was established in 1992 by the three universities located in eastern Finland: University of Joensuu, University of Kuopio and Lappeenranta University of Technology. The ECSE co-ordinates the post-graduate studies in computer science of the departments and laboratories of these three founding universities. The graduate school is co-ordinated by Lappeenranta University of Technology, and it has a Director, School Board and a Secretary. It organizes graduate level courses for all students studying in the universities. The goal of the ECSE is to produce doctors of philosophy and doctors of technology within the areas of expertise of the school. These areas include adaptive and intelligent systems, software engineering, education technology and data communications. Similar collaborative structures are found in Sweden. We note that typically this approach is found in small countries where critical mass is more difficult to establish within a discipline area(s) in a single university. It also appears to be the case that in the examples given here national governments are more closely involved with the activities of individual universities. As the regional agenda develops and the challenges of concentration and selectivity increase, this is one model which the UK regions might care to examine.

Many institutions are now developing what we might refer to as split PhD programmes in which the delivery of individual programmes is shared between two institutions. This model is frequently used in the case of overseas students, particularly members of academic staff, where the costs of three years' residence in the UK and the staff absence is a barrier to study. Typical models involve an initial period of study of up to a year in the UK in which the programme of work is developed and associated training courses are undertaken, followed by a period at the home institution. The final period, culminating in writing-up and examination, is normally spent in the UK.

The model is particularly attractive in overseas institutions' development programmes as it both reduces costs and offers the originating institution the opportunity to engage in research supervision and build additional supervisory capacity.

Examinations: getting it right

We noted earlier in this book that there is significant variation in processes of doctoral examination across the UK sector and we asked if there should be a greater drive for standardization. We have also argued elsewhere that diversity is not necessarily *per se* problematic. However, in the case of the examination process, it does seem that there need to be some principles underpinning the way in which universities operate their examination processes at doctoral level. These principles need to relate (i) to the purpose of the examination, (ii) to the candidate's need to defend his/her thesis and (iii) to the university's need to uphold its standards. Much of this is revisited in the framework with which we end this chapter, but here we comment briefly on each of these needs in turn.

First, the sole purpose of the examination is to enable judgement to be made on the question of whether or not the candidate has produced satisfactory evidence to demonstrate that the criteria for the award have been met. Examiners who take it upon themselves to extend this brief in any way are at fault. For example, it is not for examiners to pursue personal hobbyhorses by way of research directions or in terms of what they think a doctoral candidate should be able to do. They are employed by the host university to measure the candidate's achievement against its published criteria.

Second, the format of the examination needs to be such that the candidate is given every opportunity to demonstrate that he/she has met the criteria. Anything that diminishes this opportunity needs to be eliminated from the process. For example, questions need to be prepared and structured by the examination panel prior to the oral examination and need to be based on a careful reading of the thesis in advance of the examination all to enable the candidate to demonstrate as suggested above. It follows from this that examiners need to be given the thesis in time for the required reading and need to be allocated time to meet as a team prior to the *viva voce*. All of this, of course, is a typical part of the process and is underwritten in the revised QAA Code of Practice. Our point here is to stress that the procedures need to be driven by the need of the candidate to demonstrate in the way described above. Therefore, if a practical illustration of particular research procedures is necessary for that need to be met, then the examination process would have to accommodate it.

Third, each university needs to be assured that doctoral awards are made only when the candidate has demonstrated that the criteria for the award have been met. It also needs to assure that those criteria relate to a level that is comparable with the sector as a whole. There is a level of international acceptance that requires this presence of an examiner from outside of the awarding institution. With reference to the former point, we note that the use of an independent chairperson to oversee the examination process is a device recommended in the revised QAA Code of Practice. However, there is no evidence available that indicates that the presence of such a chairperson will assure proper awarding of the degrees, though we would agree it may be helpful in this respect. What the recommendation in the Code illustrates is the uncertainty across the sector that fair play is being done within current regulations and common practices. In our view what is important here is the role that the chairperson is supposed to play. The chairperson is an indicator of the way in which the 'behind closed doors' approach that has been commonplace in the UK is increasingly coming under critical scrutiny. We argue at the end of this chapter that transparency of the whole examination process is the key to quality assurance. In our view, the use of an independent chair is merely a step towards a more open, public process.

In consideration of the three points made above, it is clear that the prime task of institutions is to look to the criteria that they have set against the doctoral level of award and focus their attention on the way in which their guidance to examiners (both internal and external) matches up with those criteria.

Of course, all of the above will remain wishful thinking unless institutions can ensure that candidates are adequately prepared and that internal and external examiners approach the task with both rigour and independence. Preparing candidates can be a legitimate part of doctoral training; ensuring the approach of examiners is a more complex matter. Some universities now offer training courses for internal examiners (though these are often not mandatory) but the vast majority of universities make no claim to 'train' external examiners and no national programmes are available beyond some one-off workshops run by organizations such as the UK Council for Graduate Education. We suggest that there is a need for national guidelines for external examiners at least and recognized training programmes at best. At present examiners may have subject expertise but experience of doctoral examining is gained in an unsupervised, *ad hoc*, way 'on the job' and this can have dire consequences for the candidate who is effectively the object of the unsupervised 'experience gaining'. Internal examiners should be offered training in the same way as has become commonplace for supervisors.

In summary, doctoral examination in the UK is often an anachronistic process bedevilled by the idiosyncratic approaches of individual academics operating in closed environments that are deliberately opaque under procedures that are rule-bound but lack a clear sense of purpose. The case for reform is clear.

Diversity

Diversity has been a recurrent theme in the book – whether that is diversity of student, of what universities offer, of procedures or of the award itself. In our view such diversities are to be encouraged rather than prohibited but we also suggest that they need to be both purposeful and appropriate. The danger is that some dimensions of diversity have arisen in an *ad hoc* way and are inappropriate in terms of the purposes of the award and the functions that universities and individual students serve in respect of it. By way of exemplar, we take the award and the student and suggest that diversity needs to take a different trajectory for each.

Our discussion of the Doctorate has painted a picture of diversity at the level of the award itself – its structure and purpose, its delivery, and the individual regulatory structures that universities individually adopt to manage it. While this may have been an acceptable position when numbers of doctoral awards were very small and the soubriquet 'cottage industry' could be applied, it can no longer be a satisfactory position when numbers are growing, the international market in particular is expanding and the importance to the UK's research base is becoming more evident. It is no longer possible to speak of the UK Doctorate as an award, distinctive among the international academic community. The different kinds of Doctorate available in the UK and the connectedness of some of them, in fact or in kind, to the other parts of Europe and to the USA mean that what was once unique to these shores is now one within a range of examples of the same kind of award. In our own view this is no bad thing; what is important, however, is that doctoral study within the UK can continue to be regarded as of an appropriate doctoral standard and that its various manifestations can be seen as reasoned and appropriate to purpose (not merely idiosyncratic, *ad hoc* and disconnected from purpose). It also needs to offer value for money: that is funders need to feel satisfied that money outlaid recoups an appropriate level of return in terms of doctoral level workers.

Equally, when we look at the approach taken at an institutional level to deliver this diversity of doctoral study we find significant variability across the sector in almost every aspect. Perhaps the only exception to this case is in the post-1992 universities where in most but not all cases, structures still reflect the frameworks imposed by the erstwhile Council for National Academic Awards (CNAA). Here it may seem that diversity is non-problematic – after all, allowing individual universities to develop their own practices within a common frame is likely to allow accommodation to different local needs and constraints and to encourage ownership, and hence greater understanding, of own practices. Indeed, it may be argued that those post-1992 institutions that have not moved far from the strictures of CNAA regulations have not acted strongly enough to accept fully the challenge of the changing climate of doctoral study. We suggest that regulatory frameworks within universities that have remain ossified since 1992 may now not be adequate to the task.

Whatever the case with regard to the after-effects of CNAA regulations, we need to return to the question of what kind of diversity is desirable in respect of within institutional management and control of the doctoral process. Certainly, students need to know what they are undertaking at the outset of their studies (and they need to have this understanding reinforced during those studies). Currently it is unlikely that many appreciate the differences between universities. At a simple level, we suggest that not many will be aware that at University A they as students retain the intellectual property rights from the project and that at University B they do not. Similarly, many will not fully appreciate the implications for them of 'transferring' registration from MPhil to PhD (variously referred to as: transfer, upgrade or progression) nor will they fully appreciate the weightings that may be applied to the typical components within the examination process. Such issues are well beyond the more procedural requirements of the revised QAA Code of Practice and do little to help in our concern for diversity. Equally, employers need to be aware that there are significant differences in the successful doctoral candidates that they may employ. It might be assumed that this would be less of a problem for academic employers who understand the nuances of these differences, though we would argue that even here there is a fundamental lack of appreciation of the significance of some aspects of this variability. Academic colleagues attending workshops and seminars commonly express understandings of aspects of doctoral processes as if they were common 'givens', whereas they are in fact ways of behaving that are specific to the individual's university. For example, we may assert that examiners' preliminary reports are always confidential (when some institutions routinely make them available to candidates and supervisors), or that Professional Doctorates are synonymous with Taught Doctorates (whereas some Professional Doctorates have very little or no 'taught' content).

A consistent framework for the doctoral award

It is not difficult to see how this problem has arisen. As we have seen in earlier chapters, the various demands made on the Doctorate through time have led to adjustments at the margins. The pressures for generic training, the demands of longer programmes, the apparently differing requirements of the professions and of the arts and humanities and the emergence of new research areas, have all led to the invention of new routes to a doctoral level of achievement. We would argue that it is time to draw a line under the Doctorate and ask what it is, rather than (a) redefining it according to ever-shifting notions of the audience it is attempting to satisfy or (b) leaving it to atrophy in insular understandings of its nature that relate to individual institutional practices. In this spirit we suggest some common themes that may allow us to establish a consistent framework for *all* doctoral study.

- *Contribution to an area of research*   The doctoral award is based on individual or group research that makes a contribution to thinking and/or to practice in the area of the research (we have used 'thinking' here to encompass knowledge and skills). Clearly, the assessment process needs to take account of the need for a level of contribution that is significant enough for the award to be made. But significance may be a discipline-specific notion. What is common across all doctoral study is that there needs to be a contribution to the area concerned, which means that the area is better informed, after the making public of the thesis, than it was before.
- *Viability and accessibility of the contribution*   The contribution must be in a form that is viable enough to be sustained over a period of time and readily accessible to others in the field. Lack of such viability and accessibility would deny the purpose of 'contribution' in that others cannot make use of the new understandings. The implication here is that theses should never be kept confidential; in our view, to do is to deny the key purpose of doctoral study. The only exception to this would be a limited embargo on information within the submission in order to protect commercial sensitivity such as a patent pending. Confidentiality should never be used as an alternative to legitimate ways of anonymizing data within a research report to protect participants. Where such legitimate anonymizing is deemed not possible, then the research should not be acceptable for a research degree award.

- *Professional and academic knowledge*   The area within which the programme of study is based may be professional or academic. The precedence that academia has perpetuated in terms of bestowing exclusionary status on academic knowledge is no longer sustainable. Understandings needed to advance the professions and knowledge within non-traditional, practice-based areas are equally valid where it can be determined that the basic criteria for what counts as 'knowledge' can be met. Again, the notion of what is a significant enough contribution to warrant a doctoral award may differ across areas other than the traditionally 'academic', but never-theless contribution in the terms of the specific area is what is required. 'Understanding' may be of the skills required to further progress in the field or indeed of ways of teaching those skills effectively to practitioners.

- *Differing nomenclature and commonality of level*   In our view there is strong argument for using the title of PhD (with no elaboration) for all doctoral awards regardless of the discipline or profession in which they are awarded. However, given the pragmatic need to denote the area in which the studies have fallen for the sake of marketing and for professional status reasons, then it seems to us reasonable to use titles such as EdD and DClinPsy. Nomenclature in this sense is, for us, not the prime issue. What is of import, however, is the way in which institutions treat these differing awards in terms of their quality control and general organization. We suggest that all doctoral awards should be treated in these respects as being of a kind. Criteria for the awards will differ (otherwise why should there be a different nomenclature at all?) but they should only differ within parameters. All Doctorates have to make a contribution to a field though the fields in themselves will be disparate, as will the way in which that contribution is made manifest (and is evidenced, as noted below). In pragmatic terms, then, the range of Doctorates on offer within a university should be described within a common frame, organized within a common committee structure and awarded on the basis of criteria that can be readily compared and which are thus transparently of a level. Similarly, the way in which step-off awards are used must have some commonality across the different doctoral awards (for example, if the MPhil can be used as a step-off award after two years of study on a PhD programme, then there would need to be a clear justification for it *not* similarly being available after two years of an EdD programme). Separating out some doctoral awards for different treatment in any of these respects seems to us potentially to diminish them.

- *The place of published work as evidence in doctoral submissions*   The notion that there should be a separate form of doctorate that can be described as a 'PhD by Published Work' is anachronistic when much of the rest of northern Europe works within a model where theses comprise previously published works and when many UK universities include within their doc-toral criteria that the thesis should contain material of 'publishable qual-ity'. Universities offering the separate award to a limited group (e.g. staff and alumni) are at risk of accusations of insularity at best, and of giving preferential treatment at worst. UK universities might usefully reconsider their regulatory frameworks and seek ways of breaking down the barriers between these two separate awards and treat published and non-published work (the latter being work not published but judged to be of 'publishable quality') as parts of the same continuum. Where the criteria for an award can be met, then prior publication of part or all of the evidence that was used to demonstrate that those criteria have been met is not of concern. Students enrol and are supervised with the aim of helping them to establish an intellectual position and defend it with appropriate evidence. Whether that evidence is wholly or partially published is not the issue. The published papers approach to submission should become an acceptable form of submission within the overall concept of a UK PhD rather than a discrete form of Doctorate. What is required is flexibility in regulations to enable candidates to bring a range of kinds of evidence to bear on their intellectual position – previously published or not.

- *A doctoral award signifying doctoral level* Examination at doctoral level should be solely a matter of judging whether or not the candidate has produced enough evidence in his/her thesis to meet the criteria set down for the award. In this sense there can be no interim assessments that contribute to the final award, though, of course, there might be assessments that permit progression through phases of study. Basically, one cannot have someone with part doctoral qualifications; it is essentially an all-or-nothing award. Similarly, there cannot be a mark of distinction within the category of doctoral award. The award is one of excellence and there cannot be gradations of this quality. The contradiction in terms that arises when an institution awards a Doctorate with distinction (a Doctorate *is* a distinction) gives rise to the equally implausible notion of a Doctorate without distinction – a second-rate order of excellence. One cannot have someone working in academia or the professions as a doctor but also as a 'lesser doctor' than a colleague. That is not to say, of course, that all colleagues will be equal in ability but rather that the award equates to a level; once a candidate has reached the level it does not matter how far above it he/she was, because the criterion is solely to demonstrate it has been reached. Medical degrees offer a useful comparator here. A candidate has to produce a thesis – his/her intellectual position – that must then be defended in an oral context. The thesis and its defence must contribute to knowledge in the senses described above and following from this there cannot be a partial contribution.

- *Transparency of the oral examination* The oral examination itself is solely the context in which the examiners can test out the contribution to knowledge made in the thesis and the candidate's ability to understand it within the broader intellectual context and defend it. It is not a rite of passage or an opportunity to test the candidate on anything that is not included in the criteria for the award; nor is it an opportunity to set the scene for a final, fine-tuning of the literary presentation of the submission or the reworking of some parts of the research. The testing out that we note above is best done in as public a forum as possible. Conducting the examination behind closed doors with rigorous restrictions on who may attend and how the attendees may contribute to the examination is counter-productive to its sole aim. Making the oral examination an openly public event will lead to transparency of process and hence is more likely to be both fair and rigorous. Such an approach also aids the general dissemination of research findings – which, as we have already noted, is a key purpose of doctoral study.

• *Doctoral learning and skills* Learning to operate at doctoral level within an intellectual discipline is, in part at least, a matter of learning to learn about that discipline by practising appropriate research methods and techniques within it. Learning from one's own practice in this way is an ongoing pattern of behaviour that those operating at doctoral level will necessarily continue to develop (i.e. it is an irrevocable part of being a doctor). The criteria for a doctoral award therefore need to address this kind of learning and candidates must then demonstrate their ability in this respect both in their written submission and in their defence of their theses. It is relatively straightforward to define subject-specific skills in respect of research methods and techniques, but it is less so in the case of more generic skills. Discussion about how best to develop generic skills is premature if the relationship between them and doctoral level remains unclear. A generic skill may be worth having but it is not necessarily a part of doctoral study unless it can demonstrably be related to how an individual may be seen to operate at a doctoral level within the relevant discipline. If the skill is not reflected in the criteria for the award, then it should not be part of a programme of study and it should not be part of the doctoral assessment. On the other hand, if it is part of the criteria then it should be part of the programme and of the final assessment. We are suggesting here that much of what is subsumed under the collective term 'generic skills' is not in fact a necessary part of the concept of doctoral level and therefore should not be part of the process of doctoral study. In short, generic training programmes have become, in part at least, a device for making up for inadequacies in earlier parts of the educational process. What is required, however, is a more rigorous analysis of which generic skills *are* part of the doctoral level. Is it reasonable, for example, to suggest that anyone laying claim to a doctoral title ought to be able to communicate their ideas in both written and oral form and engage with others from other disciplines in this way? Following from this it becomes a matter of embedding those skills in the criteria for the award and in turn of finding ways of assessing the candidate's ability to demonstrate them within the final examination. We suggest that neither of these steps is impossible or implausible – but current practices typified by allocating so many hours of study to generic training without considering the above are necessarily flawed. The sector needs to return to the basic notions of level of award, defined by criteria and assessed against them.

• *A supervised award* Doctoral study has traditionally involved a supervisor who guides the student through his/her research project(s). However, the role of that supervisor has never been clearly defined and has varied according to discipline and sometimes the institution. The role may be unique in higher education in as much as it involves teaching someone towards a goal within a defined intellectual field that once achieved necessarily changes that field (and potentially has knock-on effects on other related fields). The supervisor starts out leading the student in a direction (and here the supervisor needs both experience and expertise to ensure that the trajectory is reasonable in research terms and in relation to the criteria for the award) but it is the student who then needs to demonstrate to that supervisor something that the supervisor did not know at the start of the project. The leader becomes the led; the pupil becomes the master. This seems to us to be the major challenge for supervisors and indeed needs to be the main focus for those who train them. In a sense it is independent of changes in the marketplace – except perhaps that the pace of change and the growth of new knowledge is for ever increasing. The complexity of research and of the task of supervising requires teams rather than individual supervisors – but roles within teams must be transparent.

- *The form and media of doctoral evidence*   The achievement of a doctoral award is a matter of providing satisfactory evidence to demonstrate that the criteria for that award have been met. We would suggest that the outcomes of the research will be evidenced in a form and media most appropriate to the subject under consideration. In short, all Doctorates should involve the development of an intellectual argument that pushes the boundaries of knowledge but the evidence that this argument draws upon will vary according to discipline. Therefore, while all doctoral candidates need to be able to establish an intellectual position and argue from it, the kinds of evidence they use to support their argument and the way in which they argue may involve words, formulae, artefacts, actions and may be cast as hypotheses and/or interpretive, non-deductive analyses and so on. What is important is that kind of research question is appropriately matched by kind of analysis and kind of form and medium of evidence. The candidate needs to employ the appropriate questions, analyses and evidential media and, importantly, know why what he/she employs in these senses is appropriate. Following from the above, in our view, questions over the form of submission, i.e. traditional thesis or portfolio, are misleading. What is important is that the candidate marshals evidence to defend his/her position – if a portfolio is an appropriate way of presenting evidence then it must be acceptable. It is for the candidate ultimately to choose, and subsequently of course defend, the mode of presentation of evidence.

It is clear that the outcomes of the research will need to be assessed in a way most appropriate to the specific subject and the content of the period of research – i.e. the process as well as the outcomes must come under scrutiny.

- *What counts as a Doctorate.* In seminars and workshops the claim is sometimes made that there is no common definition of a Doctorate. This is not entirely the case. While it is true that there may be differing interpretations among individual academics, there is in fact clear guidance on the matter at national level in the UK. The level of doctoral outcomes must relate to the national guidelines as set out in the Framework for Higher Education Qualifications (FHEQ). There it is stated:

  > *Doctorates are awarded for the creation and interpretation of knowledge, which extends the forefront of a discipline, usually through original research. Holders of doctorates will be able to conceptualize, design and implement projects for the generation of significant new knowledge and/or understanding.*

  > (QAA 2001)

Conclusion

In this book we have tried to set down observations about the Doctorate as it exists currently in the UK and we have offered some analyses of current issues. In a sense this is non-problematic when no subsequent action is required. However, following our attempts to better understand the current position of the Doctorate, particularly in the UK higher education system, we are left uneasy about the underpinning of its status and therefore concerned for its future. Such unease may be unwarranted – the doctoral award has changed over time, as we have tried to illustrate, and clearly it will change further as the sector moves forward. But it is not clear to us that the issues facing the award (and however one wishes to argues the detail, it does seem indisputable that issues of significance do exist) are to be addressed in a coherent, unifying way. The Arts and Humanities Research Board (AHRB) is embarking on a review of the Doctorate (the survey is being undertaken by the Institute of Education, University of London for the AHRB concerning 'the UK Doctorate in the Arts and Humanities'[4] as we complete the writing of this book. We have no quarrel with this initiative; indeed it is in many ways laudable, but it is yet another example of the piecemeal way in which the development of the Doctorate has come to be typified. AHRB is necessarily taking a parochial view of the topic – a view that may be restricted to the Doctorate within arts and humanities. We do not suggest that this will cause irrevocable harm but rather that what is really required is a strategically oriented, review of doctoral awards across the piece. We question what body is able and willing to undertake such a review in the current climate, but we suggest that this is what is required if the UK is to retain a system of doctoral education that can sustain its position in the increasingly competitive international context. Other countries are facing a similar dilemma and we need in the first instance to look at the models of review they are adopting.

---

[4] www.ioe-ahrb-doctorate.org.

References

Academy of Finland (2003) *PhDs in Finland: Employment, Placement and Demand.* Publications of the Academy of Finland, 5/03, Helsinki.

Ahola, S. and Kivinen, O. (2001) Postgraduate education in Europe. Harmonising with a dissonance. Paper presented at the *Conference on Postgraduate Education in Europe – Past, present and future.* University of Linköing, Sweden, May 2001.

AHRB (2001) *Guide to the Fellowships in the Creative and Performing Arts Scheme.* Arts and Humanities Research Board, London.

AHRB (2004) *Guidance of the Research Training Framework.* Arts and Humanities Research Board, London.

Available on: www.ahrb.ac.uk. Accessed 10/08/04.

AHRB (undated) *Doctoral Awards Scheme.* Arts and Humanities Research Board, London.

Available on: www.ahrb.ac.uk/apply/postgrad/doctoral_awards_scheme.asp. Accessed 21/01/05.

Allen, C., Smyth, E. and Wahlstrom, M. (2002) Responding to the field and to the academy: Ontario's evolving PhD. *Higher Education Research and Development,* 21(2): 203–14.

Allen, S. (2003) Unpublished survey: *Writing Up Fees.* Leeds Metropolitan University.

Becher, T., Henkel, M. and Kogan, M. (1994) *Graduate Education in Britain.* Jessica Kingsley, London.

Berelson, B. (1960) *Graduate Education in the United States.* McGraw-Hill, New York.

Berkovitz, P. (2003) The long haul. *University Affairs,* pp. 8–12.

Biggs, M. (2002) The role of artefact in art and design research. *International Journal of Design Sciences and Technology,* 10(2): 19–24.

Blume, S. and Amsterdamska, O. (1987) *Postgraduate Education in the 1980s* (OECD, Paris). Canadian evidence.

Bolton, G. (2001) *Reflective Practice: Writing and Professional Development.* Paul Chapman, London.

Booth, A.L. and Satchell, S.E. (1995) The hazards of doing a PhD – An analysis of completion and withdrawal rates of British PhD students in the 1980s. *Journal of the Royal Statistical Society Series A – Statistics in Society,* 158: 297–318.

Bourner, T., Bowden, R. and Laing, S. (1999) A national profile of research degree awards: Innovation, clarity and coherence. *Higher Education Quarterly,* 53(3): 264–80.

Bourner, T., Bowden, R. and Laing, S. (2001a) Professional doctorates in England. *Studies in Higher Education*, 26(1): 65–83.

Bourner, T., Bowden, R. and Laing, S. (2001b) The adoption of professional doctorates in English universities: why here? why now? In B. Green, T. Maxwell and P. Shanahan (eds) *Doctoral Education and Professional Practice: The Next Generation?* Armidale, Australia: Kardoorair Press, pp. 39–68.

Bowen, H.R. and Schuster, J.H. (1986) *American Professors: A National Resource Imperilled.* Oxford University Press, New York.

Bowen, W.G. and Rudenstine, N.L. (1992) *In Pursuit of the PhD.* Princeton University Press, Princeton, NJ.

BPS/UCoSDA (1995) *Guidelines for Assessment of the PhD in Psychology and Related Disciplines.* Universities and Colleges' Staff Development Unit, Sheffield.

Brignall, M. (2002) Why a PhD will enrich your life as well as your career. *The Guardian*, Saturday, 6 April 2002.

British Academy (2001) *Review of Graduate Studies in the Humanities and Social Sciences.* Main report. British Academy, London.

Brown, G. and Atkins, M. (1988) *Effective Teaching in Higher Education.* Routledge, London.

Brown, K. (2002) *Inquiry into the Fee for PhD External Examiners in Modern Universities.* Modern University Research Group.
Available on: www.cwis.livjm.ac.uk/research_and_graduate/MURG/fees.doc. Accessed 20/01/05.

Brown, K. (2003) *La soutenance de thèse en France.* Unpublished report. Leeds Metropolitan University.

Burgess, R.G. (ed.) (1997) *Beyond the First Degree: Graduate Education, Lifelong Learning and Careers.* The Society for Research in Higher Education and Open University Press.

Burgess, R.G., Pole, C.J. and Hockey, J. (1994) Strategies for managing and supervising the social science PhD. In R.G. Burgess (ed.) *Postgraduate Education and Training in the Social Sciences: Processes and Products.* Jessica Kingsley, London.

CAGS (2003) *The Completion of Graduate Studies in Canadian Universities:* Report and recommendations. Canadian Association of Graduate Schools, Ottawa.

Career Development Loans (2004).
Available on: www.lifelonglearning.co.uk/cdl. Accessed 5/01/04.

CBI (1994) *OST Consultation Paper on Postgraduate Training: A Response from the CBI.* Confederation of British Industry, London.

Charbonneau, L. (2003) Councils scramble to implement new graduate scholarships. *Affaires Universitaires*, June/July.

Clegg, S. and Green, H. (1995) Training and accreditation of research award supervisors. *Proceedings of Research Student Supervision: Management and Practice. Journal of Graduate Education.* National Postgraduate Committee, Troon, pp. 14–17.

CMRST (1968) *Manpower Resources for Science and Technology: Flow into Employment of Scientists, Engineers and Technologists, 1967–68.* Cmnd 3760. Committee on Manpower Resources for Science and Technology, London.

CMRST (1996) *Interim Report of the Working Group on Manpower Parameters for Scientific Growth.* Cmnd 3102. Committee on Manpower Resources for Science and Technology, London.

Conlon, G. and Chevalier, A. (2002) *Rates of Return to Qualifications: A Summary of Recent Evidence.* Council for Industry and Higher Education (CIHE), London.

Connor, H., Court, G., Seccombe, I. and Jagger, N. (1994) *Science PhDs and the Labour Market*. Institute of Manpower Studies, Report 266, Sussex.

Conrad, L., Perry, C. and Zubert-Skerritt, O. (1992) Alternatives to traditional postgraduate supervision in the social sciences. In O. Zubert-Skerritt, O. (ed.) *Starting Research Supervision and Training*. The Tertiary Education Institute, Brisbane.

Coyle, S.L. and Thurgood, D.H. (1989) *Summary Report 1987. Doctoral Recipients from United States Universities*. National Academy Press, Washington.

Cryer, P. (1995) Training supervisors and research students through self-study booklets developed and customised for the research students. *Proceedings of Research Student Supervision: Management and Practice. Journal of Graduate Education*, National Postgraduate Committee, Troon, pp. 18–22.

Cryer, P. (1996) *The Research Student's Guide to Success*. Open University Press, Buckingham.

Cryer, P. (1997) *Handling Common Dilemmas in Supervision*. Issues in Postgraduate Supervision, Teaching and Management, Guide No. 2. Society for Research into Higher Education and the Times Higher Education Supplement, London.

Cryer, P. (ed.) (1998) *Developing Postgraduates' Key Skills*. SRHE Issues in Postgraduate Supervision, Teaching and Management, No. 3, Society for Research into Higher Education, London.

CUDAH (2002) *Doctoral Futures. Career Destinations of Arts and Humanities Research Students*. Council of University Deans of Arts and Humanities.

CVCP (1992) CVCP/CDP *Code of Recommended Practice: The Management of Higher Degrees Undertaken by Overseas Students*. Committee of Vice-Chancellors and Principals, Tavistock Square, London.

CVCP (1993) *Handbook for External Examiners in Higher Education*. UK Universities Staff Development Unit, Sheffield.

Daniels, B. and Akehurst, G. (1995) Training researchers: A multi-disciplinary approach. *Proceedings of Research Student Supervision: Management and Practice. Journal of Graduate Education*, National Postgraduate Committee, Troon, pp. 24–32.

Darwen, J. *et al.* (2002) *National Survey of Postgraduate Funding and Priorities*. Final report Summer 2002. National Postgraduate Committee, Troon.

Davies, L.W. (1992) Federal policies for industries and development in Australia. *Search*, 3: 423–6.

Dearing, R. (1997) *Higher Education in the Learning Society*. National Committee of Inquiry into Higher Education, London.

Deem, R. and Brehony, K.J. (2000) Doctoral students' access to research cultures – are some more equal than others? *Studies in Higher Education*, 25(2): 149–65.

Delamont, S., Atkinson, P. and Parry, O. (1997) *Supervising the PhD: A Guide to Success*. Open University Press, Buckingham.

Delamont, S., Parry, O. and Atkinson, P. (1998) Creating a delicate balance: The doctoral supervisor's dilemmas. *Teaching in Higher Education*, 3: 157.

Delamont, S., Atkinson, P. and Parry, O. (2000) *The Doctoral Experience: Success and Failure in Graduate School*. Falmer Press, London.

Demers, P. and Rashmi, D. (2002) *Brave New Worlds. Graduate Education for the 21st Century*. Canadian Association for Graduate Studies, Ottawa, Canada.

DfES (2003) *The Future of Higher Education*. White Paper. Cm 5735. Department for Education and Skills, London.

DTI (1993) *Realising our Potential: A Strategy for Science, Engineering and Technology*. Cmnd 2250. White Paper. HMSO, London.

DTI (2000) *The Science Budget 2001–02 and 2003–04*. HMSO, London.

DTZ Pieda Consulting (2003a) *A Study of the Career Paths of PPARC PhD Students*. A final report. DTZ Pieda Consulting, Reading.

DTZ Pieda Consulting (2003b) *A Fifteen Year Longitudinal Career Path Study of PPARC PhD Students*. A final report. DTZ Pieda Consulting, Reading.

Durling, D. and Friedman, K. (2002) *Foundations for the Future – Doctoral Education in Design*. Staffordshire University Press, Stoke on Trent.

Durling, D., Friedman, K. and Gutherson, P. (2002) Debating the practice-based PhD. *International Journal of Design Sciences and Technology*, 10(2): 7–18.

Elton, L. *et al.* (1994) *Staff Development in Relation to Research*. The UK Universities' Staff Development Unit, Occasional Green Paper No. 6. USDU, Sheffield.

EPSRC (1999) *Flexible Support for Doctoral-Level Training*. Engineering and Physical Sciences Research Council, Swindon, pp. 34–99.

EPSRC (2002) *Doctoral Training Accounts Report on the Consultation of the First Year of Operation*. Engineering and Physical Sciences Research Council, Swindon.

ESRC (1991) *Postgraduate Training: Guidelines on the Provision of Research Training for Postgraduate Research Students in the Social Sciences*. Economic and Social Research Council, Swindon.

ESRC (2001) *Postgraduate Training Guidelines*, 3rd edn. Economic and Social Research Council, Swindon.
Available on: www.esrc.ac.uk. Accessed 12/11/04.

EUA (2004) *Doctoral Programmes Project*.
Available on: www.eua.be/eua/en/Doctorates.jspx. Accessed 15/12/04.

European Commission (2003) *European Research Area, More Research for Europe – Towards 3% of the GDP*. European Commission, Brussels.

Fallows, S. (1995) Support for research students and their supervisors. *Journal of Graduate Education*. National Postgraduate Committee, Troon, pp. 40–47.

Frame, I.A. and Allen, L. (2002) A flexible approach to PhD research training. *Quality Assurance in Education, Standards and the Doctoral Award*, 10(2): 98–103.

Frayling, C. (1993) Research in art and design. *Royal College of Art Research Papers*, 1(1). Royal College of Art, London.

Frayling, C. (1998) Practice-based doctorates in the creative and performing arts. *UK Council for Graduate Education Newsletter*, Issue 17, p. 2. UKCGE, Lichfield.

Foucault, M. (1974a) *The Order of Things*. Tavistock Press, London.

Foucault, M. (1974b) *The Archaeology of Knowledge*. Tavistock Press, London.

Garrick, R. (1996) *The National Committee of Inquiry into Higher Education*. Report of The Scottish Committee.
Available on: www.leeds.ac.uk/educol/ncihe/. Accessed 01/09/04.

Gerson, M. (1989) Shortage of PhDs is foreseen for universities. *Chronicle of Higher Education*, 3 May.

Golde, C. (2000) Should I stay or should I go? Student descriptions of the doctoral attrition process. *The Review of Higher Education*, 23(2): 199–227.

Golde, C.M. and Dore, T.M. (2001) *At Cross Purposes: What the Experiences of Today's Doctoral Students reveal about Doctoral Education*.
Available on: www.phd-survey.org. Accessed 20/01/05.

Goldman, C.A. and Massy, W. (2000) *The PhD Factory: Training and Employment of Science and Engineering Doctorates in the United States*. Anker Publishing Company, Bolton, MA.

Green, D.H. (2004) Supervisors: Good, bad or indifferent. *UK Council for Graduate Education Newsletter*, Issue 47, October 2004.

Green, D.H. and Powell, S.D. (2004) The high price of good quality. *The Independent Education*, 13 October.

Green, D.H., Shaw, M. and Hammill, F. (2001) W(h)ither the MRes? *Quality Assurance in Education*, 9(4): 178–83.

Harris, M. (1996) *Review of Postgraduate Education*. Higher Education Funding Council for England, Committee of Vice-Chancellors and Principals Standing Conference of Principals HEFCE, ref: M14/.

Hartley, J. and Fox, C. (2002) The Viva Experience: Examining the examiners. *Higher Education Review*, 35(1): 24–30.

Hartley, J. and Fox, C. (2004) Assessing the Mock Viva: The experiences of British doctoral students. *Studies in Higher Education* (in press).

Hartley, J. and Jory, S. (2000) Lifting the veil on the viva: The experiences of psychology PhD candidates in the UK. *Psychology Teaching Review*, 9(2): 76–90.

HEFCW (2001) *Credit and Qualifications Framework for Wales*. Higher Education Council for Wales.
    Available on: www.elwa.ac.uk/elwaweb/elwa.aspx?pageid=1612. Accessed 20/01/05.

HEFCE (1999) *Research Assessment Exercise 2001: Guidance on Submissions RAE 2/99*. Higher Education Funding Council of England, London.

HEFCE (2000a) *Review of Research, Consultation*. Higher Education Funding Council for England, London, 00/37.
    Available on: www.hefce.ac.uk/pubs/hefce/2000/00_37all.htm. Accessed 12/09/04.

HEFCE (2000b) *Key Findings, No. 28*. Higher Education Funding Council for England, London.
    Available on: www.hefce/pubs/hefce/2000/00_37all.htm. Accessed 20/01/05.

HEFCE (2001) *Review of Research: Report on Consultation*. Higher Education Funding Council for England, London, 01/17.
    Available on: www.hefce.ac.uk/pubs/hefce/2001/01_17.htm. Accessed 12/09/04.

HEFCE (2002) *Overseas Research, Students Awards Scheme. Consultation*. Higher Education Funding Council of England, London, 02/16.

HEFCE (2003a) *Improving Standards in Postgraduate Research Degree Programmes, Informal Consultation*. Higher Education Funding Council of England, London, 2003/01.

HEFCE (2003b) *Improving Standards in Postgraduate Research Degree Programmes. Formal Consultation*. Higher Education Funding Council of England, London, 2003/23.

HEFCE (2003c) *Performance Indicators in Higher Education*. Higher Education Funding Council of England. Available on www.hefce.ac.uk/pubs/hefce/2003.

HEFCE (2004) *Funding for Research Degree Programmes (RDPs)*. Higher Education Funding Council of England, London.
    Available on: www.hefce.ac.uk/research/postgrad/rdpfund.htm. Accessed 20/01/05.

HEFCE (2005) *PhD Research Degrees: Entry and Completion*. Higher Education Funding Council for England, London, 2005/2.
    Available on: www.hefce.ac.uk. Accessed 12/01/05.

HEQC (1996) *Guidelines for the Quality Assurance of Research Degrees*. Higher Education Quality Council, Cheltenham.

HESA (2001) *Students in Higher Education Institutions, 1999/2000*. Higher Education Statistics Agency, Cheltenham.

HESA (2002) *Resources of Higher Education Institutions, 2000/2001*. Higher Education Statistics Agency, Cheltenham.

HESA (2003) *First Destinations of Students Leaving Higher Education Institutions, 2001/02.* Higher Education Statistics Agency, Cheltenham.

HESA (2004a) *Students in Higher Education Institutions, 2002/03.* Higher Education Statistics Agency, Cheltenham.

HESA (2004b) *Individualised Staff Record, 2003–04.* Higher Education Statistics Agency, Cheltenham.

Hinde, J. (1999) Science fails to fill PhDs. *Times Higher Educational Supplement,* 26 February.

HM Treasury (2004) *Spending Review 2004: Science and Innovation, Science and Innovation Investment Framework 2004–2014.*
Available from the web: www.hm-treasury.gov.uk/spending_review/spend_sr04/associated_documents/spending_sr04_science.cfm. Accessed 20/01/05.

Hockey, J. (1995) Change and the social science PhD. *Oxford Review of Education,* 21: 195.

Hodges, L. (1999) Economists fall for the lure of lucre. *The Independent Higher Education,* 10 June.

Hooper-Greenhill, E. (1992) *Museums and the Shaping of Knowledge.* Routledge, London.

Hughes, B. (2001) *Evolutionary Playwork and Reflective Analytic Practice.* Routledge, London.

Institute of Physics (1999) *Physics Policy.*
Available on: www.policy.iop.org/Policy/Statistics. Accessed 20/01/05.

Jackson, C. and Tinkler, P. (2001) Back to basics: A consideration of the purposes of the PhD viva. *Assessment and Evaluation in Higher Education,* 26(4): 355–66.

Jenkins, A. *et al.* (2003) Reshaping Teaching in Higher Education. *Linking Teaching with Research.* Kogan Page, London.

JM Consulting Ltd (2005) Costs of training and supervising postgraduate research students. A report to HEFCE by JM Consulting Ltd. February 2005. Available from the web: http://www.hefce.ac.uk/pubs/rdreports/2005/. Accessed 04/02/05.

Johnes, J. (1990) Determinants of student wastage in higher education. *Studies in Higher Education,* 15: 87–99.

Kam, Booi Hon (1997) Style and quality in research supervision: The supervisor dependency factor. *Higher Education,* 34: 81–103.

Kerr, C. (1975) Higher education in the United States in 1980 and 2000. In R.W. Hosttrop (ed.) *Education Beyond Tomorrow.* ETC Publications, Homewood.

Krechowieck, I. (2004) *Postgraduate UK – The Employment Value of a UK Postgraduate Degree.* Postgraduate UK magazine.
Available on: www.educationuk.org/pls/hot_bc/page_pls_user_article?x=86644261804&y=0&a=0&d=655. Accessed 21/12/04.

Kouptsov, O. (1994) The Doctorate in the Europe Region. *CEPES Studies in Higher Education.* CEPES, Bucharest.

Leonard, D. (2001) *A Woman's Guide to Doctoral Studies.* Open University Press, Buckingham.

Leonard, D., Pelletier, C. and Morley, L. (2003) *The Experiences of International Students in UK Higher Education: A Review of Unpublished Research.* UKCoSA, The Council for International Education, London.

Loeffler, T. (2004) *Skills Training Funding for Research Council Funded PhD Students and Postdoctoral Researchers.* Research Councils UK Training Group. March.

Lovitts, B. (2001) Leaving *the Ivory Tower: The Causes and Consequences of Departures from Doctoral Study*. Lanham, M.D.: Rowman & Littlefield.

MacDonald, K. (2000) *Skills Profile for Chemistry Post-Graduates: The Royal Society of Chemistry Postgraduate Skills Record.* Final Report of the DfEE funded Recording Achievement Project. Royal Society of Chemistry, London.

Maslen, G. (1991a) Australia eases visa requirements for foreign teachers. *Chronicle of Higher Education,* 3 April, A37.

Maslen, G. (1991b) Slow road to PhD. *Chronicle of Higher Education,* 30 August 1991, p. 10.

Maxwell, T.W. (2003) From first to second generation professional doctorate. *Studies in Higher Education,* 28(3): 279–91.

Meagher, K. (2001) Research in art and design. Paper presented to the *NCEA Postgraduate Research Conference,* Dublin, 25 April.

Metcalfe, J., Thompson, Q. and Green, D.H. (2002) *Improving Standards in Postgraduate Research Degree Programmes.* A report to the Higher Education Funding Councils of England, Scotland and Wales, HEFCE, Bristol.

Millichope, R. (2001) Doctorates awarded from United Kingdom Higher Education institutions. *Statistics Focus,* 3, Issue 2.

Ministère de la Recherche (2001) *Ecoles doctorales, Ministère de la Recherche en France.* Available on: www.recherche.gouv.fr. Accessed 20/01/05.

Morley, L., Leonard, D. and David. M. (2002) Variations in vivas: Quality and equality in British PhD assessments. *Studies in Higher Education,* 27(3).

Moses, I. (1984) Supervision of higher degree students – problem areas and possible solutions. *Higher Education Research and Development,* 3(2): 153–65.

Mullins, G. (2004a) Evaluating supervision: Can we do better? Poster presentation at *Quality in Postgraduate Research Conference.* Adelaide, Australia, April.

Mullins, G. (2004b) Student perspectives on generic skills: are we trying to sell pogo sticks to kangaroos? Poster presentation at *Quality in Postgraduate Research Conference.* Adelaide, Australia, April.

Mullins, G. and Kiley, M. (2002) 'It's a PhD, not a Nobel Prize': How experienced examiners assess research theses. *Studies in Higher Education,* 27(4): 369–86.

NPC (2001) *EPSRC Flexible Doctoral Training Accounts.* NPC/00/02. National Postgraduate Committee.
Available no: www.npc.org.uk/page/1003800955. Accessed 20/01/05.

NPC (2002) *National Survey of Postgraduate Funding and Priorities.* National Postgraduate Committee.
Available on: www.npc.org.uk/essentials/publications. Accessed 20/01/05.

Nerad, M. and Miller, D.S. (1996) Increasing students retention in graduate and professional programs. In J.G. Hayworth (ed.) *Assessing Graduate and Professional Education: Current Realists and Future Prospects.* Jossey-Bass, San Francisco, CA, pp. 61–76.

Noble, K. (1994) *Changing Doctoral Degrees: An International Perspective.* The Society for Research into Higher Education and Open University Press, Buckingham.

Okorocha, E. (1997) Supervising international students. *Issues in Postgraduate Supervision, Teaching and Management,* No. 1. SRHE and the Times Higher Education Supplement, London.

O'Neill, I. (1997) *Postgraduate Research: Student Decision-Making and Experience.* Heist, Leeds.

OST (1994) *Consultative Document: A New Structure for Postgraduate Research Trainings, Supported by Research Councils.* Office of Science and Technology, London.

OST (1997) *Research Masters Pilot Programme: Report on Progress*, Autumn. Office of Science and Technology, London.

OST (2002) *Survey of Post Graduates Funded by the Research Councils*, Office of Science and Technology, London.

OST (2003) *The Sustainability of University Research*. Office of Science and Technology, London.

OST (undated) *Survey of Postgraduates Funded by the Research Councils*. Office of Science and Technology, London.
Available on: www.ost.gov.uk/reseach/funding/postgrad_survey. Accessed 10/01/05.

Pearson, M. and Brew, A. (2002) Research training and supervision development. *Studies in Higher Education*, 27(2): 135–50.

Phillips, E.M. (1994) Quality in the PhD: Points at which quality may be assessed. In R.G. Burgess (ed.) *Postgraduate Education and Training in the Social Sciences.* Jessica Kingsley, London.

Phillips, E.M. and Pugh, D.S. (2000) *How to Get a PhD: A Handbook for Students and Their Supervisors* (3rd edn). Open University Press, Buckingham.

Phillips, M. and Howells, A. (1999) *Survey of Postgraduate Study Intentions*. Conducted by the University of Sheffield. OST, London.

Poole, M. and Spear, R.H. (1997) Policy issues in postgraduate education: An Australian perspective. In R.G. Burgess (ed.) *Beyond the First Degree: Graduate Education, Lifelong Learning and Careers*. SRHE and Open University Press, Buckingham.

Powell, S.D. (1999a) *Return to Study: A Guide for Professionals*. Open University Press, Buckingham.

Powell, S.D. (1999b) A Swedish disputation: Reflections on PhD Examination, *UK Council for Graduate Education Newsletter*. UK Council for Graduate Education, Lichfield.

Powell, S.D. (2004) *The Award of PhD by Published Work in the UK*. UK Council for Graduate Education, Lichfield.

Powell, S.D. and Green, H. (2003) Research degree examining: Quality issues of principle and practice. *Quality Assurance in Education* (Special edition: 'Assessing and Examining Research Awards'), 11(2): 55–64.

Powell, S.D. and McCauley, C. (2002) Research degree examining: Common principles and divergent practices. *Quality Assurance in Education* (Special Edition: 'Standards and the Doctoral Award'), 10(2): 104–16.

Powell, S.D. and McCauley, C. (2003) The process of examining research degrees: Some issues of quality. *Quality Assurance in Education* (Special edition: 'Assessing and Examining Research Awards'), 11(2): 73–84.

QAA (1999) *Code of Practice for the Assurance of Academic Quality and Standards in Higher Education: Postgraduate Research Programmes*. Quality Assurance Agency for HE, Gloucester.

QAA (2000) *Code of Practice for the Assurance of Academic Quality and Standards in Higher Education. Section 6: Assessment of students*, p. 4. Quality Assurance Agency for HE, Gloucester.

QAA (2001) *National Qualifications Framework*. Quality Assurance Agency, Gloucester.
Available on: www.qaa.ac.uk/crntwork/nqf/ewni2001/contents.htm. Accessed 27/08/04.

QAA (2004) *Code of Practice for the Assurance of Academic Quality and Standards in Higher Education: Section 1: Postgraduate Research Programmes* (2nd edn). Quality Assurance Agency, Gloucester.

QAA (undated) *Policy Statement on a Progress File for Higher Education.* Quality Assurance Agency, Gloucester.
  Available on: www.qaa.ac.uk/crntwork/progfilehe/guidelines/uidline.pdfd. Accessed 20/01/05.
Reichert, S. and Tauch, C. (2003) *Trends 2003. Progress Towards the European Higher Education Area. Bologna Fours Years After: Steps Towards Sustainable Reform of Higher Education in Europe,* July 2004. European University Association.
Research Councils/AHRB (2001) *Joint Statement of the Research Councils'/AHRB's Skills Training Requirements for Research Students.*
  Available on: www.grad.ac.uk/3_2_1.jsp. Accessed 20/01/05.
Research Europe (2001) France approves 10-year plan for research jobs. *Research Europe,* 1 November, No. 110, p. 6.
Research Fortnight (1999a) Alarm bells ring over vacant studentships. *Research Fortnight,* 5(9): February.
Research Fortnight (1999b) Universities choose conditions for PhDs. *Research Fortnight,* 6(2): October.
Research Fortnight (2004) New route shapes up as new standard for PhDs. *Research Fortnight,* September.
Ries, P. and Thurgood, D.H. (1993) *Summary Report 1991. Doctoral Recipients from United States Universities.* National Academy Press, Washington.
Robbins (1963) Higher Education Report of the Committee Appointed by the Prime Minister under the Chairmanship of Lord Robbins 1961–63. Committee on Higher Education Cmnd. 2. 154, HMSO, London.
Roberts, G. (2001) *Review of the Supply of Scientists and Engineers.* Key issues consultation paper. The Public Enquiry Unit, HM Treasury, London (June).
Roberts, G. (2002) *Set for Success. The Supply of People with Science, Technology, Engineering and Mathematical Skills.* HM Treasury.
  Available on: www.hm-treasury.gov.uk. Accessed 20/10/04.
Roberts, G. (2003) *Review of the Research Assessment Exercise. Report for the Funding Bodies, HEFCE Issues for Consultation May 2003.*
  Available on: www.ra-review.ac.uk/reports/roberts/roberts_summary.doc. Accessed 20/01/05.
Royal Society of Chemistry (1995) *The Chemistry PhD – The Enhancement of its Quality.* Royal Society of Chemistry, London.
Rudd, E. (1985) *A New Look at Postgraduate Failure.* Society for Research in Higher Education, Guildford.
Rudd, E. and Hatch, S.R. (1968) *Graduate Study and After.* Weidenfeld & Nicolson, London.
Sastry, T. (2004) *Postgraduate Education in the United Kingdom.* Higher Education Policy Institute, Oxford.
Science and Engineering Research Council (SERC) (1991) The Engineering Doctorate. A SERC Working Party Report, (The Parnaby Report) SERC, Swindon.
Schon, D.A. (1983) *The Reflective Practitioner: How Professionals Think in Action.* Basic Books, New York.
SERC (1982) *Research Student or Supervisor – A Discussion Document in Good Supervisory Practice.* Science and Engineering Research Council, London.
SERC (1992) *Research Student and Supervisor: An Approach to Good Supervisory Practice* (2nd edn). Science and Engineering Research Council, Swindon.
Scrivener, S. (2002) Characterising creative-production doctoral projects in art and design. *International Journal of Design Sciences and Technology,* 10(2): 25–44.

Scott, D., Brown, A., Lunt, I. and Thorne, L. (2004) *Professional Doctorates: Integrating Professional and Academic Knowledge*. Open University Press, Buckingham.

Shaw, M. and Green, H. (1996) Standards in research awards: Length, weight or quality? Developing an approach for resolving the dilemma. *Innovation and Learning in Education: The International Journal for the Reflective Practitioner*, 2(3): 4–10.

Shaw, M. and Green, H. (2001) Benchmarking the PhD – A tentative beginning. *Quality Assurance in Education*, 10(2): 116–24.

Skuse, T. (1995) Peer support for postgraduate research students. *Journal of Graduate Education*. National Postgraduate Committee, Troon, pp. 36–9.

Siegfried, J.J. and Stock, W.A. (1999) The labour market for new PhD economists. *Journal of Economic Perspectives*, 13(3): 115–34.

Simpson, R. (1983) *How the PhD came to Britain – A Century of Struggle for Postgraduate Education*. Society for Research into Higher Education, Guildford.

Spagnold, F. (1994) Students abroad sponsored by the Government. *Infoscapes*, 2(1): 10–17.

Swedish Government (2000) *Research and Renewal (2000/01: 3)*. Ministry of Education and Science, Sweden.

Thomas, K. (1990) *Gender and Subject in Higher Education*. Open University Press, Buckingham.

Thomas, L. (2001) *Widening Participation in Post-Compulsory Education*. Continuum, London.

Tinkler, P. and Jackson, C. (2000) Examining the doctorate: Institutional policy and the PhD examination process in Britain. *Studies in Higher Education*, 25(2): 167–80.

Tinkler, P. and Jackson, C. (2002) In the dark? Preparing for the PhD viva. *Quality Assurance in Education*, 10(2): 86–97.

Tinkler, P. and Jackson, C. (2004) *The Doctoral Examination Process: A Handbook for Students, Examiners and Supervisors*. Open University Press, Buckingham.

Trafford, V. (2003) Questions in doctoral vivas: Views from the inside. *Quality Assurance in Education* (Special Edition: 'Assessing and Examining Research Award'), 11(2).

Triggle, D.J. and Miller, K.W. (2002) Doctoral education: Another tragedy of the commons? *American Journal of Pharmaceutical Education*, 66: 287–94.

UCoSDA/BPS (1995) *Guidelines for the Assessment of the PhD in Psychology and Related Disciplines*. Universities' and Colleges' Staff Development Agency, Sheffield.

UKCGE (1995) *Graduate Schools Survey*. UK Council for Graduate Education, Warwick.
Available on: www.ukcge.ac.uk/report_downloads.html. Accessed 20/01/05.

UKCGE (1996a) *Quality and Standards of Postgraduate Research Degrees*. UK Council for Graduate Education, Warwick.
Available on: www.ukcge.ac.uk/report_downloads.html. Accessed 20/01/05.

UKCGE (1996b) *The Award of the Degree of PhD on the Basis of Published Work in the UK*. UK Council for Graduate Education, Lichfield.
Available on: www.ukcge.ac.uk/report_downloads.html. Accessed 20/01/05.

UKCGE (1997) *Practice-Based Doctorates in the Creative and Performing Arts and Design*. UK Council for Graduate Education, Lichfield.
Available on: www.ukcge.ac.uk/report_downloads.html. Accessed 20/01/05.

UKCGE (1998a) *Graduate Schools Survey*. UK Council for Graduate Education, Warwick.

UKCGE (1998b) *The Status of Published Work in Submissions for Doctoral Degrees in European Universities.* UK Council for Graduate Education, Lichfield.
Available on: www.ukcge.ac.uk/report_downloads.html. Accessed 20/01/05.

UKGCE (2001a) *5 Years of the MRes. UK Council for Graduate Education.*
Available on: www.ukcge.ac.uk/other-documents_downloads.html.Accessed 20/01/05.

UKCGE (2001b) *Research Training in the Creative and Performing Arts and Design.* UK Council for Graduate Education, Lichfield.
Available on: www.ukcge.ac.uk/report_downloads.html. Accessed 20/01/05.

UKCGE (2001c) *Research Training for Humanities Postgraduate Students.* UK Council for Graduate Education.
Available on: www.ukcge.ac.uk/report_downloads.html. Accessed 20/01/05.

UKCGE (2002) *Professional Doctorates.* UK Council for Graduate Education, Dudley.
Available on: www.ukcge.ac.uk/report_downloads.html. Accessed 20/01/05.

UKCGE (2003) *Research training in the healthcare professions.* UK Council for Graduate Education, Lichfield.
Available on: www.ukcge.ac.uk/report_downloads.html. Accessed 20/01/05.

UKCGE (2004a) UKCGE Response: QAA Draft revised Code of Practice for the assurance of academic quality and standards in higher education, section 1: Postgraduate Research Programmes.
Available on: www.ukcge.ac.uk Accessed 7/03/05.

UKCGE (2004b) *Confidentiality of PhD Theses.* Unpublished survey results. UK Council for Graduate Education, Lichfield.

UK GRAD Programme (2004a) *A National Review of Emerging Practice on the Use of Personal Development Planning for Postgraduate Researchers.* UK GRAD Programme, Cambridge.

UK GRAD Programme (2004b). UK GRAD Programme.
Available on: www.grad.ac.uk. Accessed 1/09/04.

UK GRAD Programme (2004c) *What do PhDs do? 2004 Analysis of first destinations for PhD Graduates.* UK GRAD Programme, Cambridge.
Available on: www.grad.ac.uk. Accessed 19/01/05.

Underwood, S. (1999) *What is a PhD? Towards a Discussion Paper.* Higher Education Development Centre, Lancaster.

University of Leeds, Faculty of Earth and Environment (2000) *Making your PhD Work for You – A Personal Profile for Research Students.* DfEE Training Research. Students for Employability Project.

University of Nottingham (undated) *Research Students and Supervisors: A Guide, 2001/2002.* Graduate School, University of Nottingham.

University of Southampton (2001) *Research Students' Handbook.* Faculty of Social Sciences, 2001/2002. University of Southampton.

Usher, R. (2002) A Diversity of doctorates: Fitness for the knowledge economy. *Higher Education Research and Development*, 21(2): 143–53.

UUK (2003) *Report of the ORSAS Policy Review Group.* Universities UK, London.

Vella, F. *et al.* (2000) *Standards for the PhD Degree in the Molecular Biosciences.* The International Union of Biochemistry and Molecular Biology, Saskatoon, Canada.

Voisin-Demery, F. and Poble, P.E. (2004) *Doctoral Studies in France.*
Available on: www.eurodoc.net/docs/phdfrance.htm. Accessed 16/01/05.

Wakeford, J. (2004) The missing links. Education Guardian. *The Guardian*, 16 March.

Walker, G. (2001) *Rethinking the Doctorate in the 21st Century.* Carnegie Initiative on the Doctorate, 650/566–5100.
Available on: www.carnegiefoundation.org/CID. Accessed 16/01/05.

Wallace, S.A. and Marsh, C. (2001) Trial by ordeal or the chummy game: Six case histories in the conduct of the British PhD viva examination. *Higher Education Review*, 34(1): 35–59.

Watkins, J. and Drury, L. (1995) Quality initiatives and the implications for PhD supervisors. *Proceedings of Research Student Supervision: Management and Practice.* [*Journal of Postgraduate Education*, National Postgraduate Committee, Troon.]

Wellcome Trust (2001) *Review of the Wellcome Trust PhD: The Supervisor Perspective.* Wellcome Trust, London.

Williams, G., Bjarnason, S. and Loder, C. (1995) *Postgraduate Education in England.* Centre for Higher Education Studies. Institute of Education, University of London, London.

Winfield, G. (1987) *The Social Science PhD.* The ESRC Inquiry on Submission Rates. Economic and Social Research Centre, London.

Wollheim, L. (1980) *Art and its Objects.* (2nd edn). Cambridge University Press, Cambridge.

Wood, E.J. and Vella, F. (2000) IUBMB updates PhD Standards. *BioEssays*, 22(8): 771–3.

Woodward, D., Denicolo, P., Hayward, S. and Long, E. (2004) *Review of Graduate Schools Survey.* UKCGE, Lichfield.
Available on: http://www.ukcge.ac.uk/filesup/Graduateschools.pdf. Accessed 20/01/05.

Working Party on Postgraduate Education (1982) *Report of the Working Party on Postgraduate Education.* HMSO, London.

Wright, T. and Cochrane, R. (2000) Factors influencing successful submission of PhD theses. *Studies in Higher Education*, 25(2): 181–95.

Yorke, M. (1999) *Leaving Early: Undergraduate Non-completion in Higher Education.* Falmer Press, London.

Zhao, F. (2003) Transforming quality in research supervision: A knowledge-management approach. *Quality in Higher Education*, 9(2, July): 187–96.

Zur-Muehlem, M. von (1987) A faculty supply crisis in the 1990s seems unlikely. *University Affairs*, 17 March.

Index

Page numbers in *italics* refer to tables, *passim* indicates numerous scattered mentions within page range.

The Society for Research into Higher Education

The Society for Research into Higher Education (SRHE), an international body, exists to stimulate and coordinate research into all aspects of higher education. It aims to improve the quality of higher education through the encouragement of debate and publication on issues of policy, on the organization and management of higher education institutions, and on the curriculum, teaching and learning methods.

The Society is entirely independent and receives no subsidies, although individual events often receive sponsorship from business or industry. The Society is financed through corporate and individual subscriptions and has members from many parts of the world. It is an NGO of UNESCO.

Under the imprint *SRHE & Open University Press*, the Society is a specialist publisher of research, having over 80 titles in print. In addition to *SRHE News*, the Society's newsletter, the Society publishes three journals: *Studies in Higher Education* (three issues a year), *Higher Education Quarterly* and *Research into Higher Education Abstracts* (three issues a year).

The Society runs frequent conferences, consultations, seminars and other events. The annual conference in December is organized at and with a higher education institution. There are a growing number of networks which focus on particular areas of interest, including:

Access	FE/HE
Assessment	Graduate Employment
Consultants	New Technology for Learning
Curriculum Development	Postgraduate Issues
Eastern European	Quantitative Studies
Educational Development Research	Student Development

Benefits to members

Individual

- The opportunity to participate in the Society's networks
- Reduced rates for the annual conferences
- Free copies of *Research into Higher Education Abstracts*
- Reduced rates for *Studies in Higher Education*

- Reduced rates for *Higher Education Quarterly*
- Free online access to *Register of Members' Research Interests* – includes valuable reference material on research being pursued by the Society's members
- Free copy of occasional in-house publications, e.g. *The Thirtieth Anniversary Seminars Presented by the Vice-Presidents*
- Free copies of *SRHE News* and *International News* which inform members of the Society's activities and provides a calendar of events, with additional material provided in regular mailings
- A 35 per cent discount on all SRHE/Open University Press books
- The opportunity for you to apply for the annual research grants
- Inclusion of your research in the *Register of Members' Research Interests*

Corporate

- Reduced rates for the annual conference
- The opportunity for members of the Institution to attend SRHE's network events at reduced rates
- Free copies of *Research into Higher Education Abstracts*
- Free copies of *Studies in Higher Education*
- Free online access to *Register of Members' Research Interests* – includes valuable reference material on research being pursued by the Society's members
- Free copy of occasional in-house publications
- Free copies of *SRHE News* and *International News*
- A 35 per cent discount on all SRHE/Open University Press books
- The opportunity for members of the Institution to submit applications for the Society's research grants
- The opportunity to work with the Society and co-host conferences
- The opportunity to include in the *Register of Members' Research Interests* your Institution's research into aspects of higher education

Membership details: SRHE, 76 Portland Place, London W1B 1NT, UK Tel: 020 7637 2766. Fax: 020 7637 2781. email: srheoffice@srhe.ac.uk world wide web: http://www.srhe.ac.uk./srhe/
Catalogue: SRHE & Open University Press, McGraw-Hill Education, McGraw-Hill House, Shoppenhangers Road, Maidenhead, Berkshire SL6 2QL. Tel: 01628 502500. Fax: 01628 770224. email: enquiries@openup.co.uk – web: www.openup.co.uk